Maxine Hong Kingston's Broken Book of Life

Maxine Hong Kingston's Broken Book of Life

---❖---

An Intertextual Study of *The Woman Warrior* and *China Men*

Maureen Sabine

HAWAI

University of Hawai'i Press
HONOLULU

© 2004 University of Hawai'i Press
All rights reserved
Printed in the United States of America

09 08 07 06 05 04   6 5 4 3 2 1

Library of Congress Cataloging-in-Publication Data

Sabine, Maureen (Maureen Alice)
Maxine Hong Kingston's broken book of life : an intertextual study
of the Woman warrior and China men / Maureen Sabine.
p. cm.
Includes bibliographical references (p.) and index.
ISBN 0-8248-2784-8 (hardcover : alk. paper)
1. Kingston, Maxine Hong—Criticism and interpretation.
2. Kingston, Maxine Hong. Woman warrior. 3. Chinese
American women—Biography—History and criticism.
4. Chinese Americans—Biography—History and criticism.
5. Kingston, Maxine Hong. China men. 6. Chinese
Americans—Historiography. 7. Intertextuality. I. Title
PS3561.I52 Z87 2004
813'.54—dc22   2003018420

Designed by the University of Hawai'i Press production staff

Printed by The Maple-Vail Book Manufacturing Group

In loving memory of my father Bob Fath and father—in—law Basil Sabine

Men with a noble and generous heart
who yielded a rich harvest through
their perseverance

Contents

Acknowledgments

I was fortunate to receive a grant from the Hong Kong Research Grants Council at a time when this book project was gathering momentum. The rigorous assessment leading to this competitive award gave me the scholarly incentive to proceed, and the grant itself gave me the wherewithal. The grant also funded a research assistant and subsidized her postgraduate place. I have known Eliza Wong since she enlivened one of my tutorial groups as a first-year undergraduate. Without the generous help of the Hong Kong RGC, this intelligent and insightful student would not have been able to continue her studies or ably assist me as she did. I am very grateful for the support that the RGC thus gave not only my book project, but also a promising young researcher.

I am most fortunate to have been helped and supported by others on the road. Like Mr. Great-heart, they often appeared when the going was most difficult and their message was the same: be of good courage. I should most particularly like to thank my longstanding friends Howard and Christabel Flight and John and Bron Walter and the staunch traveling companions who have walked some part of the way with me at the University of Hong Kong. But behind them stands my loving family—Martin, Tony, Peter, and Christopher—who have been close by my side and dispelled much grief with laughter.

Introduction

On several occasions Maxine Hong Kingston made it clear that *The Woman Warrior: Memoirs of a Girlhood among Ghosts* and *China Men* were "conceived [as] one huge book" and that she wrote much of the two books at the same time. In the end, this epic book project proved unwieldy and was broken up into the separate life stories of the male and female characters. Hong Kingston would later rationalize this gender division by arguing that the women's "lives were coherent; there was a woman's way of thinking. My men's stories seemed to interfere. They were weakening the feminist point of view. So I took all the men's stories out, and then I had *The Woman Warrior*."[1]

The parting of the ways between the women's and men's stories, and between *The Woman Warrior* and *China Men*, is the subject of this book. This parting may have made good literary sense, in light of the complicated lifelines Hong Kingston was working to unravel and then weave artistically back into one coherent text. She did not, however, foresee that her excision of the men's perspective and consequent strengthening of a feminist point of view would allow readers to focus exclusively on *The Woman Warrior* and in large part to overlook the sequel that followed with *China Men*. Though Hong Kingston herself was adamant that, to understand each book, it was necessary to read the other and appreciate how they build on one another, and though her life writing has generated sustained scholarly interest, studies of *The Woman Warrior* have shown no great imperative to bring *China Men* back into the picture. Yet the author herself felt that *China Men* rounded off her autobiographical journey through fiction and that, although she began "the quest for self by understanding the archetypal mother" in *The Woman Warrior*, she became "more whole because of the ability to appreciate the other gender" in *China Men*.[2]

Hong Kingston's mature thoughts on finishing the two books point the way for my own study. On reflection, she came to feel that "I've gone as deeply into men's psyches as I can, and I don't find them that different. I care about men . . . as much as I care about women."[3] This compassionate recognition, in turn, made her feel that a reconciliation does eventually takes place in *The Woman Warrior* and *China Men*—not only between the opposite sexes, but also between the daughter narrator and the mother and father whom she opposes throughout the two books. I therefore propose to read her divided texts in the inclusive spirit of the feminist critic King-Kok Cheung, who argued that the time had come to show similar sympathies and work with those in gender and ethnic studies to "look at women and men together."[4] My study of *The Woman Warrior* and *China Men* aims to subvert the gender separatist readings that have not only kept these two books apart, but also resulted in a disproportionate feminist emphasis on the daughter's growing relationship with her mother in *The Woman Warrior* to the exclusion of her corresponding search for greater understanding of and closeness to her father in *China Men*.

One of the central preoccupations of feminist criticism has been to look for the imprint of the absent mother in the text whether she is literally represented there or not. Even when she is unmentionable, as in the case of the "No Name Woman," the mother is a presence who haunts, troubles, or overshadows *The Woman Warrior*. However, while *The Woman Warrior* restores the maternal figure to textual prominence, it also appears to corroborate the bleak view that "barely known, scarcely knowable, the 'absence' of fathers permeates feminist stories."[5] Yet *The Woman Warrior* was not the end—or even the beginning—of Hong Kingston's life stories. *China Men* was published on the heels of this first book; and the author underlined the fact that many of the men's stories were written at the same time or, in some instances, even earlier than the women's stories that make up *The Woman Warrior*. In her men's sequel, the author tracked the history of the father who has often been ignored in feminist critiques, and who is extracted from her first book, but who nonetheless leaves traces of his original presence in *The Woman Warrior* even when he appears absent or vacant.

In her 1986 interview with Hong Kingston, Paula Rabinowitz remarked on the way the author "played with intertextuality in the two books, where an insignificant reference in one of the books will be elaborated to a great extent in the other one" (70). Yet there has been surprisingly little critical follow-up on this early insight. A notable exception is Leslie Rabine's feminist and psychoanalytic reading of the two novels, which explores the textual crossroads where the separate lives of the men and women converge or collide.[6] My project builds on the work that critics such as Leslie Rabine and King-Kok Cheung began some time ago with a close, comparative analysis of Hong Kingston's two gender companion texts. To carry out such an intertextual study, I will trace the cross-references that run through the two books and discuss the alternative readings that arise when the life story of the father or mother missing from one text is found in a passage of the other.

Such an intertexual reading of *The Woman Warrior* and *China Men* is a more ambitious and difficult project than it might first appear. Both feminist and psychoanalytic theory concur in the view that the representation of the father and mother is constructed through a complex interplay of social and psychic, inner and outer reality. In order to appreciate both books, it is necessary to consider the imaginative process by which parents and family relations are internalized, recalled, and transformed in the running narrative of self-representation. Ruptures in either text suggest not only the contingent pressures of living, but also the fact, as Hong Kingston admits, that her stories have a "constant breaking in and out of the present and past . . . but the past breaks through and changes and enlightens the present, and vice versa" (Rabinowitz, 68). The way in which the past lives on like a "ghost" in the present of her writing is also consistent with the psychoanalytic premise that psychic existence involves a continuous and edgy movement back and forward in time as the subject struggles over a lifetime to create a coherent and mature narrative account of herself. In this connection, although King-Kok Cheung recognizes the "double-voiced discourse" pervading Hong Kingston's two texts and outlines the parallels, her reading is still based on a linear model of development in which there is self-evident and implicitly steady progression from "*The Woman Warrior* . . . related primarily by an adolescent girl groping for a viable female identity [to] *China Men* . . . presented by a woman capable of grasping the tangle of race and gender in Chinese America and of extending her feminist sympathy to men."[7] Current autobiographical theory is more inclined to see self-representation as a complex synthesis of personal history, private fantasy, and compensatory fictions embedded in a larger family, social, or ethnic narrative.

As a feminist and psychoanalytic reader, I am interested in doing what such women critics have noted but not worked through in detail: trace the play of difference and resemblance, of separation and convergence, and of juvenile insight and "adult wisdom" that characterizes the daughter narrator's tangled stories of her Chinese family. For, as she admits near the end of *The Woman Warrior*, "Long ago in China, knot-makers tied string into buttons and frogs. . . . There was one knot so complicated that it blinded the knot-maker. . . . If I had lived in China, I would have been an outlaw knot-maker."[8] The reader is warned here of the risks of trying to figure out how Hong Kingston's life writing has been fabricated: that of tying oneself up in knots or being "blind" to the textual whole. Mindful of the dangers, I outline theories of intertextuality that suggest how a written work is situated in a web of textual relationships and how that network is created through the critical interchange between the reader and writer. For, as Julia Kristeva theorized, "the writer's interlocutor, then, is the writer himself, but as reader of another text. The one who writes is the same as the one who reads."[9]

Although Hong Kingston's writing has elicited a strong response from readers, it has not always been the chord of sympathetic identification that she hoped for, but, on the contrary, one of marked antipathy. In particular, the anger that drives the daughter narrator to take up her pen in revenge against her family has provoked bitter debate in the Asian American literary community between her male and female readers. My own intertextual reading of *The Woman Warrior* and *China Men* sees it as imperative to find common ground for dialogue among women and men with material cultural, ethnic, and historical differences. Hong Kingston's autobiographically inspired narrator is painfully aware that the first step forward is, paradoxically, to delve into the deeper conflicts underlying old family quarrels and grievances. Initially, the desire for revenge drives her to take up her pen in *The Woman Warrior*, but a countermove toward understanding and acceptance gradually tempers her narrative resentments. I believe that, when *The Woman Warrior* and *China Men* are read against the grain of one another, the reader becomes caught up with the narrator in the complex "translation" of the desire for revenge into a movement toward recuperation and reconciliation. This involves aghast recognition of how compassion can arise out of the strong impulse to hurt or destroy others. In a psychoanalytic sense, the corresponding moment occurs for the daughter narrator when she acquires the maturity to dispense with the coping strategies of splitting and scapegoating that lead to gender division and maltreatment in both *The Woman Warrior* and *China Men* and learns to live with the tension of entertaining both aggressive and affectionate feelings for her two parents.

Maxine Hong Kingston is an author whose life writing crosses cultural boundaries and academic disciplines. To begin with, her work was taught in English and literature departments. With the explosion of interdisciplinary studies within the academy, however, her work began to feature importantly in women's studies and Asian American studies and in courses examining identity politics, the Chinese diaspora, postcolonialism, postmodernism, autobiographical narration, family history, myth, folklore, and oral storytelling. Since *The Woman Warrior* first appeared more than twenty-five years ago, Hong Kingston has enjoyed a phenomenal rise in popularity and literary importance and has now secured a place in the American canon as the living author most frequently taught at U.S. universities. The development of women's and gender studies and the mainstreaming of feminism in literature departments have also helped to make textual interpretation of *The Woman Warrior* a "growth industry." The interest in this touchstone work is undiminished, and intertextual study of *The Woman Warrior* in relationship to *China Men* will uncover an intricately worked story/life line, one that should attract a new generation of readers to her writing.

Approach and Argument

I take the author at her word and begin this intertextual study with the opening story of *The Woman Warrior*, "No Name Woman." I read her name back into this story by speculating on the identity of the father of her child. This search leads to *China Men* and to a greater appreciation of its pivotal position in "trying to name the unspeakable" in *The Woman Warrior* (13).

In Chapter 1, I make my case for an intertextual reading of *The Woman Warrior* and *China Men*. I start with Michael Riffaterre's definition of the intertext as "one or more texts which the reader must know in order to understand a work of literature in terms of its overall significance"[10] and argue that *China Men* is a text that the reader must know for a more comprehensive understanding of *The Woman Warrior*. I proceed to set out the key ideas of intertextuality that were expounded by Julia Kristeva in the late 1960s and suggest how they correspond to Hong Kingston's own writing and reading practices as articulated in the literary interviews she has given since *The Woman Warrior* was first published in 1976. I note that Kristeva's theory of intertexuality arose out of her engagement with Mikhail Bakhtin's ideas of heteroglossia and dialogism. Whereas Kristeva muted the assumption of intersubjective communication implicit in Bakhtin and shifted attention from utterance to textuality, Hong Kingston's talk-story mediates between the Bakhtinian idea of a polyphonic interplay of voices and Kristeva's concept of writing as a "mosaic of quotations" (*Desire in Language*, 66). Indeed, one of Hong Kingston's most distinctive literary characteristics has been her willingness to experiment with different voices and translate their speech into a textual collage. As she remarked, "When I wrote *The Woman Warrior* and *China Men*, I was trying to find an American language that would translate the speech of the people who are living their lives with the Chinese language."[11] The particular challenge that she faced as an author, however, was finding words that communicated the oral character of Say Yup, a local dialect spoken by her Cantonese relatives that has no written language.

To be sure, I argue that the clash between mother and daughter in *The Woman Warrior* is not simply intergenerational or intercultural, but interlinguistic, with Brave Orchid a bard in a culture of oral storytellers and the tongue-tied daughter a scribe of her mother's talk-stories and finally literary writer in a world of English letters. Whereas the narrator's mother is a maestro of spoken language, her father is a master of sullen silence in *China Men*, and the very fact that he constitutes what Kristeva calls "an anonymity" or "an absence" is what prompts his daughter to fill in his "blank space" (*Desire in Language*, 74) with stories that attempt to reconstruct his past history and heritage. In *The Woman Warrior*, she paid tribute to her mother's "great power" (25) to talk-story; in *China Men*, she recuperated her father's lost power as a scholar poet who was trained in the intertextual practice of reading, writing, interlocution, and commentary. Together, her mother and father demonstrated that spoken and written language exist in dynamic relationship, as do the reader and writer in Kristeva's theory of intertextuality. In interviews, Hong Kingston has emphasized the fact that her identity as a writer was inseparable from that of "a person who has built my mind on what I read."[12] In fact, she understood intertextuality as the work of appropriating "these books and this language—the American language" and country, and she imagined herself as part of a far-flung dialogic community of "writers both living and dead" who call out to one another across a vast continent of cultural space and historical time.[13]

Kristeva's theories of intertextuality were linked to her own interest in psychoanalysis and her Bakhtinian perception that, if words are connected to utterance, they must also resonate with remembered voices and emotions that retain primitive life deep within the psyche. Kristeva reasoned that "we would have to turn to the psychic aspect of writing as trace of a dialogue with oneself (with another)" (74). In fact, Hong Kingston described the production of *The Woman Warrior* and *China Men* to Arturo Islas as an arduous and seven-year-long rite of psychoanalytic passage in which "you go into the subconscious by not writing and then you make it normal consciousness by writing."[14] She was also reluctant to classify *The Woman Warrior* and *China Men* categorically as either family history or fictions, but argued, "I am writing biography and autobiography of imaginative people. I am writing about real people, all of whom have minds that love to invent fictions. I am writing the biography of their imaginations."[15] In a homely anecdote, she even suggested that her extended family's oral tradition of talk-story was intertextually connected to dream narrative and analysis. "When I go to Asia—I look up my relatives. One of my aunts in Hong Kong came to pick me up. The first thing she asks is 'How is your mother and what is she dreaming?'"

(Blauvelt, 82). Indeed, Hong Kingston made it her mission to devise a new kind of writing textually woven of her people's dreams, hopes, fantasies, ghosts, illusions, and disillusionment. Yet the psychic life of her Chinese male relations was less accessible than that of the women, because, as she says, "Memory just hurts them, because they can't go home" (Rabinowitz, 69). Furthermore, their psychic defense against the pain that the memory of the past and the loss of home evoke was repression. In *The Woman Warrior*, therefore, the onus of recollection and interiority falls on the Hong family women. Indeed, one of the reasons why Hong Kingston's book of life was broken into two separate books was that the men themselves were "broken off from their background" (Rabinowitz, 69), and from the underlying family history, mythology, and gossip that give ordinary life its shimmering texture.

When Hong Kingston made the editorial decision to cut the men's stories out of her first book, she did not eradicate them altogether from her narrative. Instead, they subsided into the textual unconscious of *The Woman Warrior*. Their eventual reassembly and publication as *China Men* in 1980 would mark the return of the repressed. Accordingly, Riffaterre argues that intertextuality "repress[es] a meaning in the process of conveying one"[16] and that the relationship of an intertext to a text resembles that of the unconscious to consciousness ("Compulsory reader response," 77). Thus, the developmental relationship of *China Men* to *The Woman Warrior* can be said to resemble that of latent intertext to manifest text and of the unconscious to consciousness. Because I see *China Men* as a crucial intertext that was largely but not entirely taken out of *The Woman Warrior*, I will begin my intertextual reading in the next chapter by focusing on the traces of *China Men* that remain in the women's stories.

In Chapter 2, "*The Woman Warrior*'s Traces of a Dialogue with *China Men*," I argue that the intertextual logic of *The Woman Warrior* and *China Men* requires the reader to seek multiple entry points into the two books and to trace the men and women who do not only lead parallel lives in their respective books but occasionally surface in the textual narratives of their gender opposite. I then turn to the problem of the narrator's father, who maintains an obstinate silence in both books and who is a major stumbling block to his daughter's quest for answers. I argue that the father's silence conditions the narrator to listen for the "unspoken in all discourse"[17] and to hear what Malini Schueller calls the "Otherness of language, the potential of words to always carry echoes of other words."[18] I go on to suggest how the men and women's stories double back on one another, by a comparative reading of *Woman Warrior*'s "No Name Woman" and *China Men*'s

"The Brother in Vietnam" and by showing how the latter story shows the author's preoccupation with war—and peace—throughout the two books. In retrospect, Hong Kingston regretted naming her women's book after the warrior Fa Mu Lan and wished that she had ended "the feminist war" in *The Woman Warrior*[19] with a story of a female war veteran who becomes a peacemaker like "The Brother in Vietnam" in the closing pages of *China Men*. I argue that even a story that seems to have little to do with modern warfare such as "No Name Woman" illustrates how the birthplace can become a battlefield and depicts women as the casualties of savage infighting. "At the Western Palace," the fourth story of *The Woman Warrior*, is a comic reprise of the battle of the sexes and foretells that the women's dominance of Hong Kingston's first set of stories is nearing an end. Both this story and "Shaman," which precedes it, can be read to show that, whether male or female, the principal family members are all victims of posttraumatic stress, like the returning veterans of Vietnam or displaced refugees of war.

I then return to the opening of *The Woman Warrior* and begin to read "No Name Woman" and the father's withdrawn and guarded behavior in this and the other stories of the first book as symptomatic of a traumatized family. In response to the question of how she managed to break through the family's wall of silence and shame prohibiting her from telling the story of the "No Name Woman," Hong Kingston admitted that it was not easy. The daughter's desire to read between the lines and imagine the life story of her aunt—a narrative her father has repressed—compels her to try and rescue not only his sister, but also him, from the psychic underworld where they languish. In other words, I regard the fate of the father and aunt, brother and sister, youngest and most beloved members of their natal family, as intertextually linked through the two books. Nevertheless, in saving her aunt "from the no-nameness, the nothing, and creat[ing] her again" (Skenazy, "Kingston at the University," 119), Hong Kingston ran the risk of suppressing or even killing her father off as a character in *The Woman Warrior*. It is the work of the intertextual reader to keep the father alive, to "save" what Kristeva calls the idea of the imaginary father and to be on the lookout for his presence, if only as "the possibility of absence, the possibility of love, the possibility of interdiction but also a gift."[20] Kristeva's idea of the imaginary father can mediate between the daughter narrator's sense of her mother, Brave Orchid, as an overwhelming presence in *The Woman Warrior* and her father as a distant or absent figure in the text.

In the remaining part of this chapter, I read the traces of *China Men* back into the interpretative analysis of *The Woman Warrior* by a close reading of the passages where the father appears in each of the five interlocking stories that constitute the first book. I proceed to suggest how these readings alter critical assumptions predicated on a complete textual break between the women and men. In particular, I pursue the intriguing question of why the narrator's father was "the only brother who never went back to China having once been traded for a girl" (*WW*, 17). What prevented him from going back home? I speculate that his fate may have been intertwined with that of his no name sister, indeed that his early experience of being traded on the cheap for a girl foreshadows his Chinese immigrant experience of being cheap labor and of being identified with "women's work" that is beneath him in racist America. I argue that such an intertexual reading shows not only that there are correspondences between the lives of the men and women, but also fosters critical sympathy for the similar hardship and suffering they experience though socially kept apart and polarized by gender and racial prejudices. I further suggest, citing parallels with the nineteenth-century Chinese intertext *Flowers in the Mirror*, by Li Ruzhen, that the daughter's retrieval and reinvention of the story of her father's "little sister" in "No Name Woman" also signal her determination to bring him back to life and out of his equivalent status as no name man in *The Woman Warrior*. I argue in the conclusion of this chapter that, although the aunt's name has been struck from the family book of life, she retains the uncanny status of missing person in the family and draws continual attention to the textual unconscious where the lost loved one continues to reside as a disturbing memory, reproachful voice, or haunting face. Indeed, she is an important missing link in the intertextual process of reconstructing the original book of life composed of men's and women's stories that were broken in two and divided between *The Woman Warrior* and *China Men*.

In Chapter 3, "Traces of Incest in 'No Name Woman' and *The Woman Warrior*," I start by suggesting that the need of the daughter narrator to "remember Father's drowned-in-the-well sister" in "No Name Woman" (*WW*, 13) may have assumed a particular urgency, in light of the depiction of both parents as becoming old and as no strangers to death in the two books. "No Name Woman" depicts the aunt as an uncanny figure who violates the natural cycle of long life expectancy among the narrator's Chinese family and who ushers the reader from birth to death in the space of only a few violent pages. I cite Freud's psychoanalytic reading of "The Theme of the Three Caskets" to suggest that the aunt is depicted as both a goddess of love and death and one who remains fatalistically silent rather than disclose the name of the father of her child.

I then propose that "No Name Woman" can be read to suggest that the "private life, secret and apart" (*WW*, 19) for which the aunt is punished may be her father's incestuous love for her. I further suggest that the daughter narrator may wish to provoke her own father "to speak up with the real stories if I've got you wrong," as she does later at the start of *China Men*.[21] The word "incest" is mentioned only once in "No Name Woman" (18) before plunging down, when the aunt jumps to her death in the family well, into the textual unconscious of the two books. The young daughter narrator first hints at the "never-said" within the "crowded house" where the attractive aunt—who turns both young and old male heads—resided with her parents (17). Even as the narrator works up the courage to say the word "incest," which is taboo, she begins to retreat from the idea that the father of the aunt's child could have been someone within the paternal family. "He may have been somebody in her own household, but intercourse with a man outside the family would have been no less abhorrent" (18). Yet Sidonie Smith rightly wondered in a footnote to her reading of this story why "this married aunt [was] living with her own parents rather than with her in-laws. And who had been the stranger, or was he a stranger, who had entered her house/womb."[22] The narrator herself provides one possible explanation when she alludes to the widespread social practice of *sim-pua* marriage. "Among the very poor and the wealthy, brothers married their adopted sisters, like doves" (19). In the first part of this chapter, I explore the textual possibility that the aunt was a *sim-pua*, or "little daughter-in-law," adopted and reared to marry a foster brother in the Hong family. In his study of *sim-pua* marriages in rural Taiwan, Arthur Wolf saw proof of the so-called Westermarck effect: that early familiarity among siblings effectively prohibits incest and often discourages later sexual intimacy between individuals who are not blood relatives but have been raised together as brother and sister.[23]

In the second part of this chapter, I consider to what extent the allusion to a *sim-pua* marriage might be a smoke screen that neutralizes, but does not altogether dispel, the fears of incest in the narrative subtext. Whereas the Westermarck hypothesis is that the incest taboo expresses a natural sexual aversion between conjugal partners who have been reared intimately together since early childhood, the Freudian argument is for a naturally occurring attraction, especially between the parents and child in the triangular family romance. Father-daughter incest has been described as "the best kept secret,"[24] a crime that fathers can commit in the name of love and that daughters can confuse with parental care and attention. Because incest is often committed in stealth and requires such a comprehensive denial of sexual predation, members of the family who "name the unspeakable" (*WW*, 13) often struggle with strong feelings of guilt, shame, and disloyalty and can mistakenly feel that it is not incest, but their reporting of it, that is the crime. The narrator's mother warns her daughter, "Now that you have started to menstruate, what happened to her [the aunt] could happen to you" (*WW*, 13). She may be expressing the fears a woman's cycle carries, that sexual history will repeat itself and that incest is a story that can be transmitted intergenerationally.

The daughter narrator shows a transgressive desire not simply to repeat, but to elaborate on, the little she is told and so recover the lifeless bodies of the aunt and her child from the family well, where they drink the cold waters of oblivion. I read this well as representational of the male unconscious that keeps women down, and that becomes the textual unconscious of *The Woman Warrior*, and as symbolic at the same time of the subversive powers of women as the fount of new life. The intertextual allusions in this story to Hawthorne's *Scarlet Letter* further signal the daughter narrator's sympathetic identification with fallen women whose impure bodies were wellsprings of life.

In her study of father-daughter incest, Janet Liebman Jacobs argues that is not the daughter victim's reporting of the incestuous crime per se, but the creative reassembly of the broken pieces of her life through such therapeutic activities as writing, art, or spirituality that can be crucial for her recovery.[25] I conclude this chapter by suggesting how the narrator writes the victimized daughter back into being. I suggest how she replays and recomposes this sexual trauma in "Shaman." Janice Haaken has observed that "the trauma story [can] anoint the survivor with a heroic status—as the bearer of unspeakable truths."[26] I go on to show how the colorful fantasy of male-inspired heroism and retribution narrated in "White Tigers," with its controlling myth of the woman warrior, resembles the compensating fictions that incest victims imagine to articulate their conflicted desire to be safe from, to be saved by, and to save the father figure. I close by suggesting how the behavior, mood swings, and appearance of the narrator in *The Woman Warrior*, especially in its ending story, "A Song for a Barbarian Reed Pipe," conform in certain key respects to the pathologized coping strategies of daughter victims of paternal abuse.

In my final chapter, "The Search for the Father in *China Men*," I point out that the daughter narrator of *China Men* engaged as a child in the imaginary activity of "Talking Men" (181), and I suggest that this activity shows that she never lost interest in her father or ceased carrying on an inner dialogue with the talking men who represent lost parts of himself or are his past relations and likenesses. The men whom she now allows to talk for themselves in the narratives of *China Men* gradually restore the father to his rightful place at the heart of the family. Moreover, the narrator's recollections of "the father places" (*CM*, 240) that she secretly explored as a child make her feel or make believe that she had a hidden connection with him. These father places introduce the reader not only to the child's imaginary, but also to the textual unconscious that links *China Men* with *The Woman Warrior*. I go on to suggest that the older storyteller of *China Men* recalls the young girl's fictions with intertextual awareness of a tradition of reading children's literature seriously, and I draw parallels with *Alice's Adventures Underground* and Louisa May Alcott's *Little Women*. Indeed one of Hong Kingston's early incentives to write came from her avid reading of Alcott, recognition that she "wasn't those March girls," and sympathetic identification with the "funny-looking little Chinaman" in one of Alcott's works (Hoy, 62; Blauvelt, 83). But I argue that, although the author insisted that she wrote against the white American grain of Alcott, she in fact unconsciously appropriated a number of Jo March's key characteristics for her own narrator. What is more, Alcott's *Little Women* and *Little Men* may have planted the idea of organizing her family history into the gender narratives of *The Woman Warrior* and *China Men*.

I proceed to point out that, if the women in the Hong family orally transmitted the men's stories, the paternal grandfather was a crucial provider of their source material; however, the daughter narrator has her own mother, Brave Orchid, to thank for the fact that his reminiscences were not lost. "MaMa was the only person to listen to him, and so he followed her everywhere, and talked and talked. What he liked telling was his journeys to the Gold Mountain" (*CM*, 127). Her mother and paternal grandfather's shared gender recollections are, in turn, intertextually reconfigured in *China Men*. I go on to show how her father's father is crucial to the family saga that begins to unfold in the first story of *The Woman Warrior* and that is played out in *China Men*. I reread this grandfather's exhibitionism in "No Name Woman" to suggest that his exposure of his penis expresses a desire for a daughter that is inconceivable in traditional Chinese patriarchy and that becomes pathologized. I turn to the marital tensions between Grandfather Ah Goong and his wife Ah Po, and I speculate how the gender role of this Hong family matriarch might be factored into his sojourner life of hard labor, loneliness, and vagrancy in America. I examine Ah Po's besotted relationship with BiBi, "the little heart" (*CM*, 15) and youngest son of the Hong family—destined to become the daughter narrator's morose and forbidding father—and I suggest that he grows up to replay his own father's disappointment with life and alienation from his family.

Finally, I trace what Hong Kingston memorably described to Jody Hoy as her "search for my father, or all of us searching for our fathers" (56). I start by noting that the narrator's father, BaBa, would follow in the footsteps of his own father, Ah Goong, by sacrificing his life for the welfare of his family. The daughter's retrospective view of her father as a "good" provider is tinged with the guilty recognition that "in our role as children of our parents . . . we do kill something vital in them . . . [and] contribut[e] to their dying."[27] I argue that narration is the atonement structure in which this daughter brings together seemingly irreconcilable images of fathers, seeks "revenge," and makes restitution to them. I return to Ah Goong's pathological habits of exhibitionism and masturbation and reread these acts as a metaphor for the wasted lives of the fathers in *China Men*. I suggest that the language of these passages conveys the narrator's attempt to redeem the barren years of her grandfather's and father's history.

In an interview with Marilyn Chin, Hong Kingston revealed that she "started out a poet" (90). In "Shaman," she honored her mother, Brave Orchid, as a homeopathic poet—natural storyteller and healer—who read the beat of the pulse and listened to the rhythm of sick and healthy body language. Her father, BaBa, is dignified in the early stories of *China Men* as both a scholar and lover of poetry. Indeed, one of the most poignant hardships her father must suffer in America is that his interest in poetry no longer earns him respect, but derision. Through her life writing, Hong Kingston lifts her father out of his exile from poetry and reshapes him as an imaginative man who had the literary "power of going places where nobody else went" (*CM*, 238). I conclude by suggesting that the daughter narrator herself undergoes a symbolic rebirth through recollection and writing and determines to bring her father back from the underworld where he lies low as a character throughout *The Woman Warrior* and for long periods of *China Men*. I close with the view that she returns her father to a full and meaningful existence by restoring poetry to its once-honored place at the "center" of his life.

Notes

1. See Paula Rabinowitz's interview with the author, "Eccentric Memories: A Conversation with Maxine Hong Kingston (1986)," in *Conversations with Maxine Hong Kingston*, edited by Paul Skenazy and Tera Martin (Jackson: University Press of Mississippi, 1998), 69. (Hereinafter, I shall refer to this volume as *Conversations*.)

2. See Maxine Hong Kingston's "Personal Statement," in *Approaches to Teaching Kingston's* The Woman Warrior, edited by Shirley Geok-lin Lim (New York: Modern Language Association of America, 1991), 23. (Hereinafter, I shall refer to Lim's edition as *Approaches*.)

3. Timothy Pfaff, "Talk with Mrs. Kingston (1980)," in *Conversations*, 17.

4. King-Kok Cheung, "*The Woman Warrior* versus *The Chinaman Pacific*: Must a Chinese American Critic Choose between Feminism and Heroism?" in *Conflicts in Feminism*, edited by Marianne Hirsch and Evelyn Fox Keller (New York: Routledge, 1990), 245–246. Cheung's essay is also included in *Maxine Hong Kingston's* The Woman Warrior: *A Casebook*, edited by Sau-ling Cynthia Wong (New York: Oxford University Press, 1999), 113–133, and *Critical Essays on Maxine Hong Kingston*, edited by Laura E. Skandera-Trombley (New York: G. K. Hall, 1998), 107–124. (Hereinafter, I shall refer to the Wong edition as *The Woman Warrior Casebook* and the Skandera-Trombley edition as *Critical Essays*.)

5. Sara Ruddick, "Thinking about Fathers," in *Conflicts in Feminism*, edited by Hirsch and Keller, 223.

6. Leslie W. Rabine, "No Lost Paradise: Social Gender and Symbolic Gender in the Writings of Maxine Hong Kingston," Signs 12 (1987): 471–492. Also included in *The Woman Warrior Casebook*, 85–107.

7. King-Kok Cheung, *Articulate Silences: Hisaye Yamamoto, Maxine Hong Kingston, Joy Kogawa* (Ithaca, N.Y.: Cornell University Press, 1993), 77, 101.

8. See Maxine Hong Kingston, *The Woman Warrior: Memoirs of a Girlhood among Ghosts* (London: Picador, 1981), 33 and 147, for the previous two quotes. I shall cite this edition parenthetically throughout this study.

9. Julia Kristeva, "Word, Dialogue, and Novel (1969)," in *Desire in Language: A Semiotic Approach to Literature and Art*, edited by Leon S. Roudiez, translated by Thomas Gora, Alice Jardine, and Leon S. Roudiez (New York: Columbia University Press, 1980), 86–87.

10. Michael Riffaterre, "Compulsory reader response: The intertextual drive," in *Intertextuality: theories and practices*, edited by Michael Worton and Judith Still (Manchester: Manchester University Press, 1990), 56.

11. Marilyn Chin, "Writing the Other: A Conversation with Maxine Hong Kingston" (1989), in *Conversations*, 100.

12. William Satake Blauvelt, "Talking with the Woman Warrior" (1989), in *Conversations*, 79.

13. See Paul Skenazy, "Kingston at the University" (1989), 144; Jody Hoy, "To Be Able to See the Tao" (1986), 50–51; and Rabinowitz, "Eccentric Memories" (1986), 72; all in *Conversations*.

14. Arturo Islas with Marilyn Yalom, "Interview with Maxine Hong Kingston" (1980), in *Conversations*, 26.

15. See Rabinowitz, 75, and Kay Bonetti, "An Interview with Maxine Hong Kingston" (1986), 37, both in *Conversations*.

16. Michael Riffaterre, "The Intertextual Unconscious," *Critical Inquiry* 13 (1987), 374.

17. Julia Kristeva, "About Chinese Women" (1974), in *The Kristeva Reader*, edited by Toril Moi (Oxford: Blackwell, 1986), 156.

18. Malini Schueller, "Questioning Race and Gender Definitions: Dialogic Subversions in *The Woman Warrior*," *Criticism* 31 (1989), 422.

19. See her remarks to Bonetti, 40, and to Neila C. Seshachari, "Reinventing Peace: Conversations with Tripmaster Maxine Hong Kingston" (1993), 193, in *Conversations*.

20. "Julia Kristeva in Conversation with Rosalind Coward," *ICA Documents* (1984), 22.

21. See Maxine Hong Kingston's sequel to *The Woman Warrior, China Men* (New York: Vintage Books, 1989), 15, which I will cite parenthetically throughout this study.

22. Sidonie Smith, "Filiality and Woman's Autobiographical Storytelling," in *The Woman Warrior Casebook*, n. 7, 82.

23. Arthur P. Wolf, *Sexual Attraction and Childhood Association: A Chinese Brief for Edward Westermarck* (Stanford, Calif.: Stanford University Press).

24. Vikki Bell, *Interrogating Incest: Feminism, Foucault and the Law* (London: Routledge, 1993), 79.

25. Janet Liebman Jacobs, *Victimized Daughters: Incest and the Development of the Female Self* (New York: Routledge, 1994), 157–163.

26. Janice Haaken, "The Recovery of Memory, Fantasy, and Desire in Women's Trauma Stories: Feminist Approaches to Sexual Abuse and Psychotherapy," in *Women, Autobiography, Theory: A Reader*, edited by Sidonie Smith and Julia Watson (Madison: University of Wisconsin Press, 1998), 356.

27. Hans W. Loewald, "The Waning of the Oedipus Complex," in *Papers on Psychoanalysis* (New Haven, Conn.: Yale University Press, 1980), 394–395.

Chapter 1

———— ❈ ————

The Case for an Intertextual Reading of
The Woman Warrior and *China Men*

The Intertextual History of *The Woman Warrior* and *China Men*

This work sets out to read *The Woman Warrior* and *China Men* with heightened awareness of its intriguing intertextual history, for, as Maxine Hong Kingston has repeatedly pointed out, these two very distinct works were first conceived as one "big novel about men and women" and were drafted simultaneously. Hong Kingston's original ambition was to create an extended family saga with a grand narrative reach "from ancient feudal times up to the Vietnam War and past that."[1] The writing that eventually led to the publication of *The Woman Warrior* in 1976 and *China Men* in 1980 also reached a long way back into the author's personal past and replayed her halting developmental journey from childhood to adulthood. Hong Kingston was a late bloomer who, by her own admission, spent twenty-five years searching for her voice and did not publish her first full-length work, the female bildungsroman, *The Woman Warrior,* until the mature age of thirty-six.[2] Yet, she says that she began the struggle to find the right words and literary form to convey her epic vision of a far-flung network of Chinese ancestors and kin as a young child. In fact, the earliest stories she remembers composing sometime between the age of eight and ten were *China Men* stories, not the stories of a mixed-up young girl who would make up *The Woman Warrior* (Bonetti, 34). Indeed, one of these short stories, "A Brother in Vietnam," was the first segment that went into her intended saga and would become the last section of *China Men* (Bonetti, 35; Pfaff, 16). Nevertheless, although her artistic vision of "our larger human family" has remained constant (Hoy, 53), the center of her "one big book"—what I will call her book of life—did not hold, and Hong Kingston found that the women's and men's stories naturally "parted into two volumes."[3]

Hong Kingston's subsequent explanations for this split suggest that she felt these stories had a gender life of their own. In a 1986 interview with Kay Bonetti, she alluded to the subliminal pressures and aggressive drives that forced her hand. "The books seemed to fall into place as two separate books because the power in *The Woman Warrior* has so much to do with a feminist vision and feminist anger, and so it became a coherent work without the men's stories. The men's stories were sort of undercutting the women's stories" (35–36). She speaks here of *The Woman Warrior* as if it were a defense against disruptive and competing male forces posing a threat to the coherence of her women's stories.

A writer who draws on not only feminism, but also psychoanalysis and Buddhist spirituality, for her insights, Hong Kingston has analyzed the inner dynamics that accounted for the sexual division of *The Woman Warrior* from *China Men*. She consciously wrote *The Woman Warrior* "with the privacy of writing a diary" (Seshachari, 197) because she was trying to take her readers inside the mind of an adolescent who is wrapped up in herself. Initially, Hong Kingston perceived this young first-person narrator as someone stuck in the developmental phase of early narcissism and primary identification with the maternal feminine. As a consequence, she "only knows herself as she knows women, and . . . has very little sympathy or interest in knowing what men are like" (Bonetti, 36). In 1996, she told Eric J. Schroeder, "Writing has to do with how to get out of one's own narcissism and solipsism in order to imagine another human being and the rest of the universe."[4] Hong Kingston's remarks indicate the psychological challenge facing the young woman narrator who ties herself up in knots in *The Woman Warrior*. The girl's convoluted history of women is symbolic of not only her cognitive narcissism, but also the sociolinguistic umbilical cord in which she is entangled. This cord has bound her emotionally to the stories circulated by the women in the family, especially those told by or revolving around her mother. Indeed, her narrative often reads as if this cord is still wound tight around her throat, making speech painful and difficult, most particularly the language enabling differentiation of self and others—what Freud would call the "reality principle."[5] The woman warrior will fly this umbilical cord alongside the red flag of battle, signaling the narrator's own struggle for free and unfettered speech and a greater engagement with the world at large.[6]

The "convoluted" sentences, stories, and myths that this intense and self-absorbed "narrator girl" constructs to figure out the women's life histories make *The Woman Warrior* at once a very complicated and one-sided book of life.[7] When she finished it in 1976 and turned to the companion volume *China Men*, however, Hong Kingston experienced a sense of release and with it "a strong desire to write simple sentences" (Pfaff, 16). More than a decade later, she felt that the more lucid language of *China Men* made it "a better written book than *Woman Warrior*"[8] and, what is more, that its greater clarity reflected not only the more mature perspective of her personal narrator, but also her own growth in humanity as a writer.[9] The writing of *China Men* was a way of cutting loose from the long and strong arm of maternal influence in *The Woman Warrior,* but also a way of making amends to the men who had been cut out of her big picture of the human family. She reminded feminist readers during the 1980s and 1990s that they could not afford to valorize *The Woman Warrior* at the expense of *China Men.* She sees *China Men* as the work of a more mature storyteller who has grown up since *The Woman Warrior.* The narrator of *China Men* has greater sympathy and understanding for men and can tell their story without being judgmental. Indeed, Hong Kingston argued that the next and perhaps most radical step feminism must take if women are "to truly grow up" is to learn to "love men." After all, she added later, they are "the other half of the universe" (Bonetti, 36; Hoy, 57; Perry, 175).

Hong Kingston's repeated message to her avid women readers is "neglect *China Men* at your peril." Yet, she complained to Donna Perry in 1991, "I've been really appalled that there are a lot of students now who are writing dissertations on my work and it looks like they just read one book. They don't write about it in the context of everything, which they should do because I think *China Men* is a sequel to *Woman Warrior.* I see each book as building on the last one" (175). A few feminist readers, however, have been alert to the need to read these two works in tandem. K. K. Cheung warned more than a decade ago that their "separation has its dangers, particularly if it means that men and women will continue to work in opposing directions" (*"The Woman Warrior* versus *The Chinaman Pacific,"* 245). Indeed as far back as 1986, Paula Rabinowitz suggested that an intertextual study of these divided works might bring women, men, and their life stories closer together when they see how "some little statement that Brave Orchid makes in *China Men* had been a whole section in *The Woman Warrior* or vice versa" (70). Yet, by and large, critically informed readers have not pursued this insight, though it is central to an understanding of the powerful forces at work in the two books. One of the few essays to explore "the permeable . . . boundary between the apparently mutually exclusive experiences of men and women" is Leslie W. Rabine's "No Lost Paradise," a French feminist and psychoanalytical reading of the gender differences in *The Woman Warrior* and *China Men* that first appeared in *Signs* in 1987.[10] Rabine looked at intermediate spaces in the two books that suggest what Hong Kingston herself called the textual "play of yin and yang" and that showed how storytelling and writing cross gender borders.[11] Rabine, however, was more interested in probing the girl narrator's ambivalent relationship to her mother in *The Woman Warrior* than in pursuing the path back to the father in *China Men*. In her imaginative investigation, she thus missed the opportunity arising from the "father places" to go, in Hong Kingston's own words, "as deeply into men's psyches as I can" (Pfaff, 17).[12]

The Theoretical Use of Intertextuality and Definition of an Intertext

Hong Kingston claims that the exploratory interest in these intrapsychic gender locations brought about a change of heart in the narrator and made her "a most understanding person, a very large person [who] can understand men and encompass them and create their lives" (Hoy, 57). Intertextuality is the theoretical concept I will use to investigate such a sweeping claim, for it has enhanced interpretative understanding of how this process of literary enlargement occurs by situating the written work in a web of textual relationships.[13] Moreover, it has generated greater critical awareness of an Asian American literary tradition in which, as Sau-ling Wong suggests, texts can be read as they "build upon, allude to, refine, controvert, and resonate with each other."[14] Intertextuality assumes, as Michael Riffaterre states, that there "is one or more texts which the reader must know in order to understand a work of literature in terms of its overall significance."[15] Some of these intertexts are actually embedded within Hong Kingston's narratives, such as the legends, ghost stories, myths, anecdotes, or historical commentary interspersed between the six major sections of *China Men* or similar source material beginning the stories "White Tigers" and "Shaman" and ending "No Name Woman" and "A Song for a Barbarian Reed Pipe" in *The Woman Warrior.*[16] In insisting that *China Men* should be read to understand and interpret *The Woman Warrior*, Hong Kingston designates the men's book as an external intertext that needs to be brought back into the discussion of the women's stories. Because the overall aim of this study is to read *The Woman Warrior* and *China Men* back into a closer working relationship with one another, I am interested in other intertexts—whether external influences on the writer or internal passages in her writing—to the extent that they open intercommunicating doors between the two books and their segregated worlds of men and women.

Parallels between Intertextuality and
Maxine Hong Kingston's Writing Practice

In metaphorically likening writing to both textile weaving and social networking, intertextuality captures the style of Hong Kingston's own women's writing.[17] As she remarked to Paul Skenazy in 1989, weaving "is something that women have done through thousands of years, in all cultures . . . Also, I love it that the word 'texture,' which has to do with weaving, comes from the same root word as 'text'—'text' in writing. So weaving and writing have a connection" ("Kingston at the University," 131). Intertextuality accords as well with the mindset of the girl narrator in *The Woman Warrior*, who famously compared herself to a maker of blindingly complicated textile knots (*WW*, 147). Indeed, intertextuality has a "complicated" perception of the dense practices and links that produce the knotted fabric of the text. The question it poses for the reader of Hong Kingston is not simply *where*, as Rabinowitz notes, one text may elaborate on an allusion in another, but *how* and *why* this occurs in the case of *The Woman Warrior* and *China Men*. Of course, the *why* seems obvious when the two books were conceived in the same womb as an "interlocking story about the lives of men and women" (Kim, *Asian American Literature*, 207). Intertextuality, however, cautions that none of these questions has straightforward answers. In this chapter, therefore, I will discuss some of the key ideas that emerged when Julia Kristeva began to expound intertextuality as a theoretical tool for literary interpretation in the late 1960s. I will point out where these ideas correspond to Hong Kingston's own writing and reading practices as she articulated them in literary interviews given over a twenty-year period after the publication of *The Woman Warrior* in 1976. I have no wish to lay down these critical theories of intertextuality as new "laws" for interpreting Hong Kingston's texts. The author herself has moved in academic circles long enough to know how critics are tempted "to cut my work up in order to fit their critical theories" or want "to figure out how to categorize it."[18] I hope instead to make a case for an intertextual reading of these "separate books" (Bonetti, 35) as interconnected, mutually enhancing gender companion works.

The Theoretical Development of Intertexuality: Julia Kristeva and Mikhail Bakhtin

Among a chorus of authoritative male voices such as Bakhtin, Barthes, Derrida, Foucault, Lacan, and Riffaterre, Julia Kristeva is the sole woman theorist to be identified as a major formulator of the concept of intertextuality. Her feminist and psychoanalytic point of view, strong female voice, sinuous "feminine" writing, and ear for the poetic beauty of literary language link her in spirit with Hong Kingston and the female descent line she imagines in *The Woman Warrior*. Kristeva's theory of intertextuality arose from her engagement with Mikhail Bakhtin's ideas of heteroglossia and dialogism. In *The Dialogic Imagination*, he defined heteroglossia as a "diversity of social speech types (sometimes even diversity of languages) and a diversity of individual voices, artistically organized."[19] He defined the polyphonic interplay of voices in the novel as dialogism and argued that "the dialogic orientation of a word among other words . . . creates new and significant artistic potential in discourse" (275). This is because, just as in actual spoken conversation, the words of a dialogic novel are "entangled, shot through with shared thoughts, points of view, alien value judgments and accents"; "weave in and out of complex interrelationships, merge with some, recoil from others, [and] intersect with yet a third group"; and seek an answering word (276, 280). In her influential essay "Word, Dialogue, and Novel (1969)," Kristeva textualized Bakhtin's theory that the words of a novel retain the register of utterances exchanged in living dialogue. She introduced the concept of intertextuality as "an *intersection of textual surfaces* rather than a *point* (a fixed meaning), as a dialogue among several writings."[20] She downplayed the idea of the writer as the active agent who produces and manages this textual dialogue by declaring that "the notion of *intertextuality* replaces that of intersubjectivity" and that "any text is constructed as a mosaic of quotations; any text is the absorption and transformation of another" (66).

Intertextuality and the Agency of the Author

Statements such as these have proved problematic for both Anglo-American and Asian American feminists who are concerned that Kristeva's passive and impersonal definition of intertextuality implies not merely the death of the author as an agent but the death of the feminist dream of an individual voice and active subjectivity for women.[21] Yet, however anonymous and clockwork Kristeva's theoretical definition may appear, her arresting image of the text as constructed out of "a mosaic of quotations" does articulate the way that Hong Kingston's two works are pieced together out of a sometimes elusive network of preexisting oral and written texts. One key premise of intertextuality is that a work signifies its literariness by interacting with external or latent intertexts, by giving readers cues as to the whereabouts of such intertexts, and by suggesting that these can fill in gaps in textual meaning (Riffaterre, "Compulsory reader response," 56–57, 75). Sometimes Hong Kingston talked about the intertexts that shaped her narrative as if they materialized like ghosts, took possession of her, and made her a passive medium for their power. "I feel I am chosen by the stories. They come to me without my trying for them. There are things that haunt me, that I keep seeing and won't go away" (Hoy, 63). Yet, at other times, she described herself as actively scrambling the text to "break up the facts, break up the stereotypes, break up the static way that most of us look at the world" (Skenazy, "Kingston at the University," 149). Whether the author's relation to the text is active or passive, the result in *The Woman Warrior* is what Shirley Lim calls "a collage of family stories, Chinese and Western legends and myths, Chinese and Chinese American history, fantasy, and memoirs," and what E. D. Huntley, capturing Hong Kingston's intertextual style of writing, describes as a "mosaic of memoir, history and fiction."[22]

Intertextuality as a Balance of Divergence and Convergence

Hong Kingston has indicated that her narrative writing has not only multiform texture, but also depth. She compared *China Men* to "a six-layer cake" constructed of alternating levels of family and adventure story that are sandwiched together by intertexts from myth, legend, and history (Bonetti, 41; Rabinowitz, 69; Skenazy, "Kingston at the University," 150). This elaborate, multilayered structure makes *China Men* sound rather like a fabulous wedding cake and unconsciously suggests that there may be a desire for reunion buried intertextually in the layers of the men's text as well as in the women's companion work. Indeed, in speaking generally about the two books on another occasion, she remarked that she "wanted the reader to feel being separated from people they loved; one would be in China and one would be in America. I wanted them to feel the physical loneliness of that, and then the joy of coming together" (Hoy, 54–55). Bakhtin explained this pull by arguing that living language contains, on the one hand, centrifugal forces of transgression and heterodoxy and, on the other, centripetal forces of unification and centralization (271–272). Of course, this same pattern of separation and reconciliation, of centrifugal and centripetal force, was being played out on a larger scale when Hong Kingston divided her "big novel about men and women" (Bonetti, 35) in two and then insisted that "to best appreciate *The Woman Warrior*, you do need to read *China Men*" (Lim, *Approaches*, 23). Hong Kingston's description of *China Men* as a six-layer cake, however, also directs our attention to the psychoanalytic premise underlying Kristeva's discourse on intertextuality—that the literary text is multilayered like the psyche, operates according to the same dynamic principles, and contains a similar imperative to "transformation." Indifferent to that all-purpose academic brickbat—the charge of "essentialism"—Hong Kingston has repeatedly insisted that her writing is addressed to "everyone" and that its general appeal is deeply rooted in the psychic life. "This means going so deep inside people that I would just shatter them, then take them higher" (Hoy, 54, 63; see also Skenazy, "Kingston at the University," 149). In effect, Hong Kingston believes that the most profound transformation that can take place in her intertextual writing will occur within the reader.[23]

Intertextuality and Heteroglossia

Unlike Hong Kingston, Kristeva did not recognize the writer as the agent of this transformation. She muted the assumption of intersubjective communication implicit in Bakhtin's dialogism and shifted attention to textual activity.[24] Notwithstanding Kristeva's lack of recognition of the writer in this role, her theory of intertextuality is inflected by the sound of the multiple voices that can be heard in Bakhtin's concepts of heteroglossia and dialogism. Indeed, one of Hong Kingston's most distinctive literary characteristics has been her willingness to experiment with different voices and to engage in the intertextual work of translating their speech into writing (Perry, 179). With hindsight she realized that, "When I wrote *The Woman Warrior* and *China Men*, . . . I was trying to find an American language that would translate the speech of the people who are living their lives with the Chinese language" (Marilyn Chin, 100). Despite her efforts, she has been continually vexed by the problem that the centripetal force of language offers resistance to literary experimentation and makes writing "so static."[25]

Hong Kingston was helped to a solution by the fact that, as Susan Stanford Friedman has remarked, "American English is heteroglossic, polyglot, multivoiced, and many-tongued—a language of the rebellious, postcolonial subject that refuses the orthodoxy of its precursor" (161). The narrator of *The Woman Warrior* would hear this multivocal language at American public school when she mixed with "the Negro students . . . [who] laughed the loudest and talked to me as if I were a daring talker too" and argued politics with her Hawaiian teacher (149–151). She would hear it too in the pidgin English that her parents and first-generation immigrants used to get by in America and in the travesty of their pidgin by white "ghost" customers to the family's Chinese laundry. "No tickee, no washee, mama-san?" (98).[26] The centrifugal energy of American English would send her words flying outward. Ironically, although these were frequently words of insubordination, they would reach out to embrace "a group of people who speak a dialect of Cantonese called Say Yup" and "capture some of the sounds and rhythms and power of Say Yup" (Pfaff, 17).

Orality and Writing

Say Yup was the local language not only of her distant relatives and ancestors in a small region of southern China but of the tight-lipped immigrants and uncommunicative parents who concealed their private past in Stockton, California's, "one small block" of Chinatown[27] and yet who, contrarily, could "laugh, visit, talk-story, and holler" and make a general spectacle of themselves in public, as during a Chopin piano recital (*WW*, 155). Although Say Yup was vibrant and colorful, even raucous and assertive, it was a minor dialect that had no script and hence no official function in China. Indeed, Hong Kingston told Arturo Islas that when she wrote about characters from the Say Yup region in *China Men*, she thought of them "in the language of the peasants of this one village, and that language has not been written down" (27). The vocal instrument of a traditional underclass, Say Yup doomed the Cantonese émigrés who came to America with their heads full of "wildly imaginative . . . and revolutionary thought" (Bonetti, 43), but who never mastered English, to a double lifetime of illiteracy and frustration.[28]

Intertextual Translation and Transmission

Kristeva had asserted that Bakhtin "situates the text within history and society, which are then seen as texts read by the writer, and into which he inserts himself by rewriting them" (*Desire in Language*, 65). This is not far off the mark from Hong Kingston's intertextual agenda in *The Woman Warrior* and *China Men*, which was to devise texts *for* characters who often had no formal subject status within either Chinese or American history and society. It is important to note, however, that Hong Kingston was not engaged in the "involuntary intertextuality" that Sau-ling Wong likens critically to a Chinatown tour of the social history and anthropology of the Chinese American community (*The Woman Warrior Casebook*, 40). As a writer, she took a gamble as "wildly imaginative" as that of her Cantonese predecessors. In an interview in the *New York Times Book Review* marking the debut of *China Men*, she explained how she went about devising a method of transliteration that registered the sounds of the Say Yup dialect in English. "When I write dialogue for people who are speaking Chinese, I say the words to myself in Chinese and then write them in English" (Pfaff, 17). But, in order to bring this low oral culture with its powerful tradition of talk-story alive again in her writing, she had to create a literary language that was vigorous enough to resist the centripetal forces of standardization and stasis. In psychoanalytic terms, stasis can indicate the repression of the libidinal energy so vital to a creative writer and can produce the neurotic reaction of the girl narrator in *The Woman Warrior*, who spends eighteen months of her life in sickbed, content that nothing happens (163). As we have already seen, the author was aware of the tendency to stasis in a print culture and understood that "the tension in my writing is that the oral tradition is very different from the written . . . . I see the oral tradition as being very alive, very immediate. It has the impact of command; it has the impact of directly influencing action. Also the oral stories change" (Islas and Yalom, 31).

In describing the process of writing as an exhilarating, but also stressful, interface with an oral tradition of commands and directions, Hong Kingston was locating *The Woman Warrior* and *China Men* within an intertextual network that Jay Clayton and Eric Rothstein aptly described as "simultaneously creating and disciplining the text's ability to signify" (27). On balance, she thought it likely that "writing books would get all kinds of neuroses straightened out because of the intense examination." She did not, however, see any "direct relation" between the dictums she heard when she spoke colloquial Chinese language to herself, the tense struggle she felt as she endeavored to translate the dynamic words resounding in her mind into English writing, and the change that oral stories could have brought about in her own "psychology" (Bonetti, 35). Linda Ching Sledge believes that Hong Kingston succeeded in investing "idiomatic English with the allusive texture and oral-aural qualities of Chinese," whereas Debra Shostak argues that her indeterminate storytelling resists "the fixity of the written word" and shimmers with "the fluidity of oral transmission."[29] Indeed, she was so successful that her intertextual work of appropriation, translation, and transmission acquired a life of its own in mainland China. When the Beijing Language Institute finished translating her two books into standard Chinese, they sent their work south to Canton University. As Hong Kingston told Kay Bonetti, the scholars there decided *The Woman Warrior* and *China Men* "would have to be retranslated because it was obvious from reading the English that I was writing in Cantonese. That I meant my people to be speaking Cantonese. And they could pick up those rhythms in the English language. So they retranslated it into Cantonese."[30]

Yet, by her own admission, Hong Kingston was striving to convey the vital energy of Cantonese culture, of its Say Yup dialect and idiomatic pidgin English, which she described as "the language used at home, the language of childhood and the sub-conscious" (Lim, "Chinese American Women's Life Stories," 265). This led her to try and translate not simply Chinese dialectal speech and talk-stories, but also the "emotional life" that is the undercurrent of intertextual transmission. As she said to Marilyn Chin in 1989, "They carry on their adventures and their emotional life and everything in Chinese. I had to find a way to translate all that into a graceful American language" (100). Hong Kingston was also conscious that in writing *The Woman Warrior* and *China Men* she was dealing with real people, some still alive and kicking, who played an active and even an interfering role in the intertextual process. "In writing the other two books—finding the form, finding the language—I didn't always feel that it was me who was the most powerful. Some of the characters helped shape it, the way they spoke." Pressed by her interviewer, Paula Rabinowitz, she made the extraordinary admission that Brave Orchid not only influenced *The Woman Warrior,* but "dictated it, dictated it" (76).[31]

Feminist readers will ruefully recognize the controlling mother behind this pushy voice; however, the logic of the writer's intertextual dialogue with oral culture suggests that Brave Orchid should not simply be read as a dictatorial mother in a clash of wills with her daughter. Their intergenerational drama is also a cultural clash of Chinese dialectal orality and standard English literacy, a clash that Hong Kingston translated from her own early life. "My first language is Chinese, and I only knew people who spoke Chinese" (Seshachari, 207). To be more precise, Say Yup was her mother tongue. She first heard and talked-story in her parents' local Cantonese dialect but admitted that she "had problems speaking" as a child (Bonetti, 34). As Rabine was among the first to observe, *The Woman Warrior* associates talking "with the most painful memories of childhood," while *China Men* links writing with some of "the most pleasant memories" (490). The author herself also identified talking with a restricted oral dialect that had no Chinese script and writing with second language English. Hong Kingston herself would speculate that Chinese may have been difficult because "oral expression is so different from writing, it's almost like a different language." In any case, oral expression was not her natural medium. Even when she went to Chinese language school, she studied Cantonese, not her parents' "peasant, village dialect," and the Chinese writing she learned did not correspond to the first language spoken at home (Perry, 187). Recalling how she attended "three hours of Chinese school" after "six hours of American school," Hong Kingston commented that she learned the Chinese and English language "as two separate things, and there was no bridging or getting them mixed up." In effect, she was taught Chinese as a third language with "many words that you don't hear used" and so did not acquire a compensating sense of verbal power in the written language. "I don't understand why I wouldn't write in the Chinese language, but it was when I learned English that I started writing down the stories." The English language and alphabet gave her "miraculous feelings" (Skenazy, "Kingston at the University," 122, 128) that she never felt when she "spoke only Chinese." Indeed the textual scrabble of the twenty-six letters of the English alphabet into endless word combinations would be "the most powerful tool," freeing her at last to express herself (Seshachari, 207).

The Intertextual Relationship of Mother and Daughter

The Woman Warrior dramatizes an intergenerational, intercultural, and interpersonal clash between a mother and daughter, and it is one that creates a knot in intertextual transmission. For an intertextual network of absorption and transformation presumes a relatively smooth "coming-and-going movement between subject and other, between writer and reader" and between oral and written culture (Kristeva, *Desire in Language*, 75). Once she had established herself as a successful writer, Hong Kingston was able to acknowledge that a crucial link between the two was the fact that "my mother and I are both artists" (Hoy, 49). Yet they were artists who employed different forms of communication and expression. The mother is a performer from a Chinese world of oral communication and has a gift of tongues that meant, to Hong Kingston's amazement, "stories just kept coming out of her" (Hoy, 60). The daughter is a writer in the English world of literature and letters that set her free as a tongue-tied child. But, as we have also seen, the set print of the written text made her feel disadvantaged vis-à-vis an oral culture where storytellers like her mother have greater "freedom to change the stories" (Bonetti, 38; Islas and Yalom, 31). Neither mother nor daughter has power in the world of the other. Hong Kingston's mother, Ying Lan Hong, did not speak or write English (Islas and Yalom, 23). Although Say Yup was the daughter's mother tongue, Hong Kingston could not express herself easily in this spoken dialect or in written Chinese,[32] and the narrator of *The Woman Warrior* is the inarticulate double who rises up from her incoherent childhood.

How was the author to overcome what Kristeva would call a "splitting of the writer into subject of enunciation [which I take here to mean written expression] and subject of utterance?"[33] One solution was an act of intertextual appropriation in which the power of oral performance is gradually transferred to her writing. Hong Kingston romantically reminisced that she "was raised in a storytelling culture" and that her mother taught her to speak through the talk-story that would form the nucleus of her first book *The Woman Warrior*. "I learned to talk with the chants of *The Woman Warrior*—she chanted it, and I just copied whatever I heard" (Skenazy, "Kingston at the University," 122). In *The Woman Warrior*, her mother is transformed into the champion talker Brave Orchid. The five stories of the book show cumulatively, however, that the skills of this maestro of utterance are not valued in a modern society obsessed with written evidence. If any trace of Brave Orchid is to survive, she must "dictate" her words to her daughter, as bards began to do in an age of increasing literacy. The unforthcoming father of *China Men* makes talk-story sound a test of blood, race, and descent. "If you are an authentic Chinese, you know the language and the stories without being taught, born talking them."[34] This is a test set in China that the daughter is born to fail in America. Ironically, it is the acquisition of a second language, English, that enables the daughter to become her Chinese parents' scribe.[35] "It was when I learned English that I started writing down the stories." Transcription, however, was not simply a rote exercise in which she repeated what her mother told her. Writing copy evolved into a longtime intertextual experiment in which she played with different forms of giving literary expression to oral talk-story. To begin with, her writing efforts brought her closer to the bardic role of her own mother, and eventually they led to the mature artistic production of *The Woman Warrior* and *China Men*. "At first it was poetry, and it always rhymed. Oh, I just thought it was a miracle. It was almost like I heard it and wrote it down. And I just kept writing from there, trying all different forms. The stories in *The Woman Warrior*, but especially the ones in *China Men*—I had already seen visions of those stories . . . . But it wasn't until I was in my thirties that I found the form" (Skenazy, "Kingston at the University," 122).

The mother storyteller's relationship to oral culture posed a conundrum for Hong Kingston as a writer, but it also stimulated a creative, intertextual response involving, if I may paraphrase Kristeva, a putting-into-process of literary identity in relationship to the different forms, voices, and linguistic systems at play in the text.[36] The mother's versatile voice could even have had some influence over the literary decision to divide *The Woman Warrior* and *China Men* in two, for oral storytellers adept at improvisation sometimes created different narrative endings for a male and female audience (Doane, 82).

The Intertextual Relationship of the Father and Daughter

The outstanding question that remains is the relationship of Hong Kingston's father, Tom Hong, to the intertextual process that would eventually produce *The Woman Warrior* and *China Men*. In *The Woman Warrior* the narrator's father exists as a "shadow creature in the world and in the book of the other sex" (Rabine, 475). In *China Men*, he is introduced as a man of curse words, savage screams, and dreadful silences who refuses to communicate or talk-story. "I want to hear the stories about the rest of your life, the Chinese stories. I want to know what makes you scream and curse, and what you're thinking when you say nothing, and why when you talk, you talk differently from Mother" (15). The daughter's pressing need to fathom the dark void alienating the father not only from his family but also from himself prompts her to reconstruct his past, and it is this act of storytelling that draws her into the past histories of other *China Men*. He resembles the writing subject whom Kristeva placed "at the very origin of narration" as "an anonymity, an absence, a blank space" (*Desire in Language*, 74). He does not, however, corroborate her theory that the writer disappears in intertextuality. On the contrary, it is the father's "emptiness" as a character that compels the daughter to step into the breach at the outset of *China Men* as a narrative and dialogic writer. "I'll tell you what I suppose from your silences and few words, and you can tell me that I'm mistaken. You'll just have to speak up with the real stories if I've got you wrong" (15).

In 1989, Hong Kingston admitted to the interviewer Paul Skenazy that these lines were written to provoke a reaction from her father. Her challenge did indeed elicit a response, one that was literary and intertextual, in which her father inserted himself into *China Men* by writing "responses, corrections, additions" in the margins of the text ("Kingston at the University," 155). These annotations had a symbolic importance exceeding their textual position as marginalia. They constituted both a translation and a rewriting of *China Men*. For her father's notes were, in effect, amendments to a pirated, Cantonese version of Hong Kingston's English publication. In making revisions to a cheap pirate edition of her text, Tom Hong was reclaiming his own lost identity and dignity as a Chinese writer, defending his daughter's artistic integrity, and entering into that "dialogue of two discourses" (Kristeva, *Desire in Language*, 75) that is a defining structure of intertextuality. Hong Kingston herself felt she was reclaiming her father when she read what he wrote. "But what makes me feel really good is that this is communication between me and my father, and maybe this is the best and only way that we will ever communicate; maybe it serves us right because we're both writers" (Skenazy, "Kingston at the University," 155).

China Men begins with a profound sense of failure and frustration at the breakdown of communication. The personal relationship that is rebuilt intertextually occurs through writing but requires the engagement of each side in the textual activity of the other. The emotionally charged nature of these intertextual relations can be measured by the subsequent actions of father and daughter. Hong Kingston displayed her father's annotated Hong Kong edition of *China Men* at a Bancroft library reception held at Berkeley to showcase their collection of her papers. When her father was shown his notations, she poignantly recalled how "he looks and he's really surprised, wide eyes, big smile, and this joy, this joy." She beheld a face that she barely recognized as a child, and that readers only glimpse in an early, fleeting sentence of *China Men*. "Father, I have seen you lighthearted" (11). While Hong Kingston saw the imagined father of childhood, Tom Hong saw a wished for life that he never achieved in America. "And he starts turning around to all these people and he says in English, 'My writing, my writing!'" (Skenazy, "Kingston at the University," 155). Most noteworthy for his daughter were the "wonderful" comments about women he wrote in the margins of the sexist passages of *China Men*. When she finished this book back in 1979, she described it as "written with a man's point of view. There are hardly any women in it" (Horton, 7). Her father's commentary introduces a more balanced gender perspective onto the textual page and indicates that the men and women in Hong Kingston's stories may have had more sympathy for each other's point of view than is first apparent in the two books. Tom Hong's "wonderful" comments may also have had private meaning for the writer because they heal the rift the father figure leaves behind in *China Men* of pathological misogyny. "That you did not mean to make me sicken at being female . . . . I want you to say to me 'I didn't mean you or your mother. I didn't mean your sisters or grandmothers or women in general'" (14). Thus, the intertextual dialogue can engender a movement of reconciliation. Writing brings not only father and daughter, but men and women back in touch with one another on the same page, and it further suggests that the texts that kept them apart, *The Woman Warrior* and *China Men*, need to be understood in relationship to one another.

Intertextual Reading and Writing

As Jody Hoy noted in her interview with Hong Kingston, the author became a storyteller like her mother, and a writer and teacher like her father (60). In *The Woman Warrior* she paid tribute to her mother's "great power" to talk-story (25), and in *China Men* she recuperated her father's lost competence as a scholar poet. Indeed, as both E. D. Huntley and Diane Simmons suggest, her highly educated father was the exception who challenged American preconceptions of the illiterate and uncultured Chinese "coolie."[37] His mandarin education in China included training in the intertextual practice of reading, writing, interpreting, and rewording classical verse. She explained, "What they used to do in the old days is a poet would write a poem and then another one would do a response, or one would do a part of a poem, somebody else finish it, or you write commentary on various texts" (Skenazy, "Kingston at the University," 155). Although neither of her parents was literate in English, they were both highly literate in Chinese.

Indeed, the daughter narrator proudly tells the reader of *China Men* that her BaBa and MaMa "were exceptionally smart, the proof being their literacy" (30). Hong Kingston recalled that her mother and father frequently read Chinese poetry and recited it at home (Bonetti, 41; Marilyn Chin, 98–99; Horton, 7). They thus showed their young daughter that utterance and text, reading—whether in silence or aloud—and writing, an oral and written tradition, all existed on a dynamic continuum. They also demonstrated the interchangeable nature of the relationship intertextuality generates between the writer and reader. Kristeva proposed that in intertextual dialogism, the writer's main interlocutor "is the writer himself, but as reader of another text. The one who writes is the same as the one who reads" (*Desire in Language*, 86–87). In her theory, both the reader and writer are eventually swallowed like Jonah by the whale and absorbed into a textual digestive tract where they become "no more than a text rereading itself as it rewrites itself" (87); however, Anglo-American theorists, especially feminists, have resisted this depersonalization of literary activity. Hong Kingston herself ironically observed to Laura Skandera-Trombley that English departments sometimes forget that "there's a life that's not the text" (*Critical Essays*, 36). On the whole, these critics have felt less of a need to engage in Harold Bloom's Oedipal rivalry with the author for textual authority and have seen that intertextuality leads to a merger of the writer and reader. The text and its dynamic meanings are produced by all the intertexts that the writer/reader brings to it.[38]

In interviews, Hong Kingston has emphasized the fact that her identity as a writer is inseparable from that of reader and that "what I am is a person who has built my mind on what I read" (Blauvelt, 79). Her intertextual understanding of literary creativity is evident in the course she taught at Berkeley on "Reading for Writers" (Skandera-Trombley, *Critical Essays*, 38). She recalls first hearing and emulating the rhythmic language of her mother as she chanted the legend of Fa Mu Lan[39] and of her parents as they sang poetry in unison (Horton, 7; Marilyn Chin, 99; Skenazy, "Kingston at the University," 122). As we have seen, it was not Chinese spoken language and literature, but written English, that she learned to use "in a very poetic way," yet so as to preserve the oral cadences of her natal tongue (Skenazy, "Kingston at the University," 128). In fact, her earliest writing was poetry, and this was an intertextual beginning and act of enlargement in which she elaborated "the rhythm and rhyme of language" in the remembered voices of her mother and father and felt her literary power grow "bigger and bigger and bigger" (Perry, 177). Although her writing evolved and diversified, she has continued to "read a lot of poetry. I keep up, as much as possible, with modern American poetry and I think that I'm very influenced by its rhythms" (Islas and Yalom, 25).

Intertexts That Cross Genre and Gender in
The Woman Warrior and China Men

If Hong Kingston's "greatest enjoyment in life is to read" (Perry, 171), and if she has read widely, poetry has remained a source of the indescribably intense and sensual pleasure that Kristeva names feminine *jouissance* and traced to the semiotic rhythms of the maternal body.[40] It has been a powerhouse of the complex feeling that her own creative writing consciously strives to "translate well" (*WW*, 186), and it has furnished some of the intertexts that left so deep an impression on her as a reader that she felt compelled to find some way of working them into *The Woman Warrior* and *China Men*. For example, Walt Whitman's vision of men and women singing harmony in *Leaves of Grass* helped shape Hong Kingston's first major writing project—the inclusive gender narrative that finally separated out into two books. This rhythmic coming-and-going movement of the two sexes is horribly parodied in "On Discovery," the opening intertext of *China Men*. Here women servants sing a lilting refrain to their bound male captive, Tang Ao, emblematic of the over-and-under pattern of a traditional footbinding song—"toes over and under one another like a knot of ginger root"[41]—and the occasional knots and ligatures of intertextual transmission "as they wound the bandages tight and tighter around his feet" (4). Yet, in general, her intertextual parody of Walt Whitman afforded more moments of pleasure than pain. This male poet would return to life as the comic character Wittman Ah Sing, and the liberating play of gender language in *Leaves of Grass* would resonate in the zing, yin, and yang of Hong Kingston's later novel *Tripmaster Monkey*.[42]

Likewise Ezra Pound's poetic experimentation with Chinese ideograms would inspire Hong Kingston to "paint little ideograms out of myth" in *China Men*, as she confirmed to Kay Bonetti in 1986 (39, 41). These myth stories, rich in visual symbols, are interpolated between the men's stories and function as allegorical interlocution on their actions. As E. D. Huntley has pointed out, *China Men* is "a literal translation of the Chinese ideograph for the word Chinese" and was pejoratively used as a racial denomination. Hong Kingston gives this ideograph a prominent and honored place on the title page of the book's six main chapters. Indeed, Huntley argues that the author uses this ideograph as her personal "chop" and so claims the character for both Chinese men and women (115–116). David Leiwei Li further argues that Hong Kingston's use of Pound's ideogram can be seen as a reappropriation of Chinese pictographic script from the Orientalist discourse of the West, a reappropriation that is perfectly consistent with the backward-and-forward, coming-and-going movement of intertextuality. Lee Quinby even suggests that *The Woman Warrior* constructs an "ideographic subjectivity" that is intricate, dialogic, and interconnected like the Chinese "I" with seven strokes that the narrator first learned as a character in *The Woman Warrior*. This ideographic character projects a more multiformed point of view than the straight up-and-down-and-across "I" of American English that the girl puzzles over as she learns to read (*WW*, 150).[43] Just as the unconscious knows no negation, so the ideographic "I" resists the separation and truncation that led Hong Kingston to split *The Woman Warrior* off from *China Men* in the first place.

Other Intertextual Influences

Hong Kingston has also spoken admiringly of modern writers who traverse the formal divide between poetry and prose, such as Grace Paley and Cynthia Ozick (Islas and Yalom, 25). In *The Woman Warrior*, her narrator struggles to break out of the categories in which she felt pigeonholed not only as a young woman and a Chinese American, but also as a writer. On reflection, as she told Eric J. Schroeder in 1996, she saw that both *The Woman Warrior* and *China Men* led a literary trend with their textual synthesis of different forms—from oral and written storytelling, to poetic myth, fantasy, and history, to imaginative biography, autobiography, and fiction (216). Yet, she complained to Laura Skandera-Trombley, in 1998, that critics still carried on trying to categorize her work (34).

In an earlier interview with Donna Perry, in 1991, there is evidence of a keen interest in writing that crosses borders and divisions: "Isn't it interesting that a lot of poets lately seem to be writing prose and prose poems, and then you see short-story writers who are writing novels, novelists who are writing nonfiction, nonfiction people who are writing fiction" (179). In fact, one of the most influential books that Hong Kingston read was *In the American Grain*, a mythic and elegiac history of America written by the poet William Carlos Williams, friend of Ezra Pound, in 1925. She has repeatedly described the huge impact that his narrative made on her. Indeed, her active reader response to his text motivated her as a writer and suggested the form that *China Men* should take. "I thought that [*In the American Grain*] was the truest book of American history I had ever read. And he did it mythically, and I wanted to do American history in that same way, especially for *China Men*" (Bonetti, 38–39; Pfaff, 15; Seshachari, 211–212). The other work to which Hong Kingston was "strongly attached" (Bonetti, 38) and that was linked in her mind with *In the American Grain* was Virginia Woolf's *Orlando*. Although Woolf's narrative was far more outlandish than Williams' history, what caught her imagination was the idea of "a person who could be a man and a woman, a person who could live for hundreds of years" (Bonetti, 39). However far apart they may have appeared culturally and artistically, both Woolf and Williams produced intertexts that showed her how to crisscross genre, gender, time, and history.

The energy driving their narratives made her feel free and alive as a reader and gave her the raw courage to imagine that "I can now write as a man, I can write as a black person, as a white person; I don't have to be restricted by time and physicality" (Fisher Fishkin, 161). Williams told the story of early American history up until the Civil War, but did so poetically as well as mythically. He represented President Lincoln through a leap of imagination akin to Woolf's—as both a mother and father to the nation. After Hong Kingston had finished writing the checkered history of mothers in *The Woman Warrior*, she had to find a format that would allow fathers to emerge from the shadow of forceful women in a book of their own. It may have helped her get *China Men* "out from under" *The Woman Warrior* by imagining it as volume 2 of Williams' *In The American Grain* (Marilyn Chin, 100–101). She remarked on several occasions that she "directly continued" this history, picking up where he left off in 1860, by telling the story of the Chinese Americans who came after the Civil War and thus carrying his narrative forward into the present.[44] As her title indicates, however, *China Men* is no simple extension or sequel to his work, but an intertextual act in which she further complicates his story and makes restitution to her excluded male ancestors. She depicts Chinese railroad builders as the next wave of pioneers to "band the country back together again" and help forge a new nation, and so advances the claim of her people to a crucial place in American history (Bonetti, 39; Marilyn Chin, 101). In her own Chinese American restatement of Lincoln's Gettysburg Address, she famously declared, "We're not outsiders, we belong here, this is our country, this is our history, and we are part of America. We are part of American history. If it weren't for us, America would be a different place. When I write I also claim America in a literary way, an artistic way" (Islas and Yalom, 25).

Intertextuality and Appropriation of America

Hong Kingston was clearly laying claim here to her own special niche as a pioneer writer in the history and the canon of American literature.[45] Whereas Sau-ling Wong notes that critical comparativists may now wish to develop "cross-readings of 'ethnic minority' literary works, bypassing the dominant center of the Anglo-American canon,"[46] Hong Kingston shows little inclination to follow this course either as a reader or writer. Despite her own recognition in both *The Woman Warrior* and *China Men* that her family "landed in a country where we are eccentric people" (*CM*, 15), her intertextual approach is to try and expand—not bypass—the center. In this, she resembles the ex-riverboat pirate, Great-Uncle Kau Goong, who refuses to return to China and declares defiantly, "California. This is my home. I belong here" (*CM*, 184). As she was telling the story of her Chinese kin in *The Woman Warrior* and *China Men*, she became conscious that she "was building, creating, myself and these people as American people. . . . Also, I am creating part of American literature . . . . The critics haven't recognized my work enough as another tradition of American literature" (Rabinowitz, 71–72). She also echoes the ethical stance of her brother in Vietnam, who enlists in the Navy rather than "live the rest of his life a fugitive and an exile. The United States was the only country he had ever lived in. He would not be driven out" (*CM*, 283).[47]

Hong Kingston's productivity as a creative writer derived from ambitious reading activity in which, as Kristeva theorized, "the one who writes is the same as the one who reads" (*Desire in Language*, 87). As a writer simultaneously reading other texts, Hong Kingston understood intertextuality as preeminently the work of "appropriation" and was determined to appropriate "these books and this language—the American language. I'm going to appropriate this country" (Skenazy, "Kingston at the University," 144; Rabinowitz, 72). On a cautionary note, the concept of "appropriation" has become a loaded gun in Asian American critical studies, and it has sometimes been cocked and pointed at the head of Hong Kingston herself because she dared to adopt and adulterate Chinese and American cultural sources.[48] Perhaps because she first spoke a "vulgar" tongue, Hong Kingston was not linguistically predisposed to read China or America as pure, monologic cultures and saw their respective literary traditions as offering opportunities for "appropriation, parody and play" (Shapiro, 6). She absorbed, responded to, and sometimes reinvented what she read in her own writing. Yet her uppermost aim in appropriation was to expand the definition of the language and the literature so that it stretched from the Old World to the New, and from a Western to a Chinese canon of influential intertexts, and developed the textual capacity to tell the story of Chinese as "my fellow Americans." Cognizance of this intertextual exercise of appropriation and enlargement will enable readers to reconcile the author's statement that she is "telling a human story" that is "very specifically Chinese American" in *The Woman Warrior* and *China Men* with the view that these same "books are much more American than they are Chinese" and the assertion that she was claiming a literary stake for Chinese in America, with the proviso that she didn't "have just a Chinese American audience in mind" (Perry, 178; Rabinowitz, 71; Islas and Yalom, 24–25). Indeed, Elliott Shapiro argues that Hong Kingston "is less interested in writing a novel which is authentically Chinese-American," according to the terms of cultural essentialists, "than in writing a novel which is, on her own terms, authentically American" (6).

Intertextuality and the Creation of a Literary Family

Hong Kingston felt she was "writing for everyone" (Hoy, 63), but the intertextual corollary was that she was also reading everyone. She remarked that "one of the first things I ever noticed and loved about reading is that words can get through all kinds of barriers; they can get through skin color and culture" (Fisher Fishkin, 163). The conviction that serious reading is a discriminating activity that it can break down racial, gender, and ethnic discrimination lies behind the following personal statement. "I never thought of myself as a Chinese writer. I feel that I am descended from Walt Whitman and Nathaniel Hawthorne and Virginia Woolf, and then a Chinese man told me how much *Tripmaster Monkey* reminded him of the *Dream of the Red Chamber*—and so they showed me that I have my roots in Chinese writing" (Fisher Fishkin, 166–167). Notably, it is a Chinese reader engaged in intertextual dialogue with the author who shows her a new way of reading her own work and who precipitates her circular movement from simple denial of being a "Chinese writer" to a more complex politics of literary and cultural identity.[49] We have already seen that Woolf's *Orlando* "broke through constraints of time, of gender, of culture." The woman writer Woolf enabled Hong Kingston to forget the "he and she" that produced binary divisions in language and society, as did the male poet Whitman, who further constructed the connectives that joined "man and woman" in a common cause (Seshachari, 212).

It is interesting to note that Hong Kingston positions Nathaniel Hawthorne (1804–1864) as the nonsequential middle link in a literary descent line that runs from Whitman (1819–1892) to Woolf (1882–1941). Most readers of *The Woman Warrior* become aware that Hawthorne's portrait of the wronged adulteress Hester Prynne is one of the intertexts that they should know in order to fully understand the first of Hong Kingston's women stories, "No Name Woman." The more perceptive have the intertextual awareness that "reading [her] story in relation to Hawthorne not only changed *The Woman Warrior* but changed the Hawthorne novel as well."[50] There has been little awareness, however, that this intertext is equally important for a reading of the father passages of *China Men*. Hawthorne named his novel after the scarlet letter that Hester must sew during the course of her pregnancy and then wear on her breast after the birth of her illegitimate child and release from prison as the public mark of her sexual transgression. For the intertextual reader, the scarlet letter is a reminder of the ambiguous and multiform nature of the textual sign. Hester is a highly skilled embroiderer, and her elaborate cross-weave and "fantastic flourishes of gold thread"[51] give the textual surface of the letter *A* hidden dimensions. Moreover, her needlework incites alternative readings that defy the censor of a judgmental Puritan community, release what is unsaid and taboo, and eventually lead to reconciliation between her and the man who wronged her, for the *A* is also a secret reminder to Hester of Arthur Dimmesdale, the father that her child Pearl wants to know, claim, and love. If the intertext points to something that is missing from the text, then Hawthorne's *Scarlet Letter* with its hidden allusion to a daughter's need to name her own father and obtain his recognition is as important for understanding the development of *China Men* as it is the opening of *The Woman Warrior*.

Like Williams' *In the American Grain*, Hawthorne's narrative weaves a lyric subtext into the prose as it gradually transforms Hester's scarlet letter into a poetic and pictorial ideogram. This ideogram grows in emblematic complexity like the woman who weaves it and wears it over her heart. For it is the symbolic handiwork of a mother-to-be who broods on the lives that go into its making and sees that they are joined forever more in a secret family. Eventually this richly embroidered *A* ceases to be seen as a brand of adultery altogether and instead becomes a blazon that embodies her passionate inner life, textual creativity, and tangible connection to her daughter and the father of her child. Beyond this, the scarlet letter signifies the reconciling power of poetry—which Audre Lorde called the power to "give name to the nameless so it can be thought."[52] Hong Kingston herself recommends that the readers of her work "let [such] images come inside of themselves for the images to do their work. Something amazing happens with images and metaphor: we see these pictures, and they go inside of our imaginations, and our imaginations change. So I hope that people will allow themselves to change as they are reading the books" (Perry, 185).

Successful male novelists who created extraordinary women characters such as Hester Prynne could triumphantly proclaim, in the unforgettable words of Flaubert, "Madame Bovary, c'est moi." Kristeva's retort in "Women's Time" (1981) is that "today many women imagine, 'Flaubert, c'est moi'" (*Kristeva Reader*, 207). No contemporary woman writer would understood her burning remark about female literary ambition and appropriation of male authorial identity better than Hong Kingston. Indeed, Kristeva's intertextual rejoinder to Flaubert can function as an interpretative commentary on *China Men*. As the author said herself, "When I was working on *China Men*, I remember reading a critic who was praising the great male writers, like Flaubert and Tolstoy and Dostoevsky and Henry James, who were able to write great women characters . . . . I remember thinking that to finish myself as a great artist I'd have to be able to create men characters" (Perry, 178).

These European novelists join Hawthorne, Whitman, Woolf, and Williams in a far-flung dialogic network that Hong Kingston melodiously describes as "voices calling out to one another across a vast continent." She imagines these voices as those of a vast dialogic community of "writers both living and dead" whose words are still audible to readers and whose sounds carry across barriers of time, convention, culture, country, race, and gender (Hoy, 50–51). Members of this community she mentions by name and describes as if they constitute an extensive support group include mainstream American male writers such as John Steinbeck, Ernest Hemingway, Herman Melville, William Faulkner, Allen Ginsberg, Jack Kerouac, Garrison Keillor, Norman Mailer, Philip Roth, and Gary Synder; Asian American writers such as Jade Snow Wong, Amy Tan, Frank Chin, Tony Chin, Laurence Yep, David Hwang, Ruth-Anne Lumm McKunn, Jessica Hagedorn, and Steven Lo; Asian writers in English such as Bharati Mukherjee and Kazou Ishiguro; women writers of color such as Toni Morrison and Alice Walker; the black "roots" writer Alex Haley; and traditionalist, high cultural, or canonical Western writers such as Louisa May Alcott, James Joyce, Rainer Maria Rilke, Charles Dickens, William Butler Yeats, and William Shakespeare.[53] The polyphony reverberating through this intertextual network gave her the license to write English differently, so it captures the intonations of dialectal Chinese spoken "with an American accent" (Pfaff, 17; see also Marilyn Chin, 100, and Islas and Yalom, 27). The narrator of *The Woman Warrior* "can see the disgust on American faces" as they observe her Cantonese community "make guttural peasant noise," "everybody talking at once," "spit flying" (154). But she develops the acuteness to hear the poetry in the commonplace and sometimes harsh-sounding language of her own people.

Intertextuality and the Art of Listening

Hong Kingston's intertextual practice is also distinguished by the belief that the aspiring writer could only "go the distance" as "reader of another text"

(Kristeva, *Desire in Language*, 86) if she learned to be a good listener. In writing "About Chinese Women (1974)," a subject in which she was a novice, Kristeva nonetheless made a valid general observation that women must take this further step "by listening; by recognizing the unspoken in all discourse" (*Kristeva Reader*, 156); however, she had not made this step explicit earlier in her elegant intertextual equation, where "the one who writes is the same as the one who reads" (*Desire in Language*, 87). Hong Kingston insists that "we listen for what is said, but also what's not said" and invoked "the Bodhisattva of compassionate listening, Kuan Yin, the goddess of mercy" to help her in reading and listening for what can be heard beyond the words.[54] She also acknowledged that the oral and poetic culture of her family made her "open to hearing talk-story" (Skenazy, "Kingston at the University," 149) and thus taught her early the importance of receptivity. She listened to her mother and female relatives "for what is said"—not only in *The Woman Warrior*, but also in *China Men*. "A great many of the men's stories were ones I originally heard from women" (Pfaff, 18; Rabinowitz, 70). But she heard the "not said" by straining to listen to her father's sounds of silence. At the end of *China Men*, she felt that the struggle to hear the inaudible other and become a compassionate listener also made her a better reader and narrator (Blauvelt, 81; Marilyn Chin, 91). For this reason, she counsels the college readers who only skim the surface of *The Woman Warrior* and *China Men* or "speed read" in order to meet a writing deadline that they should be more receptive and reflective "I want them to have their hearts and their minds and their eyes open as they are reading . . . and to read with their feelings. It's not just an intellectual book" (Perry, 185).

Few scholars have been trained to read in this spiritual way or are inclined to give the critical mind a rest for a while, to let the words sink in and stir deeper feelings and insight. For academics who take theoretical pride in probing critique, interrogation of texts, and resistance to their meanings, Hong Kingston's advice will be especially hard to swallow. "Some people resist feeling by trying to understand my work as a Chinese book. . . . And they understand it intellectually that way, but I see that as a sign of a person who's denying their own identity and their own feelings" (Perry, 178). She thus strongly recommends that we read in intertextual sympathy with the spirit of her writing—which is that of imaginative contemplation open to the inspiration, change, and transformation inherent in a vital storytelling tradition. Indeed, she insisted that "the way I keep the old Chinese myths alive is by telling them in a new American way" (Pfaff, 18).[55] As we will recall, the oral culture of talk-story taught her structural openness. "Talk-story actually reverberates. These stories don't end, they didn't have a beginning. I just wrote down parts of them. In talk-story, every time you tell a story it changes, it grows" (Skenazy, "Kingston at the University," 149). Indeed, she acknowledged to Neila Seshachari, in 1993, that she deliberately left the close of both *The Woman Warrior* and *China Men* unfinished and open ended (192–193), like the talk-stories she heard as a child. Two years earlier, she had disclosed the fact that, in rereading these two books, and their provisional endings, she felt an intertextual impulse to "rewrite them, but in a different way." Her lament—"I don't mean to rewrite; it's just that, as I'm reading it, I see what I ought to do" (Perry, 174)—bears out the internal law of intertextuality that writing and reading are overlapping relational or palimpsestuous activities (Genette, 399). It is also consistent with her own conviction as a writer that "reading . . . finishes this act of creativity" (Skenazy, "Kingston at the University," 119).[56]

Hong Kingston also insists that the writer must be open minded and make an effort "to understand things from other peoples' point of view" in order to "arrive at being able to love the people you write about and resolve the angers" (Skenazy, "Kingston at the University," 121). Though this may sound overly sentimental, it is important to remember how highly charged the intertextual relations between writer, reader, and creator of texts can become. The flamboyant literary quarrel that flared up between the talented writer Frank Chin and Hong Kingston after Alfred A. Knopf decided to publish *The Woman Warrior* under the classification of nonfiction autobiography is a melodramatic case in point. Chin attacked her autobiographical writing as a travesty of authentic Chinese culture and Chinese American experience. He argued that she had appropriated a Christian confessional form that gave white feminist readers, in particular, the voyeuristic pleasure of seeing Chinese males depicted as sexist oppressors of women. The publication of *China Men* led to an escalation in the "pen wars" that had begun over the way genre could lead to a misrepresentation of gender. In *The Big Aiiieeeee!* (1991), Chin ridiculed textual narratives constructed on the confident feminist assumption that "all women are victims. America and Christianity represent freedom from Chinese civilization. In the Christian yin/yang of the dual personality identity crisis, Chinese evil and perversity is male," but women are unconscious of their racist reading of Asian American men as degenerate or emasculated.[57] Though Hong Kingston initially tried to address Chin's charges in personal correspondence, arguing that she did not want to write polemical literature rebutting the racism and so simply "provide the other half of the dialogue, the yin to his yang, as it were (Leiwei Li, *Critical Essays*, 183), she claimed that he sent her threatening letters in reply (Simmons, 40). Just as the narrator of "No Name

Woman" claims that "my aunt haunts me" and does not "always mean me well" (22), so Hong Kingston concluded in almost identical words that "I think [Chin] does not mean me well" (Seshachari, 202). In response to his "hate mail," she conceived *Tripmaster Monkey* as "a kind of big love letter" (Blauvelt, 81). As Nora Ephron did in the 1998 film *You've Got Mail*, she made a comedy of their sexual politics by creating a central character in Wittman Ah Sing who has components of both her own and Chin's personality. Like the love-hate relationship of the principal characters in the Ephron film, there is also on Hong Kingston's part, at least, a flickering recognition that she and Chin might be alter egos. She told William Satake Blauvelt, in 1989, "I do resemble him in real life." Indeed, like the men and women of *The Woman Warrior* and *China Men*, Hong Kingston and Chin appeared to lead separate but parallel lives. "We were born exactly the same year, we identify with being dragons and come from northern California. . . . We went to school [at Berkeley at] exactly the same time . . . and had the same teachers. I think he may have been the only Chinese American male English major of that period. I may have been the only Chinese American girl English major" (80). Nevertheless, she later maintained to Neila Seshachari that they "never met" and could not be more different (202–203). It is clear that Hong Kingston and Chin love to hate, read, parody, and ventriloquize each other in their writing. As Skandera-Trombley points out, "Both are locked in a continuing response to each other" (6), one that dramatizes how intertextuality can develop into a full-blown passion play.[58] The capacity to read with feeling and to write with compassion is, then, an important safety device when intertextuality gets personal—that is to say, when powerful emotions are triggered in the dynamic transference and interchange of roles.

Intertextuality and Psychoanalysis

Hong Kingston's reading and writing techniques are consistent with Kristeva's view that "the concept of intertextuality encompasses both novel and poetry" (Waller, *Interviews*, 192). Kristeva reserves her special admiration for "the modern novel which incorporates the poetic experience in an intertextual manner" (194).[59] *The Woman Warrior* and *China Men* are prime examples of such a syncretic form and offer considerable scope for intertextual study. Notably, Kristeva also believed that the writers of such a form may sometimes "manage to lead us as deeply as possible into our malaises, where we seldom go except in dreams" (195). In both her books, Hong Kingston leads us down into the underworld of dreams where, as Freud saw, nothing is impossible and everything can mean its opposite.[60] Indeed, she thought that one of her most important undertakings as a life writer was to "know what the other person dreams and how her imagination works" (Seshachari, 198).

Kristeva's theoretical interest in intertextuality led her into the realm of psychoanalysis, because she saw that, if words are connected to utterance, they must also resonate with remembered voices and associated feelings that still have primitive life deep within the core of the psyche. For this reason, she argued, "We would have to turn to the psychic aspect of writing as trace of a dialogue with oneself (with another), as a writer's distance from himself, as a splitting of the writer into subject of enunciation and subject of utterance" (*Desire in Language*, 74). Hong Kingston has been frank about the fact that she talked to people in her head as a child and, what is more, that her psychic aptitude for introjection, where things, events, and persons are taken into the mind and become objects of primal fantasy or principals in internal dialogue, gave her the gift of literary invention (Hoy, 64). After her father's death, in 1991, she drew comfort from her writer's habit of imagining a dialogue in the mind and felt that it kept her relationship with him alive and ongoing (Seshachari, 201). The critical theorist Seán Hand further defines this interior dialogue as a "listening process in which a narrative is composed from an interaction between at least two persons, who in fact always turn out to be more than two."[61] Moreover, he sees this listening process as the activity that links psychoanalysis and intertextuality and that makes the relationship of the reader to the writer in intertextual exchange analogous to that of the analyst and analysand in psychoanalytic transference.

In the dynamics of psychoanalytic transference, the analysand talks-story and, in the process, projects inner dialogues or fantasies onto the listening analyst. Hand argues that this act of transference "creates an intertexual space in which the story changes as it is listened to and worked on" (79). Hong Kingston also summoned words to her aid as "a medium to get to the seemingly subconscious" (Rabinowitz, 68). The Cantonese pidgin English of talk-story was a natural medium because, as we have already seen, it was "the language used at home, the language of childhood and the sub-conscious, the language used in emotion" (Lim, "Chinese American Women's Life Stories," 265). Indeed, she described the production of *The Woman Warrior* and *China Men* as a seven-year process, akin to a long and arduous rite of psychoanalytic passage, in which "you go into the subconscious by not writing and then you make it normal consciousness by writing. Then you rewrite until you are working almost mechanically" (Islas and Yalom, 26). And, like Kristeva, she understood that the mystique of words derives from the radioactive traces they emit of a past that is never dead and buried. This past carries on a subterranean life in the unconscious but can well up into the conscious present through dreams, word association, automatic writing, and what Ana-Maria Rizzuto memorably sums up as "the ceaseless creativity of the human mind."[62] In response to Paula Rabinowitz, who noted how her words in the two books function as active memory traces, she explained, "My stories have a constant breaking in and out of the present and past. So the reader might be walking along very well in the present, but the past breaks through and changes and enlightens the present, and vice versa. The reason that we remember a past moment at all is that our present-day life is still a working out of a similar situation" (68).

Intertextual Traces of the Parents

Freud made the memorable comment in *The Interpretation of Dreams* that "being in love with the one parent and hating the other are among the essential constituents of [formative] psychical impulses" (362). More particularly, Hong Kingston's words in *The Woman Warrior* and *China Men* contain Oedipal traces of the parents and family relations who first arouse powerful, primary emotions of love and hate. Doris Lessing reminisced that "we use our parents like recurring dreams, to be entered into when needed; they are always there for love or for hate."[63] In "Revolution in Poetic Language," Kristeva explored the psychical traces of the mother that were still to be found in language and textuality (*Kristeva Reader*, 93). Hong Kingston felt that her foremothers gave her the magic of words with their "power to remind" in *The Woman Warrior* (26). As she exclaimed to Jody Hoy in 1986, "Those women who are so marvelous, so magic, so overwhelming took my life and my abilities and said, 'Write about us'" (64). Although male critics have traditionally focused on the role of forefathers and the paterfamilias in the Oedipal struggle of the writer with the past (Worton and Still, 28–29), Hong Kingston here describes the mother as the dominant figure who demands words of her as a writer. But the correlative of this is that her father fades into the background of *The Woman Warrior* and it is hard work to recover his traces in *China Men*.

The critical modifications that Riffaterre makes to Kristeva's theory of intertextuality can prove helpful in locating the father figure in *China Men*, for his work foregrounds the active role that the reader plays in the recovery of the traces of an intertext (Clayton and Rothstein, 23; Worton and Still, 26–27). Riffaterre suggests that syllepsis is one of the figures of speech that can alert the reader to the presence of an intertext. He defines syllepsis as a word "that has two mutually incompatible meanings, one acceptable in the context in which the word appears, the other valid only in the intertext to which the word also belongs and that it represents at the surface of the text, as the tip of an iceberg." He emphasizes the fact that, "as a word, the syllepsis has two meanings, each of which generates its own derivation in its separate text; yet as a connective, it has no meaning of its own" ("Compulsory reader response," 71).[64]

The tenuous link of resemblance in syllepsis is homophony or a homonym, where words are either pronounced or spelled the same but have different meanings. As Linda Ching Sledge notes, "Written Chinese is pictographic and homonymic, a language of visual symbols and aural puns continually pointing away from the visible surface of linguistic signs to meanings lying deeper than the signs themselves" ("Oral Tradition," 145). In fact, Hong Kingston described her father's command of classical Chinese as a mastery of the "music of homonyms. You can have a sound and then maybe ten words are the same sound, but the way you get meaning is by the tone, the pitch. And the other way that you get the meaning is the context, meaning does come from relationships, which are not just linguistic but familiar as well" (Skenazy, "Kingston at the University," 147). Riffaterre evocatively calls syllepsis "a lexical Janus, one word with two faces" ("Compulsory reader response," 72). But in *China Men*, this is a figure with many more faces, like Joseph Campbell's mythical hero.[65] Indeed, this father figure sometimes takes delight in the aural punning that characterizes syllepsis. In "The Making of More Americans," the narrator of *China Men* recalls how her "Fourth Grandfather," Say Goong, explained syllepsis to her as a child. "'A field chicken?' I repeated. 'Field chicken,' he said. 'Sky chicken. Sky toad. Heavenly toad. Field toad.' It was a pun and the words the same except for the low tone of *field* and the high tone of *heaven* or *sky*. . . . How odd that a toad could be both of the field and of the sky. It was very funny" (166). But it could also be very sad, as in an intertext like *The Scarlet Letter*, where Arthur Dimmesdale represents both a heavenly and earthly father. Hong Kingston has been accused of mistranslating such Cantonese words.[66] In this linguistically rich and instructive Shakespearean scene, Hong Kingston transforms the toad intertextually from a language lesson into an object lesson that human nature can be "ugly and venomous" but noble proof that "sweet are the uses of adversity."[67]

"Father" and "Grandfather" are homonyms frequently employed in *China Men*, not only for male relatives from the same family, but also for paternal characters split in two as in syllepsis and given different starting points, journeys, adventures, and meanings in Hong Kingston's male narrative.[68] As she stated when *China Men* was first published, "I have a father character who comes up in various guises throughout the book. He is really only one character, but I call him different things, like 'the legal father,' 'the illegal father,' 'the father from China' and 'the American father.' In the course of the book, I have him coming into this country in five different ways" (Pfaff, 16–17). Yet, as she also acknowledges, not all of these figures are "blood relatives" or indeed fathers at all. Some are addressed politely as "uncles"; others are brothers, distant relatives, or villagers. As LeiLani Nishime observes, there are "more grandfathers [in *China Men*] than is biologically possible," and this is because these "grandfathers" are not simply the eccentrics who give her narrative its rich and complex character, but "a type or a generic forefather whose story is representative of many Chinese-American immigrants" (3). With its tension of apparent likeness and inherent dissimilarity, closeness, and distance, syllepsis becomes a good metaphor for the strained relationship between the daughter and the father in *The Woman Warrior* and *China Men*.

Following the logic of syllepsis, Hong Kingston's "father" also illustrates Riffaterre's paradox that the sylleptic figure is "both represented and missing" ("Compulsory reader response," 73). In *The Woman Warrior*, he is the someone or "something . . . missing from the text" (Riffaterre, "Compulsory reader response," 56) and is a silent reminder of a succession of characters who have "something missing" and whose lives appear as jigsaw pieces in *The Woman Warrior* and *China Men*. The urge to understand the father's puzzling and pointed absence "compels readers to look to the intertext to fill out the text's gaps [and] spell out its implications" (Riffaterre 57), as indeed Hester's daughter puzzles out the identity of her father from the intertext woven into an A on her mother's breast. In other words, there are good theoretical grounds for the insistence that *China Men* is the essential intertext that readers must familiarize themselves with in order to more fully understand *The Woman Warrior*—and vice versa. In intertextual relationship to one another, *The Woman Warrior* and *China Men* represent the father as a figure who is lost but can eventually be found. Poignantly, Hong Kingston lost her father shortly before her home and previous book were destroyed in a California firestorm. "I am sure that our relationship with those people continues to grow and I will continue to resolve my relationship with my father even though he's dead. I can still think of things to say to him. It's too bad that he can't answer, but sometimes he can even answer" (Seshachari, 201). For Riffaterre, syllepsis is at once both the question in the text and the answer in the intertext. The "father" is an enigma in *The Woman Warrior*, and the daughter narrator attempts to figure him out in *China Men*. Death did not end that dialogue in the mind where the writer worked to repeat, remember, and resolve old issues and conflicts.[69]

Intertextuality, Intersubjectivity, and Psychic Reality

Kristeva had maintained that "the notion of intertextuality replaces that of intersubjectivity" (*Desire in Language*, 66); however, it is evident from Hong Kingston's above disclosure about her own father that her intertextual practices are inextricable from an intersubjective concern with "what happens between individuals, and within the individual-with-others."[70] Indeed, her famous narrative declaration—"'I' am nothing but who 'I' am in relation to other people. In *The Woman Warrior* 'I' begin the quest for self by understanding the archetypal mother. In *China Men* 'I' become more whole because of the ability to appreciate the other gender" (Lim, *Approaches*, 23)—underlines the self's intertextual and intersubjective construction.[71] The play of separation and connection that is compressed in syllepsis is also a central drama of psychic life as the individual continually calibrates the distance or closeness, difference or similarity, that should define relations to other people. Jessica Benjamin has helpfully suggested that we imagine inner life as a "continuum that includes the space between the I and the you, as well as the space within me" (95). On this continuum, psychic reality and material reality are not mutually exclusive but interrelated worlds that move toward or away from one another—like the coming-and-going movement of intertextuality—depending on the subject's character and personal needs.[72] The awareness that reality is a tangled web of real and fantasy life explains Hong Kingston's reluctance to classify *The Woman Warrior* and *China Men* categorically as fiction or nonfiction, personal memoir or family history, and to insist, when pressed, that "I am writing biography and autobiography of imaginative people. I am writing about real people, all of whom have minds that love to invent fictions. I am writing the biography of their imaginations" (Rabinowitz, 75; Bonetti, 37). Hong Kingston realized, however, that it was not only how the individual was temperamentally predisposed, but socially constructed, that would determine their take on reality. Indeed, she pointed out that traditional Chinese society gave cultural recognition to invisible realities that Western, empirical thinkers were trained to regard with incredulity. "In our culture the mythic is real. There are people who are people, and there are people that are ghosts doing real things . . . . And there is always the exciting possibility that I will break through into another world that's about to happen" (Hoy, 61; Skenazy, "Kingston at the University," 156).

As Malini Schueller observantly noted, "ghost" is "perhaps the most dialogically used term" in *The Woman Warrior* (430). The Cantonese *kuei* for ghost refers at different points in the book to the restless spirits of the dead, the unmentionable or unfathomable mysteries of the past, white devils or "demons" who make American life so strange and threatening for Cantonese immigrants, and the fears, alarms, and phobias that prey like devils or looming phantoms on the mind. Whereas Hong Kingston's free translation has not found favor among cultural critics or Sinologists, who make authenticity the standard of ethnic autobiography,[73] it has remained true to the intertextual state of mind of the writer/reader—which must be one of give and take. Ghosts keep the passages open between Chinese and American culture, and between the world of women in *The Woman Warrior* and of the menfolk in *China Men*. They enable Hong Kingston to talk, like Virginia Woolf, about silence—the things that people can't say, see, and hear —and that they are dying to know.

Intertextuality, Talk-Story, and Dreams

Hong Kingston's association of intertextuality with intersubjectivity grew out of her sense of a Chinese community where she felt "that we're part of something, that when we're alone writing we're not alone—that the imaginative life and the real life intertwine" (Skenazy, "Coming Home," 110). More specifically it is the social importance that her own family attributed to dream life that helped to build her "faith in the imaginary world" and "in talk-story" (Skenazy, "Kingston at the University," 149; Bonetti, 43) and her confidence in their power to build "a bridge toward reality" and create truth (Rabinowitz, 71; Fisher Fishkin, 160). In a homely anecdote, she even suggests that her family's tradition of talk-story was intertextually connected to their daily dream narratives. "We would wake up in the morning for breakfast, and everybody tells what each other's dreams are. This was confirmed for me when I go to Asia . . . . One of my aunts in Hong Kong came to pick me up. The first thing she asks is 'How is your mother and what is she dreaming?'" (Blauvelt, 82). She incorporated this nostalgic recollection into *China Men* in order to articulate the homesickness of her brother in Vietnam as he wakes to the memory of "mornings in another life, his family had told their dreams while eating breakfast" (292).

Chinese American immigrants like Hong Kingston's parents who made a home for themselves near Stockton's Skid Row lived with the ugly social reality of "stoned people, hoboes, dealers, and criminals." Yet daring feats of imagination embellished and inwardly transformed this reality. Dreams were recounted and interpreted inside the family house, while outside on the dingy streets, vibrant "talk-story [was] going on everywhere" (Skenazy, "Coming Home," 114–115). Hong Kingston made it her "mission" to devise a new kind of writing that would express the unseen creativity of her community and commemorate their capacity for deeper perception of beauty and truth. "I do think it's especially important for minority people, because we're always on the brink of disappearing. Our culture's disappearing and our communities are disappearing" (Fisher Fishkin, 163; Skenazy, "Kingston at the University," 157). True to her community's own spirit of improvisation, she invented the form as she went along in *The Woman Warrior* (Schroeder, 216). It was a textual form woven of dreams, hopes, fantasies, and delusions, fabricating stories that stretched to elaborate the spirit of a people and her girlhood among their ghosts. In the wake of September 11, Hong Kingston's words seem especially haunting. "I think part of what we have to do is figure out a new kind of autobiography that can tell the truth about dreams and visions and prayers. I find that absolutely necessary for our mental and political health. I think the standard autobiography is about exterior things, . . . big historical events that you publicly participate in—and those kinds of autobiographies ignore the rich, personal inner life" (Fisher Fishkin, 163).

Intertextuality and the Inner Life

Hong Kingston's goal as a writer was to get inside of real people, show how their minds worked, and bring their latent drive, energy, and vision to manifest consciousness in her text (Schroeder, 215). When she planned her first major work, however, it soon became apparent to her that the inner man was less accessible than the inner woman. The Chinese men she wanted to write about had, she felt, repressed the memories, myths, and affects that are necessary for a "rich, personal inner life" and cultivated a thick skin to survive the hardships of exile, exploitation, and legal disenfranchisement in America. "Memory just hurts them, because they can't go home. So the myth story and the present story become separated" (Rabinowitz, 69). But she also realized that as manual workers they were forced to be unceasingly active in the external world and did not have much energy to spare for an inward journey.[74] She depicted her own father in *China Men* as a reflective man who toiled until midnight in the New York laundry he ran with his immigrant partners and who paid dearly when he took time off from work. "They had ganged up on him and swindled him out of his share of the laundry. 'You were always reading when we were working'" (73). Such a man could not afford the time to "suffer from reminiscences" as in Kristeva's "Women's Time" (*Kristeva Reader*, 192) and indeed might have come to regard heightened consciousness as a superfluous burden, and introspection as a sign of emasculating inactivity (Holland 48, 74). Hong Kingston explained to Paula Rabinowitz that "the character of my father, for example, has no memory. He has no stories of the past. He is an American and even his memories are provided by the mother. . . . He is so busy making up the present, which he has to build, that he has no time for continuity from the past. It did seem as if the men were people of action" (70).

Whereas Shoshana Felman has argued that the historical oppression of women makes it likely that that they "have no real memory of their auto-biography," the gender problem of narrative before Hong Kingston was quite the reverse: it was the men whose life was largely "a story of amnesia."[75] Their psychical defense against the pain that memory evokes was repression, and this required a more taxing expenditure of energy than hard labor, for repression is a persistent inner battle in which the mind fights to block the torment of conscious awareness by digging defenses in the unconscious.[76] The onus of recollection, storytelling, and finally interiority therefore fell on the women. In *The Woman Warrior*, they possess insight—what Kristeva memorably called "a certain knowledge and sometimes the truth itself about an otherwise repressed, nocturnal, secret and unconscious universe" ("Women's Time," *Kristeva Reader*, 207). China men are held bound prisoners in this universe, awaiting release through the narrative agency of the women. Hong Kingston suggests that this is possible because the women consciously integrate their inner vision into their actual life stories. Indeed, she has remarked on several occasions that the "women's myths were more intertwined and inside their lives," that "the women are aware of them and living them out" while "the men's myths and memories are not as integrated into their present-day lives" (Schroeder, 217; Rabinowitz, 69). In effect, she describes the women as creators of "coherent" life stories out of the intertextual weave of everyday lore—often dismissed as nothing more than old wives' tales or old men's pipe dreams.

Intertextuality and Repression

One of the avowed reasons why *The Woman Warrior* and *China Men* finally emerged as two separate books was "history." Hong Kingston's book of life was broken in two because, as she sadly admits, the men themselves were "broken off from their background" (Rabinowitz, 69). We can now see that she was not simply referring to their homeland but to the underlying family history, mythology, and gossip that give ordinary life its rich and shimmering texture. The fact that the men were separated from the Chinese family's traditional sources of strength and that their lives of grinding work in America cut them off from their roots led Hong Kingston to conclude that "the men's stories were . . . undercutting the women's stories" (Bonetti, 35–36); however, her remarks also convey the sense that the men's lives of repression sapped her own narrative powers and had to be removed in order to make way for *The Woman Warrior.* "My men's stories seemed to interfere. They were weakening the feminist point of view. So I took all the men's stories out, and then I had *The Woman Warrior*" (Rabinowitz, 69). The decision to cut the men's stories out may have been a more "aggressive storytelling act" than Hong Kingston initially realized (Bonetti, 40), for, in giving the "strength" of the male stories to women, she was not only casting female characters as viragos but also representing China men by default as figuratively emasculated. The "feminist anger" (Bonetti, 35) that empowered *The Woman Warrior* would be surpassed by the indignation of affronted Chinese American male readers. Hong Kingston wondered whether "they feel that they have been castrated by American society" or if "the novel is castrated out of them and all that's left is tremendous anger at women" (Rabinowitz, 73).[77] In actuality, she participated in this unmanning by excising male gender narratives from her first book and by reducing the few men who remain in *The Woman Warrior* largely to caricatures or to nonentities.

Although she cut the men's stories out of her large narrative project, she did not eradicate them altogether. Put to one side as latent material, they subsided into the textual unconscious of *The Woman Warrior.* Their eventual regrouping and publication as *China Men,* in 1980, would mark the return of the repressed. Riffaterre argues that intertextuality "repress[es] a meaning in the process of conveying one" ("The Intertextual Unconscious," 374). In calling attention to what is missing, hidden, or taboo, intertextuality is paradoxically the X that marks the spot of repression. He further holds that "we are justified in drawing a parallel between intertextuality and the unconscious, since the text plays the role of a screen. Thus the intertext is to the text what the unconscious is to consciousness" ("Compulsory reader response," 77). In support of this theory, there is Hong Kingston's famous account in *The Woman Warrior* of how both parents and teachers misread her narrator's silence and apparent denseness as a young girl. "My silence was thickest—total—during the three years that I covered my school paintings with black paint." The educators suspect her opaque paintwork is a sign of mental disturbance, while her father fears both genetically and socially implanted deviance. "'The parents and teachers of criminals were executed,' said my father." In fact, the girl is creatively struggling to express her crude awareness that the mind constructs defensive screens that act like the unraised curtain of a theatre. The narrator explains: "I was making a stage curtain, and it was the moment before the curtain parted or rose." But even when the curtain rises, she is conscious that there are corners of her mind that are beyond the spotlight, "black and full of possibilities" (149). This is because, as Juliet Flower Maccannell explains in defining the unconscious, "what is being played on stage is prompted by 'another scene,' the fantasies and wishes of which are reconfigured in the consciousness."[78]

I thus argue that Hong Kingston's formative decision to split her jumble of men's and women's stories in two calls for a reading of psychoanalytic intertextuality in response. In order to convey the women's stories she first had, as Riffaterre theorized, to repress the men's stories. She recalls the mounting mental pressure she experienced "at one point [when] all those stories from *The Woman Warrior* and *China Men* were coming to me at the same time" (Schroeder, 217). In fact, as we have already seen, Hong Kingston's literary practice was to allow her ideas to build up in the unconscious and then release them through automatic writing. Riffaterre equates such automatic writing with the intertextual process of representing the unconscious through analogy, homophony, and association of ideas ("Compulsory reader response," 58–59). In effect, Hong Kingston found herself in the eye of the intertextual storm—where, according to Kristeva, there was "the intersection of this plurality of texts on their very different levels" (Waller, *Interviews*, 190). The organization of these stories into "two different books" (Schroeder, 217) may have helped Hong Kingston to manage the dialogic narratives that flooded the mind and to screen out the competing voices that clamored for her attention and perhaps threatened to block her writing. Above all, I would suggest that the uncoupling of the women's from the men's stories replays the developmental split, rooted for Freud in the turbulent drives and defenses of the Oedipal phase, when the subject is divided between conscious and unconscious motivations.[79]

Intertextuality and the Textual Unconscious

When Hong Kingston split her gender narratives in two, she also followed the dynamic laws of psychic organization that are implicit in Kristeva's theoretical writing on intertextuality. As Susan Stanford Friedman has noted,

Kristeva's *Revolution in Poetic Language* presumes that the text is structured like the psyche; that it traverses the borderline between the conscious and the unconscious, childhood and adulthood, mental and somatic affects; and, furthermore, that it maintains equilibrium by employing mechanisms like those decoded in Freudian dream interpretation and psychoanalysis (150, 162–163). Kristeva specifically regards intertextuality's "transposition of one (or several) sign-system(s) into another" as an amalgamation of the unconscious processes of displacement and condensation ("Revolution in Poetic Language," *Kristeva Reader*, 111). Condensation posits that single words, images, or ideas compress a cluster of deeper and more obscure impulses, as is the case, for instance, with "toad," "ghost," and "father" in Hong Kingston's two books. Condensation goes hand in hand with the overdetermination that Freud saw at work in dreams. Texts coproduced by conscious and unconscious forces, such as dream narratives, are described as overdetermined because they condense a variety of latent desires and motives into "deceptively simple displays."[80] In other words, the minimalist dreams screened in sleep have complex, underlying intertexts. Displacement, like repression, operates to relieve the psychic pressure of intolerable thoughts and feelings, but it does so by shifting disturbing ideas to other representational symbols or figures rather than pushing them down into the unconscious.[81] These and other defenses such as denial, silence, repetition compulsion, parapraxis—those mistakes or slips of the tongue that are inadvertently revealing—and syllepsis juggle the intertextual tension in the text-as-psyche between the desire to forget and remember, repress and express, release and censor desire.

Thus, the developmental relationship of *China Men* to *The Woman Warrior* can be said to resemble that of latent intertext to manifest text and of the unconscious to consciousness. Hong Kingston herself regarded the two books as a psychological chart of the "growth from a young woman to an adult woman . . . able to tell the story of men" (Bonetti, 36), but she later acknowledged that her texts encompassed a much larger learning curve. Indeed, she urged the women who read *The Woman Warrior* and identified with her young narrator to turn and "face the Other . . . whether it's men, the rest of the world, people of other races—whatever . . . in your psyche, the Other is"—and as she had done in writing about "the other half of the universe" in *China Men* (Perry, 175). Psychoanalytic intertextuality starts with the Freudian premise that the child's fantasies and primitive passions persist, unrecognized, beneath the textual surface. But it represents literary writing and reading as an interplay that "range[s] up and down the entire keyboard of our prior development" and so opens up the possibility for deeper growth in understanding (Holland, 82). According to Kristeva, intertextuality requires of all readers a "putting-into-process of our identities, capable of identifying with different types of texts (and) voices . . . at play in a given text" (Waller, *Interviews,* 190). Hong Kingston hoped that her readers would discover what Norman Holland aptly called "the face of a larger, wiser self" (103) in her two books. As Kristeva makes clear, the source of her hope was the dynamic process that lies at the heart of intertextuality. This is not simply the transformation of one text by another (Kristeva, *Desire in Language,* 66), but the change that literature can promote in readers who are allied with the writer in the arduous textual work of transforming unconscious and infantile fantasies into mature, conscious meaning.[82]

The unconscious is an underworld where women and men of all ages, races, and cultures have been held mute prisoner and where they have repeated the infantile experience of not being able to speak, comprehend, or articulate their desires.[83] Psychoanalytic intertextuality explores writing, reading, and interpretative practices that endeavor to express this unconscious predicament and make it intelligible and significant. For this reason, Kristeva imagines intertextuality as "a kind of repeat descent and reemergence such as Orpheus could not achieve" (Waller, *Interviews,* 194). Orpheus endeavored to rescue his wife Eurydice from the underworld but lost her forever because he looked back. His consolation was the posttraumatic gift of poetry that gave him the illusion of "male mastery over nature, death, the unconscious, and woman" (Steele, *Influence and Intertextuality,* 290–291). In direct opposition to this male myth, Hong Kingston urges her readers to turn and face their dark "other" side, in *The Woman Warrior* and *China Men*—whether that be the fear, chaos, destructiveness, gender anger, or racial hatred within.[84] We shall see in Chapter 4 that her narrator revises this male myth of the underworld journey by drawing on the ancient female mystery of Demeter and Persephone as "ancestral help," when she sets out as a daughter to rescue the aunt who is both beloved daughter and loathed mother from oblivion in "No Name Woman" (16). Her journey into the land of the shades culminates with "A Song for a Barbarian Reed Pipe." In this final story of *The Woman Warrior,* she commemorates the power of poetry to raise the human spirit from the dead. Her final words—"It translated well" (186)—affirm the intertextual character of her narrative writing. In turn, the intertextual process of translation and transformation leads her on a "repeat descent" to *China Men.* One of her first textual acts there will be to try and wake the father with her words from a living hell. "You screamed wordless male screams that jolted the house upright and staring in the middle of the night. 'It's BaBa,' we children told one another. . . .

MaMa would move from bed to bed. 'That was just BaBa having a dream'"
(13–14).

Hong Kingston regarded the writing of (auto)biographical fiction as an outlet for the "implosions and crazinesses" that the reader can see in BaBa and she thought "take place when you keep important energies and forces locked up inside of yourself" (Fisher Fishkin, 162). The conflict between repression and expression, creative and destructive drives, irrational and sane behavior can be more marked in autobiographical texts because they "ride the dragon," that is to say, straddle the division between the conscious and unconscious.[85] Her woman warrior seeks "adult wisdom to know dragons," but it advised that she will have to "infer the whole dragon from the parts you can see and touch" (33), for, like intertextuality, "sometimes the dragon is one, and sometimes many" (34), and its undulating body appears in different shapes at the textual surface. She glimpses higher consciousness in the mountains that resemble the dragon's head and a more cunning nether world in its tail. The break in the clouds, the fissures in the ground, and the lull between thunder and lightning are the points where desire breaks through the gaps between consciousness and the unconscious.

Susan Stanford Friedman suggests that it might be instructive to regard both the earlier and later versions of a book "as part of a larger composite text whose parts remain distinct, yet interact according to a psycho/political dynamic to which we have some access with the help of Freud's theory of repression and grammar for the dream-work" (165–166). Of course, what makes the intertextual study of *The Woman Warrior* and *China Men* more compelling is that they began life as "a larger composite text," and were subsequently divided along gender lines into two distinct books that continue to "interact" with one another both above and beneath the textual surface. If I see *China Men* as a crucial intertext, it is one that was largely but not completed taken out of *The Woman Warrior* and so retains intratextual as well as extratextual features. For this reason, I would like to begin by focusing on the traces of *China Men* that were left in *The Woman Warrior* and then consider at length what was left out by shuttling back and forth between the two books. I use the word "begin" advisedly because, by her own admission, Hong Kingston "wrote very convoluted stories" that often double back on themselves, provide an alternative or inconclusive account of events, and generally "set up the possibility that nothing happened at all" (Hoy, 50). My starting point is the first story of *The Woman Warrior*, which is the end of the road for the "No Name Woman" and a going "out on the road" for *China Men*. T. S. Eliot's cautionary advice to the traveler is worth bearing in mind at the outset: "What we call the beginning is often the end/And to make an end is to make a beginning. The end is where we start from" ("Little Gidding," v. 216–218).

Notes

1. See Bonetti's and Pfaff's interviews with the author in *Conversations with Maxine Hong Kingston*, edited by Paul Skenazy and Tera Martin (Jackson: University Press of Mississippi, 1998), 35, 16, respectively. I shall refer throughout this chapter to the comments Hong Kingston made in interviews, especially those collected in *Conversations*. As the editors note in their introduction (xv), this volume covers an almost twenty-year period and contains about two-thirds of the known interviews the author has given, constituting important source material.

2. See Hong Kingston's reply to Jody Hoy ("To Be Able to See the Tao," 62) and Paul Skenazy's ("Kingston at the University," 122) compilation of the exchanges Hong Kingston held with students and faculty at the University of California, Santa Cruz, in 1989, both in *Conversations*.

3. See Pfaff (16). See also Maxine Hong Kingston's "Personal Statement," in *Approaches to Teaching Kingston's The Woman Warrior*, edited by Shirley Geok-lin Lim (New York: Modern Language Association of America, 1991), 24. (Hereinafter, *Approaches*.)

4. Eric J. Schroeder, "As Truthful as Possible: An Interview with Maxine Hong Kingston" (1996), in *Conversations* (221).

5. See Nancy Chodorow's chapter "Early Psychological Development," in *The Reproduction of Mothering: Psychoanalysis and the Sociology of Gender* (Berkeley: University of California Press, 1978), 57–76, and esp. 61–69.

6. See "White Tigers," *The Woman Warrior* (43). Hong Kingston pointed out to Skenazy that "my people had a ritual for the umbilical cord which honors your coming into the world" ("Kingston at the University," 157).

7. See Phyllis Hoge Thompson, "This Is the Story I Heard: A Conversation with Maxine Hong Kingston and Earll Kingston," *Biography—Hawai'i* 6.1 (1983), 6; and Karen Horton, "*Honolulu* Interview: Maxine Hong Kingston" (1979), in *Conversations*, 11. Hong Kingston was unapologetic to Horton. "Oh, I'm very proud of being convoluted. I try to be convoluted. Life is convoluted." Ever the teacher, she thought the readers who found her book complicated should "work harder."

8. Donna Perry, "Maxine Hong Kingston" (1991), in *Conversations* (181).

9. She remarked to Marilyn Chin, "For 30 years I wrote in the first person singular. At a certain point I was thinking that I was self-centered and egotistical, solipsistic, and not very developed as a human being, nor as an artist, because I could only see from this one point of view" ("Writing the Other: A Conversation with Maxine Hong Kingston," in *Conversations*, 87).

10. Leslie W. Rabine, "No Lost Paradise: Social Gender and Symbolic Gender

in the Writings of Maxine Hong Kingston," *Signs* 12 (1987), 471–492. This essay is still cited as a major influence and is also included in the Wong edition of *The Woman Warrior Casebook*, 85–107.

11. Although Hong Kingston was talking to Perry in 1991 about the spirit of *Tripmaster Monkey*, she spoke to Paula Rabinowitz in a similar vein about the play of the animus and anima in her first two books. See *Conversations* (172 and 70, respectively). For fifteen years, Rabine's essay has had a respected place in critical studies of Hong Kingston. Recently, however, Yuan Shu has challenged Rabine's feminist psychoanalytic reading of *The Woman Warrior* as reflecting a preoccupation with "an Orientalist unconsciousness which privileges Western cultural traditions and historical developments as the standard, and construes Asian and Asian American social realities only as a psycholinguistic function." Terms such as "yin" and "yang"— especially when used uncritically by white women reviewers—might fall into this Orientalist category, though Hong Kingston employs the terms seriously herself. See Yuan Shu, "Cultural Politics and Chinese-American Female Subjectivity: Rethinking Kingston's *Woman Warrior*," *MELUS* 26 (2001), 200. This reading reflects not only the cultural war that has divided the Asian American literary community, but also the adversarial culture of the academy in general, where the formula for asserting a different theoretical or personal vision of a work is to attack the contribution that an established scholar has made to textual understanding. See Linda Hutcheon, "Creative Collaboration: Introduction," in *Profession 2001* (New York: Modern Language Association of America), 4–6.

12. See Rabine's discussion of the child's hiding places from the father and those that are perceived as the father's hideout in *China Men* (480–481, 491). Rabine notes a crucial proviso Hong Kingston made when *China Men* was published. "Given the present state of affairs, perhaps men's and women's experiences have to be dealt with separately for now, until more auspicious times are with us" (476). Hong Kingston is quoted in Elaine H. Kim, *Asian American Literature: An Introduction to the Writings and Their Social Context* (Philadelphia: Temple University Press, 1982), 207. Later comments, in 1986, to Bonetti (36) and Hoy (57), and in 1991 to Perry (175), however, suggest much more optimism.

13. See Jay Clayton and Eric Rothstein's lucid survey of the theoretical history of intertextuality, "Figures in the Corpus: Theories of Influence and Intertextuality," in *Influence and Intertextuality in Literary History*, edited by Jay Clayton and Eric Rothstein (Madison: University of Wisconsin Press, 1991), esp. 3–4 and 18–22.

14. See Sau-ling Cynthia Wong's discussion of intertextuality in her introduction to *Reading Asian American Literature: From Necessity to Extravagance* (Princeton, N.J.: Princeton University Press, 1993), 10–12.

15. See Michael Riffaterre, "Compulsory reader response: The intertextual drive," in *Intertextuality: Theories and practices*, edited by Michael Worton and Judith Still (Manchester: Manchester University Press, 1990), 56. What Riffaterre calls "intertextuality," Gérard Genette names "transtextuality" and defines as "all that sets the text in a relationship, whether obvious or concealed, with other texts." Genette

breaks down the concept into five types of transtextual relationships. Although Genette's work is important, he uses competing terms that can confuse readers who are trying to arrive at a clear overall definition of intertextuality. Therefore, I will refer to his theories only where they are consistent with the main intertextual arguments outlined in this chapter or where they offer singular insight into Hong Kingston's mode of writing. See Gérard Genette, *Palimpsests: Literature in the Second Degree*, trans. Channa Newman and Claude Doubinsky, foreword by Gerald Prince (Lincoln: University of Nebraska Press, 1997), 1–2.

16. Shu-mei Shih discusses some of the intertexts "lurking inside" *China Men*—"On Discovery," "The Ghostmate," "On Mortality," and "The Li Sao: An Elegy" —in "Exile and Intertextuality in Maxine Hong Kingston's *China Men*," in *The Literature of Emigration and Exile*, edited by James Whitlark and Wendell Aycock (Lubbock: Texas Tech University Press, 1992), 65–77. E. D. Huntley, *Maxine Hong Kingston: A Critical Companion* (Westport, Conn.: Greenwood Press, 2001), succinctly defines the intertexts of *China Men* as "minichapters" that "reinforce through doubling and paralleling similar accounts of the cultural predicament of the *China Men*; . . . [that] serve as ironic commentary on crucial events; . . . [that] dismantle the hierarchies of power that disenfranchise the immigrants; . . . [and that] confront the complexities of meaning inherent in Kingston's recasting of narrative forms" (123–124).

17. Tilottama Rajan draws attention to Derrida's notion of the interweaving that goes on within texts in "Intertextuality and the Subject of Reading/Writing," whereas Susan Stanford Friedman draws on Nancy K. Miller's feminist theory of arachnology—woman as weaver of texts, intertextuality, gendered subjectivity, and intersubjectivity—in "Weavings: Intertextuality and the (Re)Birth of the Author, both in *Influence and Intertextuality in Literary History*, edited by Clayton and Rothstein (62–65, 157–159, respectively). See also Nancy K. Miller's "Arachnologies: The Woman, the Text, and the Critic," in *The Poetics of Gender*, edited by Nancy K. Miller (New York: Columbia University Press, 1986), 270–295. Hong Kingston told Paul Skenazy that sewing was one of her important creative outlets, and was sometimes sacrificed when her "writing was going very well" ("Kingston at the University," 125).

18. Hong Kingston made this remark in Laura E. Skandera-Trombley's "Conversation with Maxine Hong Kingston," in *Critical Essays on Maxine Hong Kingston*, edited by Laura E. Skandera-Trombley (New York: G. K. Hall and Co., 1998), 33–34 (hereinafter, *Critical Essays*). She also complained later in the same interview that literary critics can get so caught up in "talking about Derrida and Lacan" and their high theory that they lose sight of the text and "then where am I in all this?" (41).

19. M. M. Bakhtin, *The Dialogic Imagination: Four Essays*, edited by Michael Holquist, translated by Caryl Emerson and Michael Holquist (Austin: University of Texas Press, 1981), 262. A number of Hong Kingston's critics have noted the Bakhtinian heteroglossia and dialogism in her writing. Sometimes they have referred to her intertextuality in the same breath, but they have not used these theories for a comprehensive study of *The Woman Warrior* and *China Men*. See, for example, Shu-mei

Shih's essay "Exile and Intertextuality," esp. 76; Amy Ling, "Maxine Hong Kingston and the Dialogic Dilemma of Asian American Writers," and Jeanne R. Smith, "Cross-Cultural Play: Maxine Hong Kingston's *Tripmaster Monkey*," in *Critical Essays* (172–179 and 334–335, respectively); Joseph Fichtelberg, "Poet and Patriarch in Maxine Hong Kingston's *China Men*," in *Autobiography and Questions of Gender*, edited by Shirley Neuman (London: F. Cass, 1991), 168–169; Ning Yu, "A Strategy against Marginalization: The 'High' and "Low' Cultures in Kingston's *China Men*," *College Literature* 23 (1996), 73–87 [reprinted at http://vweb.hwwilsonweb.com, 1–7, esp. 6]; Yuan Yuan, "The Semiotics of China Narratives in the Con/texts of Kingston and Tan," *Critique* 40 (1999), 292–303 [reprinted at http://vweb.hwwilsonweb.com, 1–6, esp. 3–5]; Malini Schueller, "Questioning Race and Gender Definitions: Dialogic Subversions in *The Woman Warrior*," *Criticism* 31 (1989), 421–422; Shirley Geok-lin Lim, "'Growing with Stories': Chinese American Identities, Textual Identities (Maxine Hong Kingston)," in *Teaching American Ethnic Literatures: Nineteen Essays*, edited by John R. Maitino and David R. Peck (Albuquerque: University of New Mexico Press, 1996), 281; and Donald C. Goellnicht, "Father Land and/or Mother Tongue: The Divided Female Subject in Kogawa's *Obasan* and Hong Kingston's *The Woman Warrior*," in *Redefining Autobiography in Twentieth-Century Women's Fiction: An Essay Collection*, edited by Janice Morgan, Colette T. Hall, and Carol L. Snyder (New York: Garland, 1991), 120.

20. See Kristeva, *Desire in Language: A Semiotic Approach to Literature and Art*, edited by Leon S. Roudiez, trans. Thomas Gora, Alice Jardine, and Leon S. Roudiez (New York: Columbia University Press, 1980), 65. Kristeva expands Bakhtin's eighteenth- and nineteenth-century examples of the carnivalesque, parodic, and polyphonic novel to include twentieth-century writers that Hong Kingston admired and read, such as James Joyce (71). See also Clayton and Rothstein's analysis of Kristeva's textualization and implicit depersonalization of Bakhtin's intersubjective construction of dialogized heteroglossia, in "Figures in the Corpus," 18–21. Genette categorizes Kristeva's theory of intertextuality as the first type of transtextuality, where there is "a relationship of copresence between two texts or among several texts." He defines the fourth and most significant type of transtextuality as hypertextuality and sees it as involving the textual *transformation* that Kristeva also highlights. Though Genette acknowledges that all texts are hypertextual, he adds that "some works are more so than others," depending on the extent to which they are self-transformative. See *Palimpsests* (1, 5, 7, 9, and 394–395).

21. Sau-ling Wong cautions, in *Reading Asian American Literature* (11), that the French theory of intertextuality can "take such an extreme deconstructive form that it not only dissolves the autonomous, intentional subject but also precludes the validity of an extratextual reality."

22. See Lim's account of "Other Works by Maxine Hong Kingston" in *Approaches* (6). Huntley is talking specifically about *The Woman Warrior*, but her remarks are well put for *China Men* as well (77).

23. See the perceptive comments of the undervalued psychoanalytic and

reader-response critic Norman N. Holland in *The Dynamics of Literary Response* (New York: Oxford University Press, 1968). He memorably remarks that, "at one level of our being, a very primitive level, we feel the process of transformation the literary work embodies as a transformation in us. We have introjected the literary work; it has become a subsystem within our own egos" (87).

24. Kristeva comments, in "Word, Dialogue, and Novel," in *Desire in Language*, that "Bakhtinian dialogism identifies writing as both subjectivity and communication, or better, as intertextuality" (68). Whereas she goes on to argue that "confronted with this dialogism, the notion of a 'person-subject of writing' becomes blurred," Clayton and Rothstein argue in "Figures in the Corpus" that it is Kristeva who does the blurring (18–21). She textualizes and depersonalizes Bakhtin's intersubjective construction of dialogized heteroglossia. Malini Schueller sees *The Woman Warrior* as a dialogic text that valorizes communication and intersubjectivity but does not acknowledge that Kristeva theorized intertextuality as a replacement for the intersubjectivity implicit in Bakhtinian dialogism (421–422).

25. Arturo Islas with Marilyn Yalom, "Interview with Maxine Hong Kingston," in *Conversations*, 31. As a close and complex textual reader, Rabine sees that "read by many different people, in many different contexts, writing also changes every time it is read" (490), but for Hong Kingston, it does not have the chameleon qualities of oral literature and storytelling.

26. See Shirley Geok-lin Lim's interesting footnote on Hong Kingston's use of pidgin, in "The Tradition of Chinese American Women's Life Stories: Thematics of Race and Gender in Jade Snow Wong's *Fifth Chinese Daughter* and Maxine Hong Kingston's *The Woman Warrior*," in *American Women's Autobiography: Fea(s)ts of Memory*, edited by Margo Culley (Madison: University of Wisconsin Press, 1992), 265; and Susan Brownmiller, "Talks with Maxine Hong Kingston, Author of *The Woman Warrior*," in *The Woman Warrior Casebook*, edited by Wong (178). See Hong Kingston's interview with William Satake Blauvelt in *Conversations* (78) and the discussion of *Tripmaster Monkey*, where her textual use of "Chinese, Chinese American, Japanese, and Hawaiian pidgin" is considered. Linda Ching Sledge argues that Hong Kingston's China Men do not use pidgin but "a formal, generally grammatically correct diction" ("Maxine Kingston's *China Men*: The Family Historian as Epic Poet," *MELUS* 7.4 [1980], 18).

27. Commenting on her trip to China with other American writers in 1984, Hong Kingston remarked that the "whole journey was a linguistic adventure . . . because we traveled from the north to the south, and the closer we got to my home village the more I could communicate." See Perry (186–187) and her discussion with Skenazy on how Stockton formed her as a writer, in "Coming Home" (1989), in *Conversations* (114).

28. Hong Kingston told Pfaff that Say Yup was a Cantonese dialect "spoken by people many of whom historically have been illiterate and many of whom are still illiterate today" (17). Later, she told Islas that it was "the dialect of one little village . . . and that language has not been written down. I write about illiterate peo-

ple whose language has not even been Romanized. So it's a matter of starting with a language that has no writing and yet writing about people who talk-story in that language" (27). It is important to note, however, that her parents were literate in Mandarin or Putonghua (Horton, 7).

29. Linda Ching Sledge, "Oral Tradition in Kingston's *China Men*," in *Redefining American Literary History,* edited by A. LaVonne Brown Ruoff and Jerry W. Ward Jr. (New York: Modern Language Association of America, 1990), 145; Debra Shostak, "Maxine Hong Kingston's Fake Books," in *Critical Essays* (54–55).

30. See Bonetti (45) and similar remarks made to Shelley Fisher Fishkin, "Interview with Maxine Hong Kingston" (1990), in *Conversations* (166). It is not clear what university in Guangdong province Hong Kingston is referring to by the old name of Canton.

31. In 1977, Hong Kingston told Nan Robertson of the *New York Times,* "My mother is the creative one—the one with the visions and the stories to tell. I'm the technician. She's the great inspiration. I never realized it until I finished the book." See Robertson's "'Ghosts' of Girlhood Lift Obscure Book to Peak of Acclaim," in *Critical Essays* (90).

32. Hong Kingston told Donna Perry, "The only Chinese language that I have is the dialect that my parents speak, . . . a real minority dialect in the southwest." This was not the Cantonese widely used in Hong Kong or the Pearl Delta region—which she studied for seven years at Chinese language school—but a local "peasant, village dialect" (Perry, 187; Skenazy, "Kingston at the University," 128).

33. There are times when Kristeva reads like the Delphic oracle, and this is one of them. Further down in the same passage (*Desire in Language,* 74), she seems to identify the writer as the subject of enunciation and the character as the subject of utterance. Friedman thinks that the subject of enunciation refers to the author and the subject of utterance to the writing subject (148). To enunciate, ironically, means to express an idea or theory in definite terms, which Kristeva most definitely does not do here. I take her statement at its simplest to mean a split between written and oral expression, and between writing and utterance or dialogue, which is consistent with her shift from Bakhtin.

34. See *China Men* (256). In *Reading Asian American Literature,* Sau-ling Wong discusses the cultural conflict for American-born Chinese between the democratic rhetoric of "consent" and a Confucian patriarchal ideology of "descent" through blood ties (41, 44). In *The Woman Warrior,* Hong Kingston writes, "A family must be whole, faithfully keeping the descent line by having sons to feed the old and the dead, who in turn look after the family" (19–20).

35. See A. N. Doane's illuminating discussion, "Oral Texts, Intertexts, and Intratexts: Editing Old English," in *Influence and Intertextuality,* edited by Clayton and Rothstein, 75–113. Although Doane tackles a subject that is commonly regarded as far removed from the "cutting edge" of literary or critical theory, he brilliantly uses it to explore a dynamic intertextual moment "when the oral text and the technology of literacy are capable of penetrating and interpreting each other" (79). Whereas Doane argues that oral texts tend to be more "homeostatic" and do not "confront

change as such" (78), Hong Kingston admired the oral tradition of talk-story in her family for its capacity to grow and change and did not feel writing naturally had the same mobility. In "Oral Tradition," Sledge argues similarly that Hong Kingston "consciously assumes the role of tribal bard in the guise of various storytelling personae" (145).

36. I paraphrase Kristeva's discussion of her theory of "Intertextuality and Literary Interpretation" with Margaret Waller, in *Julia Kristeva Interviews*, edited by Ross Mitchell Guberman (New York: Columbia University Press, 1996), 190.

37. See Huntley (3, 49) and Diane Simmons, *Maxine Hong Kingston* (New York: Twayne, 1999), 108–110.

38. See Michael Worton and Judith Still's opening remarks in their introduction to *Intertextuality: Theories and practices* (1–2). Both Clayton and Rothstein, as well as Friedman, locate Bloom's critical work on literary transmission and influence within debates about intertextuality. See Clayton and Rothstein, eds., *Influence and Intertextuality* (9, 156).

39. "Fa Mu Lan" is the Cantonese transliteration of the standard Chinese *Hua Mulan*. This medieval Chinese mythical figure would be popularized by Disney as "Mulan."

40. In her literary discussion at the University of California, Santa Cruz, Hong Kingston remarked that, through her writing allusions, she was claiming "the Joycean soul, this Rilkean romantic poetic soul" as her own. She also added that "maybe the greatest joy of my life is to read. I love it, it's pleasurable, it's sensual" (Skenazy, "Kingston at the University," 144). In "From One Identity to an Other" (1975), Kristeva cites Joyce as a writer whose rhythmic and polyphonic language should be listened to in order to experience this extreme pleasure of *jouissance* (*Desire in Language*, 142).

41. I am indebted to Sledge's "Oral Tradition" (149) for this point.

42. See Hong Kingston's discussion of Whitman with Paul Skenazy ("Kingston at the University," 145), Fisher Fishkin (160–161), and Neila C. Seshachari, "Reinventing Peace: Conversations with Tripmaster Maxine Hong Kingston" (212), and his alter ego Wittman Ah Sing with Blauvelt (79–80) and Perry (172), in *Conversations*.

43. See David Leiwei Li, "Re-presenting *The Woman Warrior*: An Essay of Interpretative History" and Lee Quinby, "The Subject of Memoirs: *The Woman Warrior*'s Technology of Ideographic Selfhood," in *Critical Essays* (185 and 126–133, respectively).

44. In fact, Hong Kingston is somewhat inconsistent on the dates. She told Pfaff, when *China Men* was published in 1980, "The earliest episode in my book is about 1850, which is roughly where Williams left off" (15). She told Rabinowitz, in 1986, that Williams "stopped in 1860 and I pick up in 1860 and carry it forward" (72). Elliott H. Shapiro notes the same discrepancy in "Authentic Watermelon: Maxine Hong Kingston's American Novel," *MELUS* 26 (2001), 12, n. 6, 25, but he opts, as I do, for 1860 as the "more plausible date."

45. Hong Kingston proudly told Marilyn Chin in 1989 that she understood

she "was the living author whose books are most taught in colleges" across America, in *Conversations* (97).

46. See Sau-ling Wong's introduction to *The Woman Warrior Casebook*, 9.

47. In "Exile and Intertextuality" (66, 69, 76), Shu-mei Shih discusses the politics of "center" and "margin" in *China Men*. (I will be saying more about this later.) While Shih see Hong Kingston's vision as the product of "an exilic imagination," I think she reflects the "exilic imagination" of her parents and Chinese relations and that she writes with a conviction that she has a right to belong.

48. For some sense of the critical debate, see Sau-ling Wong's "Autobiography as Guided Chinatown Tour? Maxine Hong Kingston's *The Woman Warrior* and the Chinese American Autobiographical Controversy," in *The Woman Warrior Casebook* (35–36); and Frederic Wakeman Jr., "Chinese Ghost Story," in *Critical Essays* (207, 214). In the same volume, Debra Shostak argues (57), wrongly in my view, that Hong Kingston valorizes and distinguishes assimilation from appropriation. In fact, the author told the editor, Laura Skandera-Trombley, (33) that she was shocked to be labeled "an assimilationist writer." David Leiwei Li argues (184) for Hong Kingston's "deliberate accommodation, adaptation, and appropriation of some familiar orientalist geopolitical imagination." In *Reading Asian American Literature*, Sau-ling Wong explores the vexed issues of appropriation and assimilation in terms of the culture of eating and observes that "disagreeable food puts to the test [the Asian American immigrant] capacity to consolidate one's self by appropriating resources from the external environment" (26).

49. Genette concludes in *Palimpsests* that "hypertextuality is only one name for that ceaseless circulation of texts without which literature would not be worth one hour of exertion" (400).

50. See the question put to her by Paul Skenazy ("Coming Home," 109) and remarks made to Paula Rabinowitz (72), in *Conversations*.

51. Nathaniel Hawthorne, *The Scarlet Letter and Selected Tales* (London: Penguin Classics, 1986), 80.

52. See Audre Lorde, "Poetry Is Not a Luxury," in *Sister Outsider: Essays and Speeches* (Freedom, Calif.: Crossing Press, 1984), 37.

53. Hong Kingston's interviews in *Conversations* are studded with references to the writers she has read, admired, and generously acknowledged. See, by way of example, her remarks on American writers in Hoy (50), Rabinowitz (72), Marilyn Chin (100), Perry (173), Schroeder (219–220); Chinese and Asian American writers in Islas and Yalom (28), Hoy (62), Marilyn Chin (98), and Skenazy ("Kingston at the University," 156); Asian writers in English in Marilyn Chin (96, 98); American women writers of color in Perry (177); the black "roots" writer Alex Haley in Seshachari (206); and Western canonical writers in Islas and Yalom (25), Hoy (62), Skenazy ("Kingston at the University," 144), and Perry (171, 176, 186). Intertextuality was perceived as a theory that would oust the traditional concept of influence in author-centered works. But, as Clayton and Rothstein have observed in their subtle introduction to *Influence and Intertextuality in Literary History*, intertextual theorists

can ironically affirm the concept of influence by the very fact that they so vehemently deny or reject it. They note the position taken by American feminists who "have worked to recover the notion of agent" abandoned in Kristeva's impersonal operation of intertextuality and who have tried "to broaden the notion of influence, at times coupling it with an intertextuality that augments rather than substitutes for influence theories" (11). I believe this is closer to Hong Kingston's own position as a writer. As Friedman rightly reminds readers, "The discourses of influence and intertextuality have not been and cannot be pure, untainted by each other" (154).

54. Hong Kingston was talking to Eric J. Schroeder about the writing community that she formed with Vietnam War veterans. Her workshop is characterized by its intertextual exercises of reading, writing, and spirituality as evident from her remark that "everyone takes a turn reading, and then we do a walking meditation" (226). See Huntley's remarks (30–31), and King-Kok Cheung's discussion of some of the virtues, consolations and strengths that world religions have drawn from silence, in *Articulate Silences: Hisaye Yamamoto, Maxine Hong Kingston, Joy Kogawa* (Ithaca, N.Y.: Cornell University Press, 1993), especially in her introduction (1–26).

55. Genette would describe hypertextuality as "the art of 'making new things out of old'" (398), but it is clear from Hong Kingston's remarks that this can be said of intertextuality in general.

56. In her conversation with Laura Skandera-Trombley about *Tripmaster Monkey,* Hong Kingston again underlined this point when she remarked that her intention was to make the reader "finish this story . . . . I was trying to replicate in text what happens in talk story and in music where you tell your version of the story. I've told this far, I've told my version, now you go on with it" (*Critical Essays,* 42).

57. See A. Noelle Williams' discussion of this Chin quotation from "Come All Ye Asian American Writers of the Real and the Fake" in *The Big Aiiieeeee!* and the issue of white/feminists' orientalist reading of Hong Kingston's two books in "Parody and Pacifist Transformations in Maxine Hong Kingston's *Tripmaster Monkey: His Fake Book,*" in *Critical Essays* (319–322). See King-Kok Cheung's groundbreaking discussion of the same issues in *"The Woman Warrior* versus *The Chinaman Pacific,"* which first appeared in *Conflicts in Feminism,* edited by Marianne Hirsch and Evelyn Fox Keller (New York: Routledge, 1990), and was reprinted in *Critical Essays* (107–124, esp. 108–114). Sau-ling Wong covers some of the same ground in "Autobiography as Guided Chinatown Tour," in *The Woman Warrior Casebook* (29–36), and notes that "a complex autobiographical tradition does exist in Chinese literature" (35) (also reprinted in *Critical Essays,* 146–167), a point that is taken up by LeiLani Nishime, "Engendering Genre: Gender and Nationalism in *China Men* and *The Woman Warrior,*" in *Critical Essays,* 264–267. See David Leiwei Li, "Re-presenting *The Woman Warrior,*" in *Critical Essays* (183–193); and Huntley (57–61).

58. See Elizabeth D. Harvey's remarks, in *Ventriloquized Voices: Feminist Theory and English Renaissance Texts* (London: Routledge, 1992), that "ventriloquism and intertextuality overlap" because, among other things, "an intertextual allusion opens a text to other voices and echoes of their texts, just as ventriloquism multiplies

authorial voices, interrogating the idea that a single authorial presence controls an utterance" (10). Simmons believes that "Wittman, despite superficial resemblances, is not Frank Chin but Maxine Hong Kingston herself" (38). Amy Ling, in *Critical Essays*, spoke to one of Chin's associates, Shawn Wong, who remarked on how accurately Hong Kingston captured Chin's voice in *Tripmaster Monkey* (71). For his part, Chin famously mocked *The Woman Warrior* in "The Most Popular Book in China," in Wong's *The Woman Warrior Casebook* (23–28).

59. See Genette's interesting discussion of whether the meaning of poetry is so inseparable from its language as to be essentially untranslatable (214–216).

60. "Only think of fairy tales and of the many daring products of the imagination, which are full of meaning and of which only a man without intelligence could say: 'This is nonsense, for it's impossible'." See Sigmund Freud, *The Interpretation of Dreams*, vol. 4, edited by Angela Richards, trans. James Strachey (London: Penguin Freud Library, 1991), 418–419.

61. Seán Hand, "Missing you: Intertextuality, transference and the language of love," in *Intertextuality*, edited by Worton and Still, 79.

62. Ana-Maria Rizzuto, *The Birth of the Living God: A Psychoanalytic Study* (Chicago: University of Chicago Press, 1981), 47.

63. Doris Lessing, "What Good Times We All Had Then," in *Fathers: Reflections by Daughters*, edited by Ursula Owen (London: Virago, 1983), 80.

64. Genette takes issue with the definitive importance Riffaterre gives to syllepsis because he thinks it is a reductive reading of the ambiguity present in the hypertext (397).

65. Jody Hoy asked Hong Kingston whether she read Joseph Campbell's *The Hero with a Thousand Faces* and was aware of his theories when she wrote *The Woman Warrior*. Hong Kingston said that, although she had not read his book, she was aware of "his idea of the journey and the quest" (59).

66. Sau-ling Wong discusses the critical dispute over Hong Kingston's translation of words like toad and ghost in "Autobiography as Guided Chinatown Tour?" in her *The Woman Warrior Casebook* (32–33).

67. See Shakespeare's *As You Like It*: "Sweet are the uses of adversity, / Which, like the toad, ugly and venomous, / Wears yet a precious jewel in his head" (2.1. 12–14).

68. See Riffaterre's further discussion of syllepsis and critical demonstration of how it can be at play in the literary text in "The Intertextual Unconscious," *Critical Inquiry* 13 (1987), 376.

69. In 1980, when *China Men* was published, Hong Kingston told Pfaff, "If I'm writing well, by the end I have come to a resolution, a kind of love for a character based on my experience of the way that person sees the world" (18).

70. Jessica Benjamin, "A Desire of One's Own: Psychoanalytic Feminism and Intersubjective Space," in *Feminist Studies/Critical Studies: Issues, Terms and Contexts*, edited by Teresa de Lauretis (Bloomington: Indiana University Press, 1986), 92.

71. I am grateful to Jeffrey Steele's essay "The Call of Eurydice: Mourning and

Intertextuality in Margaret Fuller's Writing," in *Influence and Intertextuality*, edited by Clayton and Rothstein (275, 277), for setting out the writing subject's intertextuality and intersubjectivity.

72. See Ana-Maria Rizzuto's brilliant refutation of Freud's view that reality and illusion are necessarily contradictory terms, in *The Birth of the Living God* (209). Joanne S. Frye develops the same point with respect to Hong Kingston, in "*The Woman Warrior*: Claiming Narrative Power, Re-Creating Female Selfhood," in *Faith of a (Woman) Writer*, edited by Alice Kessler Harris and William McBrien (Westport, Conn.: Greenwood Press, 1988). She asserts "Kingston's reaction to female experience is centered in simultaneously claiming new possibilities and integrating a knowledge of actual lived reality—claiming fantasy not as a separate inner world of the imagination but as a powerful tool for reshaping lived experience beyond the repressions of personal daily life" (294).

73. See, for instance, Wakeman's charge that Hong Kingston's *China Men* is an "inauthentic" retelling of Chinese myth and lore, in "Chinese Ghost Story," and Laura Skandera-Trombley's discussion of his remarks, in *Critical Essays* (207–215 and 15, respectively). What Hong Kingston meant by "ghosts" has been the subject of extended critical debate. Most critics are less interested in the reality of ghosts in Cantonese culture than their symbolic importance. See Jeffrey Paul Chan's reply to Diane Johnson's "Ghosts" in "The Mysterious West," John Leonard's review of *The Woman Warrior*, "In Defiance of 2 Worlds," Lee Quinby's "The Subject of Memoirs," and David Leiwei Li's "Representing *The Woman Warrior*," all in *Critical Essays* (86, 77, 128–129, and 192–193, respectively). See also Huntley (95–97) and Teresa C. Zackodnik, "Photography and the Status of Truth in Maxine Hong Kingston's *China Men*," *MELUS* 22 (1997), 55–69 [reprinted at http://vweb.hwwilsonweb.com, 4], who cites Amy Tan's salient point that "in China . . . a ghost was anything we were forbidden to talk about."

74. Garrett Hongo writes movingly in "Introduction: Culture Wars in Asian America," in *Under Western Eyes: Personal Essays from Asian America*, edited by Hongo (New York: Doubleday Anchor Books, 1995), 9–10, of the stoicism of Japanese American internees in World War II and the cost of survival that was an equivalent stifling of the emotional life.

75. See Shoshana Felman, *What Does a Woman Want? Reading and Sexual Difference* (Baltimore: Johns Hopkins University Press, 1993), 15–16.

76. See Elizabeth Grosz's definition of "repression," in *Feminism and Psychoanalysis: A Critical Dictionary*, edited by Elizabeth Wright (Oxford: Blackwell, 1992), 382–384.

77. Hong Kingston—perhaps unconsciously—continues to use sexually emasculating metaphors of adultery and cuckolding to articulate the accusation that Chinese American men have leveled against women writers like herself: that "we are in bed with the white literary establishment" (Marilyn Chin, 95). In a later interview with Perry, she compared these hostile male critics who attack her work to abusive partners who take their sense of frustration and impotence as minority men out on

their women. Indeed she claimed that Frank Chin threatened to beat her up when he ran into her at a conference (184).

78. See Maccannell's definition of the "unconscious," in *Feminism and Psychoanalysis: A Critical Dictionary*, edited by Wright (442).

79. See Leon S. Roudiez's introduction to Kristeva, *Desire in Language* (6), and Norman N. Holland's discussion of the Oedipal phase of development when intense love and hate for parents and caretakers can provoke the powerful defenses indicative of splitting, in *The Dynamics of Literary Response* (46–53).

80. I am indebted to Peter Gay's neat formulation in *Freud: A Life for Our Time* (New York: Doubleday Anchor Books, 1988), 91. See also Holland's useful glossary of key psychoanalytic terms, in *The Dynamics of Literary Response* (361–365).

81. See Angelika Bammer, "Introduction," in *Displacements: Cultural Identities in Question*, edited by Bammer (Bloomington: Indiana University Press, 1994), xiii.

82. See Holland's comments (27–32, 79–87, 103, and 337).

83. In "Place Names" (1976–1977), Kristeva asserted that the Freudian theory of infantile sexuality "allows for the examination, not of he who does not speak *(in-fans)* but of what within the speaker is not yet spoken, or will always remain unsaid, unnamable within the gaps of speech" (*Desire in Language*, 272).

84. Hong Kingston agrees with Skandera-Trombley that the stories of *The Woman Warrior* are "trying to create order out of the chaos, and that makes critics and readers uncomfortable" (*Critical Essays*, 41).

85. Friedman argues that, "when the novel is autobiographical, this negotiation [between desire and repression]—which may be conscious or unconscious—is further heightened" (164).

Chapter 2

———◆✳◆———

"You Say with the Few Words and the Silences"
The Woman Warrior's Traces of a Dialogue with China Men

Duality in The Woman Warrior and China Men

"'The Brother in Vietnam" was the first story that Maxine Hong Kingston wrote for her intended family saga, but it ended up as the last section of *China Men*.[1] The last story her father wanted told was "No Name Woman," yet it became the first tale to lead off *The Woman Warrior*. With the gender division of her narratives into two separate books, the women's stories took precedence over the men's; and when *The Woman Warrior* appeared in 1976, it read as a neat feminist parable that the women ordinarily heard last would come first and the men accustomed to come first would go last. However in 1980, the year that *China Men* followed as the male narrative sequel to *The Woman Warrior*, the author cautioned her readers against reading the order of publication so simply. She argued pragmatically that "given the present state of affairs, perhaps men's and women's experiences have to be dealt with separately for now." Yet she did not want *The Woman Warrior* emphasized over and above *China Men*, or seen as an afterthought and hoped, as Elaine Kim explained, that the two books would be read together "as two parts of a whole."[2] Not only did she write much of the material in the two books simultaneously, she also projected a narrator who could not always keep the stories straight and separate in her mind or "tell the difference" between them (*WW*, 180) and who was prone to the troubling double reads of intertextuality.[3]

Critics have usually interpreted the narrator's confusion as it reflects the double vision of a Chinese American girl who is raised in the shadow of Chinatown and who grows up with the contradictions, half-truths, and ghetto mentality of its elder immigrant generation (Kim, 199–200). As a female minor, she is caught in the racist and sexist crossfire that emanates from both the ethnic minority group into which she was born and the white society to which she must conform. As she matures into womanhood, she must learn to live with the pain, the paradox, and—her final insight—the poetry of her Chinese American identity. Sau-ling Wong has shown how the narrator of *The Woman Warrior* is brought face to face with her racial double when she bullies the quiet classmate of Chinese descent who personifies hated and rejected aspects of this dual identity (*Reading Asian American Literature*, 77–92).

The intertextual logic of *The Woman Warrior* and *China Men*, however, requires the reader to seek "multiple entry" into the two books and to traverse repeatedly the simplistic binary divisions that have been arbitrarily set up between high and low, Chinese and American culture, between male and female experience, the singular "I" projected in autobiography and the dialogical points of view gathered together in the memoir.[4] Indeed, Kristeva argues that such a traversal is a "truly great 'literary' achievement" because "the word 'traverse' implies that the subject experiences sexual difference, not as a fixed opposition ('man'/'woman') but as a process of differentiation."[5] In other words, intertextuality gives nuance to the definition of the double so that it can include not only "opposing selves" who result from the internal splintering or splitting of the personality, but also dyadic figures who exist separate from the self yet who may not, after all, be all "that different" from the narrator—such as the opposite sex.[6]

Although Leslie Rabine argues that the members of the opposite sex created by Hong Kingston are more often than not "shadow creatures in the world and in the book of the other sex" ("No Lost Paradise," 475), this view can encourage the reader to pay little attention to the faint traces of the men in *The Woman Warrior* or the cameo appearances of the women in *China Men* and conclude that they have no hermeneutic importance in each other's book. An intertextual reading of the two books allows us to envisage these women warriors and China men as actively shadowing one another and leading parallel lives that occasionally intersect or surface in the textual narratives of their gender opposite. The figurative traces of these dual lives may contradict or complement—and will certainly complicate—the reader's perceived understanding of the relationships between the female and male characters.

Male Silence, Female Speech, and Intertextual Listening

At first glance, the father's obstinate silence in the two books does not seem to promote this complex understanding. His taciturnity cuts him off from his family and constitutes a major stumbling block to his daughter in her narrative quest for answers. It puts him on an unequal footing as character with the mother whose outspoken voice leaves a lasting impression on the readers of *The Woman Warrior*.[7] But, as Yuan Yuan has suggested, there is indeed an intertextual relationship in *The Woman Warrior* and *China Men* between the mother's strong speech presence and the father's absence.[8] Just as one of Virginia Woolf's male characters was interested in writing "a novel about Silence, . . . the things people don't say," and Kristeva was alert to "the unspoken in all discourse,"[9] so Hong Kingston redeems the father's deadly silence by making it the context for the reader's intent listening. This listening is the intertextual corollary of the close reading that is an established practice in the Anglo-American canon.[10] Hong Kingston defined a good listener as "open to hearing talk-story" (Skenazy, "Kingston at the University," 149). The narrator of *The Woman Warrior* begins to realize that she too is a "story-talker" when she stops vying with her mother to have the last word or to get the better of this "champion talker" and realizes that there is "no higher listener . . . but myself" (184, 180, 182). Hong Kingston sees this narrator as a neophyte and represents her as somewhat unbalanced. Apart from "At the Western Palace," which is told with a forbearing detachment, she is generally more interested in her own point of view than that of other people.[11] Only when "the 'I' began to fade away" can the narrator become "the perfect listener or the perfect reader"—what Hong Kingston said she tried "to be for those China men."[12] Then, as Amy Ling has shown, the writer of *The Woman Warrior* is "in dialogue with herself." This dialogue of the self is a "composite of many voices: her mother's, her own physical voice, her imaginative voice, the Chinese culture's, American males', and American females' voices" (*Critical Essays*, 172, 179).

Paradoxically, the fact that the father hardly talks at all and is largely unfathomable to his daughter can work to her advantage as a storyteller. With her lifelong interest in core practices of spirituality such as peace, justice, and compassionate awareness of suffering humanity, Hong Kingston believes that "a writer is always contending with a great silence" (Skenazy, "Kingston at the University," 121). Her father's "great silence" throughout the two books creates the conditions of meditative quiet and attention that facilitate intertextuality's dialogism, allowing heteroglossic sounds to arise and the traces and echoes of other words to be heard in and beyond the words actually spoken.[13]

Intertextual Dialogue, Otherness, and Resemblance: "No Name Woman" and "The Brother in Vietnam"

If words convey "the Otherness of language, the potential of words to always carry echoes of other words" (Schueller, 422), this otherness weaves intertextual counterpoint into the statements that are made in one or other of the books. Occasionally it rebounds on the sender, throwing up points of hidden resemblance and suggesting—as in the case of the double—that the Other is also an I (Sau-ling Wong, *Reading Asian American Literature*, 84). A good instance of this simultaneous contrast and accord of vocal statement occurs in the respective openings of "No Name Woman" and "The Brother in Vietnam." In *The Woman Warrior*, the daughter narrator begins by speculating on the harsh end of a paternal aunt who has forfeited her claim as next of kin in the Hong family. "We say that your father has all brothers because it is as if she had never been born" (11). The suicide of the aunt with her infant daughter in her arms is not good enough for this patriarchal clan. They want her to have a fate worse than death—to be nothing, not even a no name woman, and to be deprived retroactively of any trace of existence, even that "tenuous hold on life" which the narrator of *China Men* anxiously recognizes as the uncanny state of the newborn (207).

In dramatic contrast, "The Brother in Vietnam" brings the birth of the narrator's two youngest brothers to the fore. It is one of her most happy and impressionable memories. "The baby had been born . . . . We heard him cry. Joy swelled the world" (265). This jubilant reminiscence closely recalls her description of her father's birth, "the youngest and the smartest of four brothers," near the beginning of *China Men* (15). In this case, as critics have noted, she employs narrative analogy, using the memory of her brothers being born to imagine in retrospect the birth of her father.[14] The narrator must look back many years, at an event that happened a long way off in China, to the remote figure of her father, about whom she knows little or nothing, like the figure of her no name aunt. "You say with the few words and the silences: No stories. No past. No China" (14–15).

The narrator of *The Woman Warrior* is aggrieved that the birth of sons is celebrated in patriarchal Chinese culture while that of daughters is greeted with dismay. Yet, in fact, one of the quirkier patriarchs in *China Men*, her paternal grandfather Ah Goong, is depicted as bitterly disappointed to have not fathered a daughter and "puckered all over with envy" when he beholds his neighbor's "loveliest dainty of a baby girl" (18). His tender solicitude toward this "pretty little sister" whom he brings fruit and flowers (19) may be exceptional—or it may be his granddaughter's wistful attempt to rewrite patriarchal history. Whatever the cause, his behavior warns readers not to presume that all Chinese fathers are misogynists. Ah Goong and his grand-daughter narrator also provide a double take on the birthday of daughters. Through her words of protest in *The Woman Warrior* and his compensating actions in *China Men*, the reader learns that newborn girls do not start life as they should, with their fair share of the oranges, red eggs, ginger, lycée packets, or sweets, but rather run the risk of being neglected, starved of food and affection, or suffocated in a box of ashes. Furthermore, there are points where the description of the aunt whom the family wishes unborn and the sons who cannot be born too often strangely coincide. One of those points of unexpected resemblance is supplied by Hong Kingston herself, when she related to Joy Hoy the impetus for writing "No Name Woman." "I was so mad at my mother for telling me a cruel tale for the joy of telling. I told her it wasn't a true story, yet part of me was really interested in hearing the story. . . . I also have that joy of telling" (49). That "joy of the telling" brought home the fact that she was a storyteller like her mother. The joint pleasure, the mother-daughter *jouissance* they manifest in both books, derives from relating what Yeats memorably called "the uncontrollable mystery on the bestial floor" ("The Magi," 1.8)—whether that is the joyful description of "MaMa . . . squatting over a basin, . . . blood . . . pouring from her" as she gives birth to her youngest sons in *China Men* (264) or the aunt in *The Woman Warrior* giving birth to "the hot, wet, moving mass" of her unwanted daughter amid the dirt and squalor of the pigsty (21).

Helicoidal Movement in *The Woman Warrior* and *China Men*

Like the double helix that maps the chain of life in DNA, we can imagine Hong Kingston's intertextual narratives as spiraling in unison through history. Indeed, if I may elaborate on Mary Slowik's evocative reading of *China Men*'s introductory intertext "On Fathers," the men's and the women's stories often double back on each other, with the ending of one the beginning of another ("When the Ghosts Speak," 247). As they do, they alternately cast light or shadow across the path of the other. I shall illustrate this movement by reading "No Name Woman" and "The Brother in Vietnam" again to suggest how Hong Kingston brings men and women from different worlds and times closer together in spirit. We will recall that she originally planned "a big novel about men and women . . . going from ancient feudal times up to the Vietnam War and past that" (Bonetti, 35). Consequently, one common view of the rationale behind her gender division is that *The Woman Warrior* is Hong Kingston's "China book" and *China Men* her "Gold Mountain book" of America.[15] It is tempting to conclude from this that the women's stories cover the past and the men's take the reader up to the present. Although it is true that *The Woman Warrior* depicts the women as the custodians of the old myths and stories, and *China Men* represents their menfolk as makers of a new history and nation, the fact remains that much of the respective writing was done simultaneously.

One of the major challenges facing the reader who wishes to trace the Hong clan history from *The Woman Warrior* through *China Men* is that the narratives are organized nonchronologically. Instead, they are built around a talk-story, or "old chestnut," that has been in family circulation for sometime, whet the interest in a relative who is a "character" or the subject of juicy gossip, are hazy when it comes not only to the order of events but corroborating details, and involve disorienting zigzags back and forth in time (Huntley, 25, 78). As Laura Skandera-Trombley observes in her introduction to *Critical Essays*, quoting Jeanne R. Smith, discussing such works "'requires culturally specific, flexible, border-crossing analysis,' a methodology for which at present there is no model" (*Critical Essays*, 25, 335). Clara Claiborne Park suggests that rather than fight "the dissolving chronology of these books," the reader go with their narrative flow.[16] For Park, as for Rabine, the model is the helicoidal symbol of the yin and yang that brings opposites together, interconnects masculine and feminine force, the active and passive principle, and, as defined by Cirlot, helps animate "the universal whirlwind," which "engenders perpetual motion, metamorphosis and continuity in situations characterized by contradiction."[17]

War as the Backdrop to the Two Books

This universal whirlwind is also set in motion by war, and, although Fa Mu Lan is a composite folk heroine drawn from ancient (fifth century) and feudal (twelfth century) Chinese source material (Huntley, 98–99) who histrionically fights mythical battles, Hong Kingston reminds her readers that *The Woman Warrior* is "not just a story about the ancient, mythic past, nor is it just a story about a present time of childhood. I remind people where I am . . . [when] I'm writing the book, which is the early 1970s. The Vietnam War is just over, and there's still a lot of fallout from it" (Skenazy, "Kingston at the University," 139). In fact, she goes on to say that many of the events recounted in *The Woman Warrior* actually take place in the 1960s during the Vietnam War. This war is a recurrent subject in her interviews, and it is evident that it taxed her conscience to the limit, as it does "The Brother in Vietnam" at the end of *China Men*. It led to student protest at Berkeley, prolonged exile with her husband in Hawai'i, where she began to write in earnest, and an expansion of consciousness that found expression in pacifist causes, Buddhist spirituality, and the establishment of workshops of meditation and creative writing for the rehabilitation of Vietnam War veterans.[18] Even when she does not specifically convey the oppressive darkness of spirit she felt during the Vietnam War, she envisages war in general as the looming backdrop to both the men's and women's stories (Seshachari, 195).

The first and third stories of *The Woman Warrior*, "No Name Woman" and "Shaman," are set largely in the 1920s and 1930s, after the collapse of the Chinese empire, when the country was torn apart by the rival fighting of warlords, civil war between the Communists and the Kuomintang, and the brutal Japanese invasion of the mainland that preceded full-scale global war (Simmons, 62). The first major chapter of *China Men*, "The Father from China," also covers this same history and dramatically depicts Brave Orchid, the Japanese enemy at her back, bribing her way onto the last ship out of Canton in 1939, with only enough time to rip the canopy border from her bridal bed as a last keepsake of old China.[19] The next chapter in *China Men*, "The Great Grandfather of the Sandalwood Mountains," portrays Great-Grandfather Bak Goong as prescient during the Taiping Rebellion that a "century-size upheaval" had begun in China and as an early draft-dodger who evaded conscription by signing on as a crewman to Hawai'i (92–93).[20] "The Grandfather of the Sierra Nevada Mountains," which begins during the America Civil War, depicts "the Driving Out" and massacre of the Chinese labor force that built the transcontinental railroad system and punctures the myth that the "new world" was free of the fighting, slaughter, and lawlessness that took place in "old" China. The tragic-comic events of *The Woman Warrior*'s "At the Western Palace" occur during the Vietnam War, whereas both "A Song for a Barbarian Reed Pipe" and "The Brother in Vietnam" also refer to the Korean War. "White Tigers" mentions the war in which "The Brother in Vietnam" enlisted (49) and, along with *China Men*'s "The Making of More Americans," alludes to the bloody birth of the People's Republic of China.

Hong Kingston herself was born into the vortex of war in 1940, the year of the so-called Angry Dragon (Skandera-Trombley, *Critical Essays*, 4), and she admits that her first, and arguably most lasting, memories were defined by World War II. As a schoolgirl during the Korean War, her narrative double writes a composition on "The War," ignorant of the fact that "there was more than one" (*CM*, 276). Her child's wartime mentality opens "The Brother in Vietnam," coloring and contextualizing the vivid memories that succeed of her two youngest brothers being born.[21] Although her representation of these births is joyful, as we have seen, blood pours from her mother in labor, with the cry of the newborn piercing the rapt silence surrounding the first moments of life. The sounds that this baby will hear in the 1960s as he goes to the Vietnam War are The Byrds' popular ballad interpretation of the song in Ecclesiastes: There's "a time to be born and a time to die, a time to laugh and a time to weep, a time to love and a time to hate, a time for war and a time for peace" (Eccl. 3:1–8).[22] Referring to her own feelings on becoming a mother in 1963, Hong Kingston remarked that "I felt very protective of not just my son but my brothers. And I didn't want my son to grow up in a world where there is going to be a draft" (Seshachari, 195–196). When she looked back to the 1960s, when both her brothers went to Vietnam, she recalled thinking, "Girls and women had it easy compared to that" (Blauvelt, 80).

WOMEN AS COMRADES-IN-ARMS OF MEN

Whatever she may have felt then, the overall impression that both books give is that women cannot afford to take it easy but must soldier on in life like the men. In *The Woman Warrior*, Fa Mu Lan is given the composite strengths, but not the weaknesses, of the principal female characters in the other stories. She is romantic and passionate like the no name woman, courageous and resourceful like Brave Orchid, courteous and graceful like Moon Orchid, an inspirational and self-sacrificing mother like Ts'ai Yen, and idealistic and inventive like the narrator. Although women do not have the same prominence in *China Men*, resilient figures such as Brave Orchid and her youngest sister Lovely Orchid appear from time to time in the male narratives and show their mettle or put "hero-fire" (*WW*, 40) into the bellies of husbands facing defeat.[23] Armed for action, they not only resemble Fa Mu Lan, but also bear out the revolutionary possibility transmitted in the original fifth-century ballad of Mulan—that when they join forces in a common cause, women and men can put aside and sometimes move beyond their differences.[24] Of course, Hong Kingston's version of the Mulan ballad is a wish-fulfilling fantasy, reflecting resentment not only of the traditional Chinese preference for boys, but also of the American cultural fact that, as she said, "guys had more interesting, adventurous, dramatic lives in the '60s than the girls did" (Blauvelt, 80). Both the story of Fa Mu Lan and "The Brother in Vietnam" end with their homecoming and welcome return to their families. In retrospect, however, Hong Kingston regretted that she did not use the occasion to end "the feminist war" in *The Woman Warrior* and transform "an aggressive storytelling act" such as "White Tigers" into a more "hopeful story" about a female war veteran who, like her male brother counterpart in *China Men*, becomes a peacemaker (Bonetti, 40; Seshachari, 193). She also regretted the fact that her editor, Charles Elliott at Alfred A. Knopf, persuaded her to name her book of women's stories *The Woman Warrior*, because it accentuates the warrior at the expense of the pacifist.

While professing not really to like warriors or be "telling the story of war," she conceded that she "was not seeing clearly about war and peace" when she wrote her first book.[25]

BRAVE ORCHID AS WOMAN WARRIOR

If *China Men* is the book of fathers, *The Woman Warrior* reads as a mother book. Indeed, though it takes its name from Mulan, the book leaves the strong impression that it was named for Brave Orchid.[26] Even in peacetime, Brave Orchid shows her warrior spirit. She loves to retell old war stories, especially those that recount social instability, mob violence, and extreme personal danger such as the account of the "No Name Woman" or her tense narration of how the sitting ghost was vaporized and the village crazy lady stoned to death in "Shaman."[27] While Hong Kingston bemoans the fact that "peace has hardly been imagined" and "is rarely dramatized" (Seshachari, 201), Brave Orchid craves the drama and excitement of a good fight, as we can see from the battle of the sexes she stages at her wedding near the start of *China Men*. This "very clever bride" is determined not to let China's oppressive laws of gender dictate her life, and she outsmarts the in-laws who want her to kowtow to the groom. To the surprise of all, "she leapt up on the bed and sat facing him so closely that there was no room for her to kowtow" (32), thus showing her initiative, her force of character, and, possibly, her strong sex drive. She is declared "the best crying bride" the women have ever heard when she improvises a mock-serious bridal song and cries to her heart's content "for boys and men drafted into armies" and for "widows and orphans" (30). Though her cries are greeted with delight by her audience—like the cries of the newborn in "The Brother in Vietnam"—they are a portentous reminder of the families devastated by war and male emigration to the Gold Mountain. Ironically, both she and her sister-in-law are also destined to become "widows of the living." "No Name Woman" opens with the two women's fate being sealed when their husbands go "out on the road" together in 1924.[28] The absence of their marital partners and a normal sex life lies behind the story of adultery and illicit pregnancy that befalls Brave Orchid's sister-in-law at the beginning of *The Woman Warrior*, but this story is set in motion by a complicated chain of historical events and circumstances recounted near the beginning of *China Men*.

WAR ON THE FAMILY

If the Vietnam War made Hong Kingston feel vulnerable as the mother of an only son, human vandalism and savagery make the aunt in "No Name Woman" poignantly aware of the "preciousness" of young life, even though her new baby is a daughter, begot out of wedlock, rather than the favored son and heir born to Brave Orchid or indeed to Hong Kingston. The aunt protects her daughter the only way she knows how—not by trying to keep her safe from war, but by saving her through death from further harm. In the narrator's opinion, "Carrying the baby to the well shows loving. Otherwise abandon it. Turn its face into the mud. Mothers who love their children take them along. It was probably a girl; there is some hope of forgiveness for boys" (*WW*, 21).[29] In fact, the mother's death pact with her daughter is a macabre version of the loving rituals that mark the birth of boys in traditional Chinese society (Rabine, 479–480).

Though the recurrent nightmare of modern warfare haunts the narrator in both *The Woman Warrior* and *China Men*, mothers and fathers are not always capable of leading their children out of its horror to safety. In "No Name Woman," the birthplace blows up into a battlefield, a Vietnam on a miniature scale. Indeed, Hong Kingston memorably told Jody Hoy that she wanted to "show the terrible problems, fights, wars within the family—even mother and daughter who love each other so much and yet have wars that tear them apart—and families fighting families. And then the fathers go across the ocean, not just because they want a better life, but because they can't stand their families" (52). In *The Woman Warrior* women are given complicated representation as the victims, the combatants, the collaborators, and the survivors of domestic violence. As feminist critics have been quick to note, the two stories that frame *The Woman Warrior*—"No Name Woman" and "A Song for a Barbarian Reed Pipe"—recount the rape, subjugation, and impregnation of gifted women. Their final indignity is that they are not allowed to raise the offspring of their sexual assault in peace (Huntley, 111). Hong Kingston depicts the no name woman as a stoical warrior who faces birth and death alone. "She got to her feet to fight better and remembered that old-fashioned women gave birth in their pigsties to fool the jealous, pain-dealing gods" (21). The *China Men* intertext "On Mortality" makes men look in horror at a cruel Chinese belief that women who die in childbirth will be sent in punishment to the bloody pit of the underworld (120).[30] The no name woman does not escape punishment in the afterlife, but her stoicism is a reminder that both giving birth and dying require courage and that, in some societies, women who died in childbirth received the hero's tribute of the warrior killed in battle.[31]

THE BATTLE OF THE SEXES

In marked contrast, battle-axes like Brave Orchid continue to fight on long past the age of childbearing, still determined to prove in their eighties that they are "brave and good" and "have bodily strength and control"

(*WW*, 70, 95), even if the minor "victories" cost lives in the family. Moon Orchid, tai-tai sister from Hong Kong, is one of the chief casualties of her art of war and tactical penchant for surprise attack. "At the Western Palace," the fourth story of *The Woman Warrior*, unfolds as a black comedy in which Brave Orchid plans an offensive against Moon Orchid's bigamist husband. She and her sister remember him as a mollycoddled boy thirty years ago in China, that is to say, as no threat to "the feminist war that's going on in *The Woman Warrior*" and to women's feats of strength over men in its stories (Bonetti, 40). Brave Orchid's madcap strategy to ambush a grown man, however, goes horribly wrong. "'So. A new plan, then,' said Brave Orchid, looking at her son, who had his forehead on the steering wheel. 'You,' she said, 'I want you to go up to his office and tell your uncle that there has been an accident out in the street. . . . You bring him to the car'" (136).

As though already anticipating a male comeback in *China Men*, the narrator shows how the startled husband proceeds to project, assert himself, and wrest command of this story from the women. She suggests that, as he does, the women involuntarily recoil and shrink in size to little old ladies who are faintly ridiculous. "The two old ladies saw a man, authoritative in his dark western suit, start to fill the front of the car. . . . Suddenly the two women remembered that in China families married young boys to older girls, who baby-sat their husbands their whole lives" (137). Having escaped his maternal minders in China, this husband built a successful new life for himself as a doctor in America, yet remained a "good provider" to his abandoned wife, the pampered Moon Orchid. Unable to cut this confident man down to the size of a young boy, all that Brave Orchid can think to say in reply is "you made her live like a widow" (138). While intended to be cutting, her retort is a feeble last defense of her sister. Now that her days as a central character in *The Woman Warrior* are numbered and she is addressed, to her indignation, as "Grandmother," Brave Orchid becomes the belated champion of the "widows of the living." As Sau-ling Wong has persuasively argued, she is defending not only her sister but herself, her vilified sister-in-law, and the many no name women of Guangdong region who did not accompany their husbands out on the road, but were left behind to make their own separate lives and stories (*Reading Asian American Literature*, 198–200). The husband's final, devastating reply as an intertextual reader—"you became people in a book I had read a long time ago" (139)—consigns Brave Orchid and all her "sisters" not simply to the past history he abandoned in China or to a book of life that is old and out of date, but to *The Woman Warrior*, a book nearing its end, shortly to be overtaken by *China Men*.

Brave Orchid's kill-or-be-killed mentality, satirized in the thud of her kitchen chopper and the screams of the animals she butchers for the family meals (*WW*, 85–86), takes a heavy somatic toll on the narrator of *The Woman Warrior*, as is evident from the frank exchange between mother and daughter at the close of "Shaman." "'I can't stop working. When I stop working, I hurt. My head, my back, my legs hurt. I get dizzy. I can't stop.' 'I'm like that too, Mama. I work all the time. . . . I know how to kill food, how to skin and pluck it. . . . I know how to work when things get bad'" (99). In an interview with Skenazy, Hong Kingston indirectly spoke of the problem of having a woman warrior for a mother and of the battle for power fought not only between the sexes but also from one generation to another. She alluded to Allen Ginsberg's *Kaddish*, in which "Mom and grandmother are arch-enemies? These are the people who are supposed to love each other the most! Same thing with mother and daughter, same thing with husband and wife" and commented that "it's a life-and-death struggle, a love and hate struggle" ("Kingston at the University," 154). This remark also seems apt commentary on the heated intertextual relationship between Hong Kingston and Frank Chin, the antagonistic reader of her two gender books. As David Eng has wittily but fittingly observed, they are the "spiritual matriarch and apoplectic patriarch of Asian American literature."[32] As we saw in the first chapter, her writer's revenge and teasing but affectionate response was to capture his militant voice and character in her third novel *Tripmaster Monkey*.

War Victims and Displaced Persons

Hong Kingston's subsequent social work with Vietnam veterans made her think again about her mother and aunt and reread them from a more forgiving perspective than she had when she wrote in the 1970s. In "At the Western Palace," Moon Orchid is the victim of her sister's laughable attempts at tactical warfare. In a revealing exchange of views with a classroom audience at the University of California–Santa Cruz, however, Hong Kingston speculated that Brave Orchid was a victim, too—of the Sino-Japanese war that flares up in "Shaman." "Lately I've been thinking about her in the way that we think about Vietnam veterans, as a victim of post-traumatic stress syndrome" (Skenazy, "Kingston at the University,"139). The daughter narrator relates how "by 1939 the Japanese had taken much of the land along the Kwoo River, and my mother was in the mountains with other refugees" (*WW*, 87). Even after she escapes to America, Brave Orchid continues to relive the traumatic wartime experience of fleeing her home on the Kwoo River in New Society Village. "I used to watch my mother and father play refugees, sleeping sitting up, huddled together with their heads on each other's shoulder, their arms about each other, holding up the blanket like a little tent" (87). As Diane Simmons observes, World War II did not begin for Chinese Americans in 1941 with the Japanese assault on Pearl Harbor, but in 1937, with the invasion of China (133). Though it is Brave Orchid who has experienced this invasion firsthand, and not the father who left for America in 1924, both parents pantomime their emotional conviction that they remain fugitives on the run from the enemy, finding temporary shelter in a large refugee camp called America. "'Aiaa,' they'd sigh. 'Aiaa.' 'Mother, what's a refugee? Father, what's a refugee?'" (87).

In *China Men* the narrator remembers this scene again, but she introduces it from the point of view of her father and shows how he sought refuge in an old army cot at home from the hostile environment of work. "When BaBa came home, he and MaMa got into the cot and pretended they were refugees under a blanket tent" (246). The two books do not provide tidy answers to the question she asked her parents as a child—"what's a refugee?"—but suggest that the posttraumatic stress suffered by victims of war and displacement is a relatively common psychological phenomenon, especially among older, first-generation Chinese immigrants to America. Indeed, with hindsight, Hong Kingston began to understand not only Brave Orchid's siege mentality, but also Moon Orchid's mental breakdown as a manifestation of refugee syndrome.[33] It is noteworthy that the daughter narrator of *The Woman Warrior* also exhibits characteristics similar to the symptoms of stress disorder in combat survivors or displaced persons. She is inhibited, withdrawn, and paranoid; she cannot cope with feelings and so oscillates between numbness and rage; she suffers from fragmented recall, intrusive thoughts, and sudden flashbacks; and she is troubled by apparitions, hallucinations, broken sleep, and nightmares in which her traumatized family suffers a living death at her hands. "I had vampire nightmares: every night the fangs grew longer, and my angel wings turned pointed and black. I hunted humans down in the long woods and shadowed them with my blackness. Tears dripped from my eyes, but blood dripped from my fangs, blood of the people I was supposed to love" (170). I therefore propose that we begin to read the "No Name Woman" as a story of a recurrent family trauma and the traces of the fathers of *China Men* as the signs of amnesia and repression gradually giving way to recollection.

FAMILY TRAUMA, AMNESIA, AND REPRESSION

When she explained to Paula Rabinowitz her rationale in *China Men*, Hong Kingston stated that she "wrote the characters so that the women have memories and the men don't have memories. They don't remember anything. The character of my father, for example, has no memory. He has no stories of the past. He is an American and even his memories are provided by the mother" (70). She depicts the men suffering from collective amnesia. Yet the narrator of *China Men* also highlights the superlative memory feats that must have won her father the accolade of "Learned Scholar or a Righteous Worthy" on "the qualifying test for the last Imperial Examination ever given" (24, 28) and gain him entry to America after being grilled at length by cunning immigration officials (60). The father's later effort to fix himself in the present (*CM*, 15) and stop China from intruding into his thoughts would have required the massive psychic shutdown of an extraordinary memory. Hong Kingston remarked in the aftermath of Tiananmen Square that she was "working against the silence of people who try to forget huge chunks of history"; and she saw remembrance, however painful, as the only safeguard against collective insensibility to the past (Skenazy, "Kingston at the University," 121).

As we saw in the first chapter, psychoanalytic intertextuality maintains that the greater the pressure to repress, the more insistent is the need to express, and that, vice versa, the conscious wish to reveal may result in further concealment. Although the narrator of *The Woman Warrior* is pressured by her mother to collude in the family secrets—"'Don't let your father know that I told you. He denies her'" (13)—her writing does not "deny the father's truth" (Rabine, 488) so much as attempt a difficult catharsis and express the truth he denies. Her mother, however, is the keeper of the memories that provide access to the father, and as the narrator famously complains near the close of *The Woman Warrior*, these are screened by riddles: "You lie with stories. You won't tell me a story and then say, 'This is a true story,' or, 'This is just a story'" (180). She must resist being waylaid by her mother's false or trick memories in *The Woman Warrior*, and in *China Men* she must try to fill the gaps between her father's "silences and few words" (15). Ironically, until such time as her father is ready "to speak up with the real stories," she has to resort to her mother's narrative technique of making up her father's past where she "can't tell what's real and what you make up" (*WW*, 180).

The Return of the Repressed—Bringing the Father and Aunt Back to Life

When asked if it was easy to begin writing about her family when confronted with a wall of silence, Hong Kingston made the emphatic and revealing response: "Oh no, no, no. I had all kinds of strictures to myself about "no name woman," of don't tell, just don't tell. Because these are shameful things" (Skenazy, "Kingston at the University," 129). Her triple denial echoes the three repeated interdicts that kick-start "No Name Woman" and that reverberate throughout *The Woman Warrior*. "'You must not tell anyone,' my mother said, 'what I am about to tell you.'"—"'Don't let your father know that I told you.'"—"'Don't tell anyone you had an aunt'" (11, 13, 21). Clara Claiborne Park, who reviewed *China Men* and *The Woman Warrior* together in 1980, suggested that Hong Kingston was in the grip of a compulsion and "had to write both books, imagining her way out of the Yin symbol she was born to and into the Yang of masculine experience. The two together complete the circle" (*Critical Essays*, 218). Let me reconfigure this helicoidal symbol of the yin-yang in terms of the daughter's family circle. The narrator of *The Woman Warrior* feels driven to tell the chilling story of the "No Name Woman" who gave nothing away about her victimizer before she jumped down the family well to her death and was sentenced posthumously to oblivion. In *China Men*, this same narrator, now older and more tolerant of others, has an analogous and equally strong need to break through her father's blanket silence. In order to do so, she will engage in the Freudian activity of interpreting his dreams, though her father is dismissive of dreamers like Uncle Bun in *China Men*.[34] "Baba snorted, 'Foolish man. Silly man. Long winded.' . . . 'Fermenting dreams,' said Baba. . . . I heard in his scorn and words how dreams ferment the way yeast and mold do, how dreams are like fungus" (193). Undeterred by these words, she will attempt to translate BaBa's terrifying dreamscape of nightmares, swearing, and nightly screams into an intelligible life story. In fact, the fate of BaBa and the no name woman, youngest brother and sister, most "precious" and beloved members of their family, are intertextually linked through the two books. In *The Woman Warrior*, the narrator sets out to rescue her aunt, and in *China Men* her father, from the psychic underworld where they languish.

Family Disclosure and Disloyalty

In response to the question of how she managed to "break through the silence," overcome the strong inhibitions against disclosure, and put the forbidden story of the "No Name Woman" into words, Hong Kingston indicated that it was not easy, and described the tortuous steps involved in drafting *The Woman Warrior*. Guilty feelings of betrayal and disloyalty are common to women who write about their parents, for as Ursula Owen remarked, "Our parents lie at the heart of our innermost feelings, and are part of our most important inner debates. For daughters writing about fathers, this difficulty seems to be acute."[35] Clearly troubled in conscience,

Hong Kingston recounted her ongoing internal dialogue with the disobedient and dissembling daughter self and the mother who had been introjected as the censoring and prohibiting voice of the superego. "Sometime I get really tricky, like a lawyer, and I think, 'My mother says, "Don't tell what I am about to tell you,"' and I think, 'Well, I'm not going to "tell," I'm just going to write.' Or she says, 'Don't tell what I am about to tell you,' and she tells it in Chinese. But what if I told it in English?" In the end, Hong Kingston writes the story "because I have to, and there's no real way of stopping that," but evades the punitive censor by telling the carping voices in her head that she "won't publish." This act of expression overcomes the repression, and she finds herself "freed" at last "to write whatever way I pleased," to write "more and more perfectly and . . . with more and more understanding." Finally, she concludes that her writing will not wrong the family but is "all right to publish," indeed, is the right thing to do (Fisher Fishkin, 162). Her inner debate highlights Kristeva's definition of intertextuality as a dialogue of the self with the other who is always more than one. It also illustrates Hong Kingston's intertextual connection with African American writers such as Alice Walker and Toni Morrison, who begin their respective novels—*The Color Purple* (1982) and *The Bluest Eye* (1970)—with similar injunctions to silence and secrecy and who break the taboos forbidding women's stories a place in literary history.[36] Hong Kingston's powerful justification for telling the forbidden, writing the "unspeakable" (Hoy, 50), and imagining the unthinkable goes to the heart of my intertextual study of her two books. She wrote the no name woman back into existence because "all these villagers are taking a living creature and saying, we're going to wipe her out of the book of life, we're going to forget about her" (Fisher Fishkin, 162).

The Pain and Price of Remembrance

"Lest we forget" is the haunting inscription on war cenotaphs reminding a present generation that they have the dead to thank for the fact that they are now alive. "Lest we forget" contains the warning that the history of bloodshed can repeat itself and reminds the living that they must fight "a battle against silence" on behalf of the dead, as the daughter narrator does in "No Name Woman."[37] Yet, as we have already seen, the telling of her aunt's life required a further act of aggression. The men had their stories taken away from them and their strength given to the women (Bonetti, 40). As we have also seen, Frank Chin took Hong Kingston and her white feminist readers to task for condemning patriarchal oppression and male abuse of Chinese women in *The Woman Warrior* while ignoring how China men have been vilified, emasculated, and generally misrepresented in America. One of the chief aims of this intertextual study is—paraphrasing the final lines of the Ballad of Mulan—to look at men and women as they "run side by side" in the two books.[38] But this requires tolerant listening to the dissenting voices of others. As Garrett Hongo astutely observes, Asian American critics may "respond with anger because of the pain released" when cultural representation does not adequately communicate their experience and inner feelings (16). Chin's virulent response to Hong Kingston's writing suggests how painfully hard men and women must struggle to arrive at common understanding over the course of *The Woman Warrior* and *China Men*.[39]

Murder and the Saving of the Family

Nonetheless, in restoring the memory of her aunt, the narrator does appear to neglect her father. She wipes all but the faintest traces of him from *The Woman Warrior* and tears his pages in the book of life out of her narrative. Hong Kingston felt passionately that her aunt had suffered "a most terrible kind of murder" (Skenazy, "Kingston at the University," 119) through the spiteful silence and forgetting of her family relatives; in redressing this wrong in her narrative, though, she commits a kind of parricide by her radical diminishment of her father's character. Indeed, his amnesia, dumbness, deadened feelings, and bad dreams at the beginning of *China Men* suggest that he is punished severely for his attempt to murder the memory of his sister in *The Woman Warrior*.

Hong Kingston tackled the forbidden subject of the "No Name Woman" head on, breaking the taboo—"you must not tell anyone"—by saying it out loud and so dispelling its secret power.[40] Her speech transgression is also a dialogic act in which she puts words that convey her mother's narrative voice and emotional register into circulation. In overcoming the obstacle that prohibits the expression of her aunt's story, however, she faces another: the repression of her father's story. For mother and daughter are so deep in talk—and thought—in this first story that the father can go virtually unheard (Leiwei Li, 196). Hong Kingston has spoken of the barriers she surmounted to make the aunt's story come to life and declared on several occasions that "she saved her . . . from the no-nameness, the nothing, and created her again" (Skenazy, "Kingston at the University," 119; see also Fisher Fishkin, 162). But she also alluded to the intertextual network of listeners and readers who "finish this act of creativity" by continuing to speculate about the no name woman's life. In giving all her attention as a storyteller to the narrative act of saving this woman's life, she inevitably runs the risk of losing sight of the father. Intertextual readers thus face the double duty of keeping him alive as they prolong the women's lives through their interpretation of *The Woman Warrior*.

The Idea of the Imaginary Father

What the intertextual reader is also being asked to "save" is an idea—the idea of the father—and Kristeva's psychoanalytic theory of the imaginary father suggests how this idea can function textually. Kristeva does not conceive of this figure as a real person, a real father, or a real man, but as a parental metaphor. This metaphor has symbolic value for the child insofar as it creates the space for the free play of language and dialogic speech. She also defines the psychic role of this metaphor, however, and in doing so elucidates the intertextual importance that the shadowy figure of the father can have for the daughter narrator in both *The Woman Warrior* and *China Men*.[41] Kristeva projects the imaginary father as "the possibility of absence, the possibility of love, the possibility of interdiction but also a gift. And which is something different from the overwhelming presence of the mother which is loving, but which is also too much desiring, too much in close proximity with the child."[42] It must be stressed that Kristeva's idea of the imaginary father is also "something different" from the idealized patriarch who traditionally habituated daughters to patriarchal dependence and hero worship of men who appear all-powerful. The imaginary father carries the promise of greater emotional autonomy and powers of differentiation. It is in this sense that the psychoanalytic feminist Jessica Benjamin claims, "The key to the missing desire in women is in one sense the missing father" (88).

Read on its own, *The Woman Warrior* certainly seems to bear out Sara Ruddick's generalization that "barely known, scarcely knowable, the 'absence' of fathers permeates feminist stories."[43] It is also true that the mother is an overwhelming presence in the book. Brave Orchid not only encroaches her daughter's personal space with her physical bulk, her loud voice, and her tireless energy for work, but also invades her mind with her talk-stories. Recalling how she envisaged her mother as a child, Hong Kingston remarked, "I thought my mother was enormous, you know, much taller, much heavier, much bigger in every way—bigger soul, bigger personality, bigger everything" (Skenazy, "Kingston at the University," 123). *The Woman Warrior* projects the child's mythology of the mother as a larger-than-life figure. In answer to Hoy's question—"What 'size' is your mother these days?"—Hong Kingston acknowledged the hold that the fabulous parents of the child's imagination can continue to have over the creative mind. "You know, just when I think things are normal, that we're just like everybody else, then she will do something immense and enormous" (61).

Nevertheless, the problem that Kristeva acutely diagnosed remains. In relation to the overwhelming figure of the mother, the child not only perceives herself as little but sees her father as diminished.[44] The father's only display of power in *The Woman Warrior* is the interdict that opens "No Name Woman" and is repeated three times with the magical authority of the prohibition in fairy tales. If, according to Donald Goellnicht, writing is the daughter's "pure gift" that will give the father the voice he lacks ("Tang Ao in America," 240), that gift is not freely given until *China Men* is finished. That leaves us to consider the imaginary father as representing "the possibility of love" in *The Woman Warrior*. In tune with the popular language, beat, and songs of the street, Hong Kingston echoes the voices of the Beatles, troubadours of the Sixties, who tongue-in-cheek proclaimed "all you need is love . . . love is all you need." Later accused by her critics of hanging out the family's dirty linen,[45] especially that of her father, the China laundryman, who spends the prime of his life "Washing out blood that stinks like brass— / Only a Chinaman can debase himself so" (*CM*, 63), Hong Kingston defended herself in terms of this "possibility of love." She argued that "it's OK to write about the very worst people in your family and worst feelings that you might have about your loved ones" (Skenazy, "Kingston at the University," 129). She gave herself permission to "let it all hang out" as a storyteller because she believed that writing was an emotional, as well as creative, process. She trusted that it would lead to love and the resolution of her conflicted feelings for the people in her stories (Pfaff, 18; Skenazy, "Kingston at the University," 121).

The Role of the Imaginary Father in Intersubjectivity and Intertextuality

In the case of the mother, we have a character who is portrayed as coming too close to her daughter narrator for comfort. In the case of the father, we have a character who is represented at the other extreme as a remote figure in *The Woman Warrior*. Kristeva's idea of the imaginary father mediates between the child's fluctuating sense of the presence of the mother and the absence of the father, of the daughter's overidentification with her mother and distance from her father, of the attachment and detachment that triangulate their relationship to one another, and of the love and hostility that circulate among them. For this reason Kristeva pointed out that the imaginary father can stand symbolically for either parent.[46] Or the idea can encompass both mother and father, as in the case of the sage old couple who train Fa Mu Lan as a woman warrior, whose life cycle turns in harmony with the seasons, the earth, and the cosmos, who move in unison with the cultural eurhythmics of "Chinese lion dancers, African lion dancers . . . high Javanese bells . . . Indian bells, Hindu Indian, American Indian" (*WW*, 31), and who keep their balance by concentrating on the "unvarying mean" at the center of the yin-yang principle (Cirlot, 380). Just as Fa Mu Lan glimpses different and mysterious sides to this old couple—but only when she looks obliquely, never directly—so the daughter narrator will detect hidden depths and undercurrents to her parents' lives. In *The Woman Warrior* her mother will show flashes of a more remarkable life in China as heroic shaman, bard, and wise woman before receding back into the demeaning role of work slave and querulous immigrant in America. Likewise, her father will emerge from the shadows of *The Woman Warrior* and give glimpses of his chameleonlike character in *China Men*. He will appear in diverse guises, as the father from China, the American father, the illegal father, and the legal immigrant. He will go here, there, and everywhere, and, like Kristeva's imaginary father, he will end up at a "here that cannot (possibly) be here" (Coward, 22). He will begin his voyage in "Canton or Macao or Hong Kong" (*CM*, 48), disembark in Cuba, make a legal trip from Cuba to New York or hide contorted like Houdini in a crate being shipped to Florida, New Orleans, or New York harbor, or sail into San Francisco Bay, be detained at the Immigration Station on Angel Island, gain legal entry into America and work his way across the continent to New York (Hoy, 53; Pfaff, 16–17). In effect, the imaginary father facilitates an open-ended intertextual journey where the reader is free, like the storyteller, to imagine what might have actually happened and how it concluded.[47] Moreover, insofar as the imaginary father corrects overidentification with the real mother and radical separation from the actual father, "he" can be seen as an agent of the intersubjectivity that personalizes intertextuality where there is an heightened dialogic awareness of self in relation to others (Benjamin, 92–93).

Traces of the Father and China Men in "No Name Woman"

THE OPENING OF *THE WOMAN WARRIOR*
"No Name Woman" begins in 1924 with a paradoxical concurrence of events: a group wedding of seventeen couples followed a few days later by the mass exodus of the Hong family men from the women's lives. These

events recapitulate the creative decision Hong Kingston took to separate the men and women, and treat their lives in two distinct books rather than consider them jointly in an extended family saga. "Your father and his brothers and your grandfather and his brothers and your aunt's new husband sailed for America, the Gold Mountain" (*WW*, 11). This is also the starting point of the journey of "The Father from China" to America and contains the nucleus of the material that would be developed into the main narratives of *China Men*. "They fed and guarded the stowaways and helped them off in Cuba, New York, Bali, Hawaii" (11). It is the end of the line, the final going "out on the road" for Ah Goong, "The Grandfather of the Sierra Nevada Mountains." "It was your grandfather's last trip" (11). It appears to be the first and last time that the aunt sees her new husband. "The night she first saw him, he had sex with her. Then he left for America" (14). Like his ill-fated wife, this husband will never be seen or heard of again. The only visual reminder the aunt has of his brief presence is a "black and white face in the group photograph the men had had taken before leaving" (14), and there is not the slightest trace of him as a male character in *China Men*. Brave Orchid will not see her own husband for the next fifteen years, and he will never again see his family left behind in China. An account of their eventual reunion will be held over until *China Men* and will be told through the father's eyes as he painfully adjusts the memory he carried of his wife during all those years apart with the sight that greets him—an older matron with "no child tugging her coat and no baby in her arms" (*CM*, 68). As for the new wives who married in haste to ensure that the men "would responsibly come home" (11), the expansion of Chinese exclusion laws in 1924 would make it virtually impossible for Chinese women to join their men working overseas in America, while male sojourners who returned to their wives in China risked loss of their reentry permit (Leiwei Li, 199; Goellnicht, 232, in *Critical Essays*; Kim, *Asian-American Literature*, 96–98).

THE PARTING OF COUPLES AND SEXUAL REPRESSION

Bereft of the men's stories, *The Woman Warrior* points to the social aftermath of Chinese immigration policy: involuntary segregation of the sexes, splitting up of families, and elimination of regular sex and heterosexual companionship. After the husbands' departure, Brave Orchid and the aunt will share the same bedroom. Her blindness to the fact that her sister-in-law develops "such a protruding melon of a stomach" and her amazed disbelief and denial—"she could not have been pregnant, you see, because her husband had been gone for years" (11)—all suggest that for the women left behind, sexuality, their female cycle, and time itself were expected to stop. In "The American Father," the narrator of *China Men* will play with the childish ignorance and folklore that were a social defense against the reality of sexual repression. She wonders if, "in 1903, my father was born in San Francisco, where my grandmother had come disguised as a man. Or, Chinese women once magical, she gave birth at a distance, she in China, my grandfather and father in San Francisco. . . . Or the men of those days had the power to have babies." She repeats her mother's wedding story: "My mother and a few farm women went out into the chicken yard, and said words over a rooster, a fierce rooster, red of comb and feathers; then she went back inside, married, a wife" (*CM*, 237). She replays this scene in *The Woman Warrior* to help her envisage how her aunt "stood tractably beside the best rooster, [her husband's] proxy, and promised before they met that she would be his forever" (*WW*, 14). Yet she endows her aunt with dignity in "No Name Woman" by imagining how she strove to be more than a hen that mates with a rooster, or a dumb animal that is mounted by a farmer who "worked an adjourning field" (14). Instead, she fantasizes how her aunt sought to make sexuality an exploratory outlet for gender-confined longings. "But the rare urge west had fixed upon our family, and so my aunt crossed boundaries not delineated in space" (15).

While "No Name Woman" suggests that the aunt's sexual transgression might have entailed a brief lifting of repression and liberation of the pleasure principle, it also hints at the economic hardship and exhausting servitude that grind her immigrant brother down in America. "After the one carnival ride each, we paid in guilt; our tired father counted his change on the dark walk home" (13). As his sister samples the forbidden delights and drives of the carnivalesque body, the brother walks down a dark road that demands the continual deferral of pleasure and an endless postponement of the return trip home to China (*WW*, 17, 60, 87, 100).[48] Desire drives his sister to her death, but it drives her brother to distraction. It finds neurotic expression in the bad dreams and night screams, curses and evil silences, apathy and rage that come tumbling out at the beginning of *China Men* as the pressures of the father's unconscious, pent up in *The Woman Warrior*, at last find release. Other China men make their way back into the narrative of "No Name Woman," whether they be the crazy grandfather who is kept locked up at home or the "many other men . . . uncles, cousins, nephews, brothers . . . home between journeys" (17). And they leave again as sojourners because of famine, floods, war, plague, greed, and the need "to send food-money home" (19). The narrator's father, however, is a conspicuous absence from their ranks though his recurrent veto of his sister makes him a brooding and inhibiting presence in this first story of *The Woman Warrior*.

His radical break with custom—he is "the only brother who never went back to China having once been traded for a girl" (17)—is a mystery that pricks the interest of the intertextual reader. What are we to make of the narrator's odd non sequitur, which inexplicably connects his adult exile in America with an event that he cannot possibly remember from his early infancy? Does the father perceive himself as less valuable than a girl, interchangeable with her, or does he feel that he is identified with the wished-for "sister" and that their fates are intertwined in some way, so that he cannot bring himself to return to China?

Traces of the Father in "White Tigers"

TRADING PLACES—A GENDER SWAP WITH AN "INFERIOR" GIRL

The thought that, as the youngest of four brothers, he might have been disposable, that he might have been traded for a baby girl worth next to nothing in Confucian society, and, worse, that his father might have preferred him to be "the precious only daughter" (17) would be a source of chagrin and possible confusion to any Chinese male acculturated to the rhetoric that women are "slaves" and if not *xiao ren*, then *nei ren*, or inferior humans for domestic work and breeding.[49] The Confucian classification of women as domestic slaves is still alive in the language the daughter narrator hears at home. "There is a Chinese word for the female I—which is 'slave'" (49). In "White Tigers," she famously lashes out at her hidebound family elders for upholding the iniquitous gender values and traditions of Chinese patriarchy when they settle in America. "When one of my parents or the emigrant villagers said, 'Feeding girls is feeding cowbirds,' I would thrash on the floor and scream so hard I couldn't talk" (48). She resents the fact that the birth of girls is not a cause for celebration or an occasion to rejoice with Walt Whitman that "of male and female . . . either is but the equal of the other."[50] Instead, she bitterly observes how her parents lose face when she and her sister walk together through Chinatown while her brothers restore the family's social prestige and are rewarded with special treatment. "I minded that the emigrant villagers shook their heads at my sister and me. 'One girl—and another girl,' they said, and made our parents ashamed to take us out together. The good part about my brothers being born was that people stopped saying, 'All girls,' but I learned new grievances . . . 'Did you have a full-month party for *me?*'" (48). The narrator's protest against patriarchy's misogyny and strong bias in favor of males, however, is preceded and qualified by the mention of an important social anomaly: that her father was once exchanged for a female and further—as we have already seen—that when her paternal grandfather "finally got a daughter of his own, he doted on her" (17). Of course, it can be argued that the father is given a brief taste of the patriarchal traffic in women. Like Tang Ao in the opening intertext of *China Men*, his symbolic gender swap may force painful and unwanted consciousness of the exploitation Chinese females have routinely experienced.

The father's early experience of being traded on the cheap for a girl also foreshadows his Chinese immigrant experience of being cheap labor in white racist America—a role customarily allocated to women in Confucian sexist ideology. Indeed, one of the father's favorite and most distasteful gender anecdotes, repeated first in "At the Western Palace" and later in "The Father from China," shows his loathing for the fact that he is treated like dirt and his visceral dislike for the unclean women whom he has come to resemble as he sorts mountains of dirty clothes in his Chinese laundry. "'When your father lived in China,' Brave Orchid told the children, 'he refused to eat pastries because he didn't want to eat the dirt the women kneaded from between their fingers'" (*WW*, 129–130). In *China Men*, he "complained about holiday dumplings: 'Women roll dough to knead out the dirt from between their fingers. Women's finger nail dirt'" (14). So deeply ingrained is the cultural message that daughters are dirt cheap and girls will grow up to be slaves (*WW*, 78) that, when the narrator later bullies her Chinese classmate in "A Song for a Barbarian Reed Pipe," she unconsciously imitates her father and imagines how she can use her dirty hands and blackened fingernails to "work her face around like dough" (158, 170). Ironically, when the father settles in America, as we learn from Brave Orchid later in *China Men*, his experience of racial discrimination leads to a perverse form of gender parity. He and his wife lose their distinguishing features of sex and character and become nothing more than faceless Chinamen who look the same in white racist America (Huntley, 115–116). They are forced to work equally hard and long hours as inferior humans. "'He was a slave; I was slave.' She is angry recalling those days" (*CM*, 244).

MALE AND FEMALE SOJOURNERS

I should, however, also like to suggest that the family hearsay portraying him as a "changeling" once traded for a girl fosters an uneasy identification with his sister's changeable and fickle subject position as a woman. Goellnicht points out that the opening intertext of *China Men*, the legend of Tang Ao in "On Discovery," has affinities with "No Name Woman," the hush-hush story that begins *The Woman Warrior* ("Tang Ao in America," 230). The aunt takes after Tang Ao in her "rare urge" to go "west" and cross the ocean that stretches out as far as the eye can see (*WW*, 15; *CM*, 3). Both wish to be sojourners and neither get very far. Tang Ao is held a housebound and footbound prisoner in the Land of Women. As a Chinese female, the aunt is perceived as a temporary sojourner who has a natural "outward tendency" (*WW*, 49). She changes her name in marriage and will raise another family for strangers.[51] Male sojourners also changed their names when they bought the right to be "paper sons" of legal Chinese American citizens (*CM*, 46–47; Goellnicht, "Tang Ao in America," 235–236). Ironically, it is the aunt's marriage to one such sojourner that leads to her regressive move back home to the role of the little daughter. "When her husband left, they welcomed the chance to take her back from the in-laws: she could live like the little daughter for just a while longer" (17). In their move inward, both Tang Ao and the No Name Woman resemble the father who not only turns against the family but also turns in on himself in *China Men*. Goellnicht believes that "BaBa's self-hatred stems from seeing his position in racist America mirrored in the subjection of women in traditional Chinese culture" ("Tang Ao in America," 238). I would go further and argue that it originates in his early switch with a girl and reluctant identification with the gender role and plight of his sister.

INTERTEXTUAL LINKS BETWEEN THE FATHER,
HIS NO NAME SISTER, AND THE NARRATOR

Indeed my intertextual study of *The Woman Warrior* and *China Men* is based on the premise that the lives of the men and women remain connected, making it difficult for the reader to take sides and fostering a critical sympathy for the suffering that sexually and racially polarized groups bring upon themselves and each other. By extension, the fate of the brother and his little sister are still linked. In fact, Simmons regards the early nineteenth-century Chinese novel *Flowers in the Mirror* by Li Ruzhen as a crucial intertext for reading the controlling myths of the two books. She compares the legendary Fa Mu Lan of *The Woman Warrior* to Li Ruzhen's filial daughter Little Hill who steps out of the traditional role of "Little Sister" to rescue her lost father. In respect of the "On Discovery" legend that begins *China Men*, she observes that this same Little Hill was the daughter who set out to find her father Tang Ao—though in the original novel it is not Tang Ao but his brother-in-law, the merchant Lin, who is held captive by women (Simmons, 3, 55, 109–111). This intertext suggests that the "little sister" has a crucial role to play in the fortunes of the father. By her own admission, Hong Kingston felt it was her family duty to give her father's little sister back her "life and a place in history and maybe immortality" (Fisher

Fishkin, 162). In a complicated take on the Fa Mu Lan myth, the narrator steps into, *not out of*, the role of this little sister.[52] Her first overt act in "No Name Woman" is to save her aunt's story and restore it to the book of life. Her second and more urgent act in "White Tigers," however, is her fantasy sacrifice of her life for the father. "'No, Father,' I said. 'I will take your place'" (37). In *The Woman Warrior*, she expresses fears that her father will lose his life, but in *China Men*, she gives vent to the fear that he will take his life, and end up "a spite suicide" like the no name woman (*WW*, 22). If his life is in the balance, then the writer's professed desire to avenge her aunt and redeem her life must apply equally to her father.

The Daughter's Intertextual Journey

Near the close of "White Tigers," the narrator contemplates the intertextual journey that she must make in order to salvage her family's broken book of life and complete her filial mission. "To avenge my family, I'd have to storm across China to take back our farm from the Communists; I'd have to rage across the United States to take back the laundry in New York and the one in California." She will have to crisscross the American continent and travel to the other side of the world. She will have to cross not only time zones but time barriers. She will have to do the impossible and be in two places at once. "Nobody in history has conquered and united both North America and Asia" (50). The only way she can accomplish the impossible, bridge the old world and the new, unite the hyphenated space between Chinese and American life history, and avenge her divided family is by the transhistorical, dual-cultural, and cross-gender writing of *The Woman Warrior* and *China Men*.[53] As if gathering her strength for this task or working herself up into a righteous "rage" on behalf of her family, the daughter narrator assembles the fragments of revolutionary history that filter back to her distraught parents from Communist China. She contextualizes her father's neurotic behavior at the start of *China Men* by suggesting in "White Tigers" that her father had good cause to "scream in his sleep" and that he was not alone. "My mother wept and crumpled up the letters" (51). If the Hong family punished the no name woman by "deliberately forgetting her" (22), they are now punished in turn by systematic torture, extermination, and mental anguish. The narrator's mother and father break down as they hear of Communist reprisals with the news that the uncles left behind in China "were all executed, and the aunt whose thumbs were twisted off drowned herself" in a brutal reprise of the "spite suicide" of the aunt. She recounts how "other aunts, mothers-in-law, and cousins disappeared" and how "the Communists gave axes to the old ladies and said, 'Go and kill yourself.

You're useless'" (51). She narrates the tragic end of the Fourth Uncle, who was killed and left hanging in a tree after climbing up to catch nesting doves to feed his starving wife and children (52). In effect, she watches in horror as the revolutionaries take an axe to the family tree and destroy it root and branch.

In "The Making of More Americans," the narrator will suggest how the cut and dismembered Hong family puts down new roots in American soil and begins to grow back together. Genette pointed the way forward when he insisted on "the fertilizing powers" of intertextuality, where one text is grafted regeneratively upon another.[54] It is not for nothing that this fourth chapter of *China Men* starts with the child's vivid synaesthetic memory of a large, redolent, heaving mound of horse manure! "This pile hummed, and it was the fuel for the ground, the toads, the vegetables, the house, the two grandfathers. . . . It smelled good" and it fertilizes the family tree (166). She will return here to a story that is only half told in "White Tigers" and recount the subsequent fortunes of the Fourth Aunt, left to fend for herself after "the grandmother escaped with the loose cash" and the Communists executed her husband (*WW*, 52). In general, as Simmons remarks, "Kingston signals her intention to make both men and women imaginatively identify with the plight of the other" (109).

Traces of the Father in "Shaman"

CONTRADICTIONS IN BRAVE ORCHID'S WOMAN CHARACTER

"Shaman," the third story of *The Woman Warrior*, opens like old family archives, and as it does, "the smell of China flies out . . . a smell that comes from long ago, far back in the brain" (57). This storage space contains the testimonials of her mother's other life as a Western-trained "lady" doctor. Sau-ling Wong sees her in part as a "'new woman' coming of age during China's turbulent modernization period" (*Reading Asian American Literature*, 28). Unlike Mao's mythologized barefoot doctor, however, Brave Orchid practiced medicine dressed impeccably in "a silk robe and western shoes with big heels" (73). Nor did she walk, but was carried in a sedan chair resembling the palanquin she rides to her wedding in *China Men* (31). She is accompanied by a sturdy slave girl who serves as an assistant nurse and a white puppy being trained as a guard dog (73–74, 78). Hong Kingston later fleshed out this scene by remarking in surprise to Skenazy that, when her mother brought her wardrobe from China out of hiding, the clothes were "so small . . . so pretty"—obviously so feminine—and they fit her own petite frame perfectly (123). In other words, Brave Orchid used to dress like her ladylike sister Moon Orchid, was clothed with the softer feminine spirit of the Mulan ballad's closing stanzas and was once tiny in size like her daughter.

As Huntley reminds us, Brave Orchid's paradoxical name pairs the qualities "of a beautiful and fragile flower with an adjective that connotes strength, sinew, and power" (91). In light of her feminist agenda at the time she wrote *The Woman Warrior*, Hong Kingston could not bring herself to follow the ending of the original chant and represent Fa Mu Lan as "a strong figure [who] turn[s] into such a feminine person with make-up. . . . She wears a silk dress and she's a classically beautiful woman" (Seshachari, 192–193). Dressed in her silk finery in "Shaman," though, Brave Orchid does not seem to be unduly "troubled by [her] feminine powers" nor perceive her stylish attire as a "weakness" (Skenazy, "Kingston at the University," 131–132). Quite the opposite, her smart appearance is calculated to enhance her professional status. "When I stepped out of my sedan chair, the villagers said 'Ahhh,' at my good shoes and my long gown. I always dressed well when I made calls" (74). Her sister, Moon Orchid, will make a similar effort to put her best foot forward when she is reunited with Brave Orchid more than thirty years later, in "At the Western Palace." She will travel from Hong Kong to San Francisco International Airport "dressed in a grey wool suit; she wore pearls around her neck and in her earlobes. Moon Orchid *would* travel with her jewels showing" (108). In present-day America Brave Orchid looks like a bag lady in comparison with the elegant and genteel Moon Orchid—or even the graceful "village crazy lady" (87)— but there are important points of resemblance in their past.[55]

PHOTOGRAPHIC TRACES OF THE FATHER

Brave Orchid's baggage from the past in "Shaman" also includes a photo album filled with the black-and-white snapshots that her husband sent her as a record of his new immigrant life as "Ed" in New York during their fifteen-year separation. The photos appear to corroborate the daughter's narrative claim at the beginning of *China Men*—"Father, I have seen you lighthearted" (11). In the first two pages of "The Father from China," she is able to recall several moments of pure magic when her normally careworn father undergoes a personality change that is metaphorically expressed in the inventive way that he plays with his children. He snatches dragonflies out of thin air and with a wave of his wand turns them into "pet airplane[s]" or transforms the killing of Hitler moths into an Allied raid against the Germans (11–12). Yet just as the games quickly deteriorate— with the clipping of the dragonflies' wings and the crushing of the moths against the walls—so the mood of this passage darkens. "But usually you did not play. You were angry. You scared us. Every day we listened to you swear, 'Dog vomit.' . . . You slammed the iron on the shirt while muttering, 'Stink pig. Mother's cunt'" (12). Indeed the disturbed and sickening portrait of her father that follows is a dark negative of the photos he sends to buck up his wife stuck in China. "Year after year my father did not come home or send for her" (WW, 60). The story these New York photos tell has been carefully stage-managed to support the sojourner fiction that the Gold Mountain is the sweet land of liberty, fraternity, and opportunity. Most have a cheesy but cheerful Hollywood stage-set quality about them that is inspired by the continuously running film shows her father attends as cheap, all-day entertainment. Indeed, the father is so impressed by *Young Tom Edison* as brought alive on the screen by Mickey Rooney that he takes the name "Ed"—"Ed-Da-Son. Son as in *sage* or *immortal* or *saint*" (CM, 71). Anyone who has seen James Cameron's blockbuster *Titanic* will also be struck by the similarity between the photos that Rose keeps from her early immigrant days in New York and the ones Ed takes and sends to his wife in both "Shaman" and "The Father from China"—the same windswept Coney Island backdrop, the same "pose in the cockpit of a biplane" (WW, 59). Fred Astaire and Ginger Roger films also offered Ed the mesmerizing self-image of a figure who cuts a dash "in his many western outfits," and who is "always laughing," "smiling," "dancing down the stairs," and making an effort, like his wife and sister-in-law, to put his best foot forward (WW, 59; CM, 66–67).

The full narrative of "The Father from China" will blow a hole in this fantasy played out on the silver screen and in dance hall mirrors (CM, 61, 65). It will expose the grueling sweat labor that, presto, produces the "wall of clean laundry" against which Ed smiles in one of the photos he sends to Brave Orchid (WW, 59). It will further show the racial hatred for exploited minority workers—whether "chinks" or "micks"—that cankers the heart of American capitalism. In "Shaman," Ed writes to his wife about the light-hearted, fall custom in New York of snatching and stomping on out-of-season straw hats. "That's the way they celebrate the change of seasons here" (WW, 59). *China Men* shows intertextually that, in actuality, Ed takes refuge from racism in pretense and in "takes" on reality as superficial as the Hollywood camera or his amateur snapshots. He cannot afford to look with the honesty and gritty realism of the documentary at the taunting of new immigrants—white as well as yellow. But his daughter, one generation removed from the first-generation American's raw deal, can. "Suddenly a band of white demons came up from behind them. One picked off Ed's straw hat and kicked its lid through. Before Ed and Woodrow could decide what to do for the shame on China Men, they saw the whites stomp on other whites' hats. 'It must be a custom,' said Ed" (*CM*, 64).

TRACES OF DAREDEVIL CHINA MEN

Brave Orchid is undoubtedly the leading lady of "Shaman," and the story recounts the high drama and adventure she had in China before her comedown in America and her final decline into the role of an old trouper, wrapped up against the cold like "a sad bear, a great sheep in a wool shawl" (93). "Shaman," however, also alludes to the colorful adventures and narrow escapes of daredevil China men. Brave Orchid compares her dangerous night calls as a rural doctor to the high risks taken by the China men who "swing over the faces of the Malayan cliffs in baskets" to harvest sea swallow nests (83). Their technique will be adopted by paternal grandfather Ah Goong and the other railroad "basketmen"—some, like Ah Goong, basket cases!—who plant highly volatile gunpowder in the rock face of the Sierra Nevada Mountains (*CM*, 130–132). Brave Orchid also delineates her own father's colorful and devil-may-care sex life by describing the black woman he brings back to China as his third wife (81). The grandson of this "barbarian" wife will later badger his American relatives for money, in "A Song for a Barbarian Reed Pipe" (183–184), and "The Great Grandfather of the Sandalwood Mountains" will open with another account of the effects this racial intermarriage had on the extended family. Indeed, this *China Men* story of "the black grandmother" who "jabbered like a monkey" until the native Chinese family cut her dead and she "fell mute," and who nonetheless, to their amazement, produced an articulate son and grandson is an important exemplum (*CM*, 85–86). The narrator employs it to explode the myth that the Chinese are racially pure, to critique Sinocentric racism, and to remind the reader of yet another no name women condemned to silence. This third wife with the black skin and "brown puffball" hair (*WW*, 81) escaped the aunt's death but perhaps did so because she produced a son who could speak and be understood as Chinese.

THE FATHER'S UTERINE FAMILY

There are also glimpses of the father's upbringing in old China with an allusion to his "tyrant mother with the bound feet" and to Brave Orchid's relief as a Canton medical student in being "free from families" and no longer at the beck and call of her mother-in-law (61). Her husband may have understood her sense of liberation as a woman and shared her need to get away from the uterine family. Indeed, this could be one explanation for the question that troubles the daughter narrator—why her "father did not come home" as expected (60).[56] The daughter narrator suggests further that her father is a highly educated, cultivated, and cerebral man who has been trained to think as a scholar and to master and "recite whole poems" (63). Despite his considerable mental powers, Brave Orchid refers near the close of "Shaman" to the withdrawal and depression that dog his life in America and that return in force after his laundry is torn down for urban redevelopment. "Do you think your father wanted to stop work? Look at his eyes; the brown is going out of his eyes. He has stopped talking" (97). In reading *China Men* we shall want to consider why he sits staring vacantly off into space.

No Name Father, Aunt, and Narrator

Like his sister, the father is an enigma, but he could also be called the no name man of *The Woman Warrior*. Neither he, his sister, nor indeed the daughter narrator is ever addressed by proper name. Hong Kingston did not want her readers to overlook this fact as they routinely do when they give the daughter narrator the name of the author and call her "Maxine." Rather, the absence of a name points to the lack of a complete identity in all three characters and underlines their very human need for recognition. (Skenazy, "Kingston at the University," 133). The daughter experiences the frustration of being told by her mother, "just give your father's name," as if it is a secret password that will give her power "to return to China where I have never been" (73). It is not clear from the final story of *The Woman Warrior*, "A Song for a Barbarian Reed Pipe," whether the narrator actually knows the father's real name or whether she has been forbidden to mention it for fear that like other Chinese American children, she will unwittingly reveal "immigration secrets whose telling could get us sent back to China" (*WW*, 164). But if one of the boys in her class makes a helpless fool of himself by demonstrating that "a son does not know his father's name" (*WW*, 159), it is unlikely that such a fearful personal secret would be entrusted to a daughter low down the pecking order. In this respect, her father is as much terra incognita as China. Indeed, for the uncomprehending child, China and the father represent the irrational and inexplicable terrors of the unconscious life. This life fouls the father's pure, oratorical voice with screams and curses, troubles the daughter's mind with "the language of impossible stories" (*WW*, 82), and disturbs the sleep of both with nightmares, freak shows, and horror movies set in old China. At the end of "Shaman," her mother's romance story of old China, Brave Orchid concedes that her husband is the last link with the old country. "Now it's final. We got a letter from the villagers yesterday. They asked if it was all right with us that they took over the land. The last uncles have been killed, so your father is the only person left to say it is all right, you see. He has written saying they can have it. So. We have no more China to go home to" (99).

Traces of the Father in "At the Western Palace"

The Father as "the Ideal in Masculine Beauty"

Yet China has formatively shaped the father's mind, his character, and even his deportment. When Moon Orchid meets him again in "At the Western Palace," he is "waiting under the tangerine tree" like a classical figure in a Chinese scroll painting. Of course, he is no longer "the young man who left on a ship" with his father, uncles, brothers, and brother-in-law in 1924, but a silver-haired old man who has lived and toiled in America for nearly half a century. Indeed, Moon Orchid recognizes him as the immigrant in the New York photos he sent Brave Orchid in "Shaman." His self-conscious pose under the tangerine tree, the Chinese New Year symbol of prosperity, however, is evocative and reminds Moon Orchid that "her sister had married the ideal in masculine beauty, the thin scholar with the hollow cheeks and the long fingers" (*WW*, 110). The reader needs reminding of his early life as well. The expressive hands that his mother proudly prophesies were made "for holding pens" in "The Father from China" are no longer prized for their connection to the "Four Valuable Things: ink, inkslab, paper, and brush" (*CM*, 16). Now they are the marks of a good for nothing. "The only thing you're trained for is writing poems," Brave Orchid complains during one of her husband's fits of depression in *China Men* (247). In "At the Western Palace, his "graceful fingers" are valued because they are "good for folding shirts to fit the cardboard patterns" in the Stockton family laundry (*WW*, 125).

Memory Lane

The portrait of the father in "At the Western Palace" depicts a dignified old man who, despite his setbacks, still cuts a stylish figure and who, despite his age, remains somewhat vain about his appearance. The debonair grace of a Fred Astaire, however, has now been replaced by the nostalgic air of a displaced Englishman greeting a person from another time and place. The sudden crosswind of memory that ruffles this scene—"his hair blowing silver in twilight"—is reminiscent of the reunion of Ronald Colman, in the role of a first-world-war veteran suffering from shell shock and amnesia, with his forgotten wife at the half-remembered gate in the 1942 film *Random Harvest*. Despite his many years in America, the father's voice sounds familiar to Moon Orchid—not the "chingchong ugly" (*WW*, 154) voice of

Cantonese refugees in the British colony but the polished voice of its white ruling class. "'Hello,' he said like an Englishman in Hong Kong" (110). It is Brave Orchid who looks like the refugee with her blanket, canned food, and thermos bottles spread out on the floor of the airport while she waits for Moon Orchid (105).

Superficially, at least, the father and Moon Orchid resemble one another in their elegant, refined, and vaguely effete manner. They are similarly built with a thin frame and slight body shape. Indeed, the surprise in this passage is that they look the part of man and wife, and certainly appear better matched physically than Brave Orchid and her husband. Once, as we have seen, Brave Orchid also kept up appearances. As she says bluntly to her daughter, "I didn't need muscles in China. I was small in China" (*WW*, 97). Once upon a time Brave Orchid dressed and was the same size as her sister Moon Orchid. The daughter holds up her mother's old wardrobe to the light in "Shaman" and notes in awe that "the silk dresses she gave me are tiny. You would not think the same person wore them. This mother can carry a hundred pounds of Texas rice up and downstairs. She could work at the laundry from six thirty A.M. until midnight" (97). Indeed Hong Kingston wistfully remarked to Simmons that "Moon Orchid is the way Brave Orchid could have been. She's softer, . . . she takes it easy, she lightens up, she doesn't have a sense of mission" (43). Whereas America wears her husband thin and breaks Moon Orchid into tiny pieces, Brave Orchid not only survives but also seems to grow in size and presence. Indeed, her life journey moves in the opposite direction to the Mulan legend where, as Hong Kingston observes, "this strong figure turn[s] into such a feminine person" (Seshachari, 192). Social femininity is an economic luxury that Brave Orchid must leave behind her in China and cannot afford to cultivate or hanker after as an immigrant. Her law of social adaptation is "whatever does not kill you, makes you strong and gives you its power." Again Hong Kingston tellingly remarked that "the women who don't die are the powerful peasant types like Brave Orchid" (Skenazy, "Kingston at the University," 132). In her metamorphosis from a small, pretty woman in feminine attire into a powerful, no-nonsense peasant type, Brave Orchid reverses the thrust of the woman warrior myth and leaves the reader with the subversive image of a feminine person who has become the strong man of the family.

O Sister, Where Art Thou?

"At the Western Palace" lampoons Brave Orchid's strong-arm tactics and recounts the comic disaster that ensues when she handles members of her family like hundred-pound sacks of Texas rice. It is worth noting that Brave Orchid complains in *China Men* that the father weighs "less than a hundred pounds" (250), and by the end of "At the Western Palace" Moon Orchid is an empty sack, "skin hung loose," "clothes bagged," "shrunken to bone" (140, 144). The poignancy of this story is that Brave Orchid really loves her sister, though she is instrumental in her mental and physical collapse. Indeed, as Moon Orchid loses touch with reality, Brave Orchid has a regressive need to follow her back into the past, and like Fa Mu Lan or Li Ruzhen's Little Hill, she tries to rescue and protect her as she once did when they were "little sisters" together in China. "She held her hand along the walk home, just as they had held hands when they were girls" (140). "I won't let anything happen to you" (141). Brave Orchid's list of things "you must not tell anyone" (11) includes telling others how much you love them, and she adheres to this immigrant's law of harsh necessity throughout the two books. Her sister's complete breakdown weakens the stout defenses Brave Orchid has erected within the family to prevent the open admission of vulnerability and neediness and brings about a return of the repressed. Moon Orchid is the only family member she ever openly tells what each one desperately needs to hear: "how much she loved her and how much her daughter and nephews and nieces loved her, and her brother-in-law loved her" (141). As her children "felt loved" when she led them "out of nightmares and horror movies" (73), so Brave Orchid tries to draw her sister out of acute paranoia by reassuring her that love can hold the women and men in the family together and keep them from falling apart (Slowik, 258).

O Brother, Where Art Thou?

When it becomes apparent to Brave Orchid that her sister is losing her mind, "the tears break inside her chest" (140). These tears bring about a momentary release of repressed emotions. For once Brave Orchid is moved to let down her guard and articulate the love that circulates unexpressed and often undetected within her family. Her husband, however, experiences no such brief lifting of repression. Although this is the only story of *The Woman Warrior* in which he has any direct communication with the women characters, his tight-lipped speech discourages dialogue and sends the disapproving message that he will have nothing to do with his wife's reckless plans for her sister. He exchanges only one word of greeting with the sister-in-law he has not seen for years—"Hello." When Moon Orchid later corners him with a direct question and asks why he keeps his desk locked and what's in it, he is again reluctant to be drawn into speech: "'Nothing,' he said. 'Nothing'" (113). "Nothing. Nothing" is the double negative both he and his wife regularly employ to keep the lid on the family secrets (112). These secrets are symbolically stowed away in the broken-down old rolltop desk, crammed with family memorabilia, that occupies a prominent place in the dining room. These "nothings" are "incredibly damaging" not only for the father who, in the words of Kristeva, remains "an anonymity, an absence, a blank space" (*Desire in Language*, 75), but also, as Hongo suggests, for the next generation who grow up "cipherously—as if everything behind us was a zero and we were the first" (10). Furthermore his repeated "nothing" gives credence to the words of denial and nullification Brave Orchid attributed to him in "No Name Woman." When he finally opens his mouth, the father has little or "nothing" to tell. In prohibiting free speech within the family, he has internalized the voice of the censor.

THE FATHER TURNS A DEAF EAR TO INTERTEXTUAL DIALOGUE

With his third direct remark—"Oh, no. I don't want to listen to this" —the father rejects the role not only of active speaker but willing listener in intertextual dialogue. Instead he leaves "to read in bed" (114). For the intertextual theorist Seán Hand, reading is a "listening process in which a narrative is composed from an interaction between at least two persons, who in fact always turn out be more than two" (79). Two is one too many for the father. Reading is a strategy he employs to hide from his family and keep his distance from their conflicts. The father wants to hear nothing of his wife's excited dialogue with her sister and niece. Reading in bed brings the promise of sleep, and sleep will bring oblivion and temporary escape from their raised voices in the realm of the unconscious; however, there will be no letup when he wakes. For much of the story, Brave Orchid volubly nags the reluctant Moon Orchid into a showdown with her bigamist husband, now settled in Los Angeles. In his fourth and longest statement, the father finally snaps at his wife: "'You ought to leave the poor man alone,' said Brave Orchid's husband. 'Leave him out of women's business'" (129). Obviously, the father's outburst reflects his own conscious wish to be left alone and out of his wife's crazy schemes. I think we can further assume that the father has refused to actively cooperate by driving the two sisters to Los Angeles. Brave Orchid pays him back here, and later in *China Men* (14), for his overfastidiousness. She tells the unflattering story of how he refused to eat pastry kneaded by women who were prepared to roll up their sleeves and get their hands dirty—as she does now pummeling and shaping her sister's life (129–130). Of course, the father's protest expresses a traditional view of the gender division between women's and men's affairs in society, but it also calls attention to the authorial decision Hong Kingston took to leave the men's side of the story out of the women's narratives in *The Woman Warrior*.

When Brave Orchid and her sister finally encounter Moon Orchid's wayward husband, he is anything but a "poor man." Unlike the father, he does not shirk confrontation or handle emotional demands obliquely. "He looked directly at Moon Orchid the way the savages looked, looking for lies. 'What do you want?' he asked. She shrank from his stare" (138). As we have already seen, this man succeeds where the father fails. Not only does he succeed in making a new and prosperous life for himself in America; he succeeds in dominating and diminishing the women, and in putting an end to Brave Orchid's plots—so central to the stories of *The Woman Warrior.* He gives her the foreboding sense that she is getting old and that he has supplanted her in power and vitality. This fear lies behind the last provocation that she gives her husband to speak up. "Brave Orchid told her children they must help her keep their father from marrying another woman because she didn't think she could take it any better than her sister had. . . . 'I am almost seventy years old,' said the father, 'and haven't taken a second wife, and don't plan to now'" (144). Brave Orchid's sympathies are with her sister, but she suspects that her husband's may lie with the errant brother-in-law, clever enough to outwit her and virile enough to take a second wife who is "very pretty and very young: just a girl"—young enough perhaps to be his daughter (135).

Traces of the Father in "A Song for a Barbarian Reed Pipe"

THE UNREPORTED CRIME OF "NO NAME WOMAN"
In the final story of *The Woman Warrior,* "A Song for a Barbarian Reed Pipe," the daughter narrator is again attacked by the fear that her father will remain a closed book. At the beginning of *China Men,* he still bewilders and intimidates her with his incomprehensible silences and mood swings, and it is only by daring him to "speak up with the real stories"—and outdaring him by telling him that she will read his "silences" and elaborate his "few words" (15)—that she can proceed with the male narratives of *China Men.* In "A Song for a Barbarian Reed Pipe," there is a strong sense of the return of the repressed, that same sense of an unreported crime in "No Name Woman." At the beginning of this story, her parents are called to school for a meeting with the anxious American teachers who suspect that the daughter narrator may be seriously disturbed. Her father speaks to them in Chinese, but his comment would be incomprehensible even if translated into English. "The parents and teachers of criminals were executed" (149). His only other direct statement in this last story is another cruel and vengeful saying: "'Chinese smeared bad daughters-in-law with honey and tied them naked on top of ant nests,' my father said. 'A husband

may kill a wife who disobeys him. Confucius said that'" (173). In *China Men* the male villagers repeat this adage and the reader learns that the father is, in fact, carrying on an old intertextual practice to ensure sexual fidelity in sojourner households. "Husbands and wives exchanged stories to frighten one another" (*CM*, 47). Ignorant of the history of male out-migration and the emotional anxiety and suffering it caused to both men and women, however, the daughter narrator, her two sisters, and three girl second cousins understandably conclude that it is simply because of their sex that "our old man hates us" (171). The intertextual reader of "No Name Woman" possesses the means to translate these hateful slogans differently. Whether they originally come from the mouth of Communists who punish misfits or from Confucian patriarchs who punish women, they accrue their emotional force in *The Woman Warrior* from the story of the aunt's sexual infidelity. The father is thinking about his sister when talking about his daughter. Indeed, he punishes his daughter for an hysterical outburst later in this story by banishing her figuratively to the "outcast table," where her aunt sat after her illicit pregnancy became shamefully apparent (14–15). "My brothers and sisters had left the table, and my father would not look at me any more, ignoring me" (182). The fate of his own sister with its terrible "power to remind" (26) is implicated in the sayings—insults really—that he trades here with the women in his family.

Of course, *The Woman Warrior* opens with the father's flat refusal to allow that his sister ever had a place at the family table. Yet the extreme vehemence of this denial and his compulsion to repeat words and actions originally provoked by her is symptomatic of a textual unconscious where the lost loved one continues to reside as a disturbing memory, imaginary idea, reproachful voice, or haunting face. Indeed, as Hand has argued, intertextual activity revolves around the search for what is missing or continues to be missed in this textual unconscious (79, 89). Hong Kingston herself conceded that she has a need to "keep writing about things that are lost because I think that readers will find them" (Skenazy, "Kingston at the University," 138). In fact, I will argue in chapter 3 that the aunt has the uncanny status of missing person in the family. Rather like Banquo's ghost at the feast, her conspicuous absence from family reminiscences and reunions calls attention to the fact that she is an invisible and dread presence among them. However tightly the narrator's immigrant parents huddle together in America or clasp their arms about each other ("I used to watch my mother and father play refugees, sleeping sitting up, huddled together with their heads on each other's shoulder, their arms about each other," 87), however much they try to close ranks, the "raw pain of separation" (21) from this little sister still pervades *The Woman Warrior.* Indeed it remains an open and angry wound that continues to weep in *China Men.*

I will further argue that though the aunt's name has been struck from the family book of life, she is an important missing link in the intertextual process of reconstructing this book of life after it has been broken in two. Though banished from collective memory and circulation, the aunt's tale is unforgettable for readers of both *The Woman Warrior* and *China Men.* The terrible and mordant beauty of "No Name Woman" has earned this talk-story canonical status in its own right, and it has been treated as a short story that not only stands out in Hong Kingston's writing but, further, can stand on its own (Leiwei Li, 198). As I shall now proceed to show, however, although "No Name Woman" can be read alone, it was fabricated out of the strong desire for connection. As the narrator memorably declares, "unless I see her life branching into mine, she gives me no ancestral help" (16). Envisaging the aunt's lost limb of the family tree will allow the narrator to "branch out" as a storyteller and, indeed, is a crucial first step for a daughter who feels cut off from the Chinese roots of her mother and cut out of the Chinese past of her father.[57] I will suggest that, in restoring the aunt to life, she finds not simply ancestral but intertextual help. Moreover, the niece's intertextual concern to "see her life branching into mine" also reflects an intersubjective interest in "what happens between individuals, and within the individual-with-others" (Benjamin, 92). Of course, on a genealogical table, the aunt would occupy a separate though parallel branch of the family tree, and the only lives that would branch directly into the narrator's would be those of her parents. This curious anomaly supports my earlier point that the aunt figures as a crucial intermediary in the daughter's narrative effort to connect with the mother's and father's stories. I will return in the next chapter to "No Name Woman," a story where the father and mother converged in their reading of events and yet where they also parted company and went their separate ways in the narratives that would be divided between *The Woman Warrior* and *China Men.*

Notes

1. Hong Kingston told Timothy Pfaff, "The final chapter in *China Men* began as a short story that I was working on before I even started *The Woman Warrior*" (16). She said much the same thing to Kay Bonetti (35). Both in *Conversations with Maxine Hong Kingston,* edited by Paul Skenazy and Tera Martin (Jackson: University Press of Mississippi, 1998). Hereinafter, I shall refer to this volume as *Conversations.*

2. She is quoted further by Elaine Kim, *Asian American Literature: An Introduction to the Writings and Their Social Context* (Philadelphia: Temple University Press,

1982), 207, as hoping that the books would "be boxed together" but remarked in her "Personal Statement," in *Approaches to Teaching Kingston's* The Woman Warrior, edited by Shirley Geok-lin Lim (New York: Modern Language Association of America, 1991), 24, that only "the Quality Paperback Club printed *The Woman Warrior* and *China Men* as a boxed set, the most correct presentation." Had this become a common publishing practice, *China Men* might routinely have been read as the companion volume to *The Woman Warrior.*

3. See Kristeva's discussion of the double character of intertextual language in "Word, Dialogue, and Novel," in *Desire in Language: A Semiotic Approach to Literature and Art*, edited by Leon S. Roudiez, translated by Thomas Gora, Alice Jardine, and Leon S. Roudiez (New York: Columbia University Press, 1980), 66–69.

4. In "The Subject of Memoirs: *The Woman Warrior's* Technology of Ideographic Selfhood," in *Critical Essays on Maxine Hong Kingston*, edited by Laura E. Skandera-Trombley (New York: G. K. Hall, 1998)—hereinafter *Critical Essays*—Lee Quinby argues that, while "autobiography promotes an 'I' that shares with confessional discourse an assumed interiority . . . memoirs promote an 'I' that is explicitly constituted in the reports of the utterances . . . of others" and is dialogical in a "Bakhtinian sense" (*Critical Essays*, 126).

5. Fichtelberg quotes from a Kristeva interview with Xavière Gauthier in "Poet and Patriarch," in *Autobiography and Questions of Gender*, edited by Shirley Neuman (London: F. Cass, 1991), 169. He cites an excerpt from "Oscillation between Power and Denial," translated by Marilyn A. August, in *New French Feminisms*, edited by Elaine Marks and Isabelle de Courtivron (Hemel Hempstead, Herts.: Harvester Wheatsheaf, 1981), 165.

6. In "Questioning Race and Gender Definitions: Dialogic Subversions in *The Woman Warrior*," *Criticism* 31 (1989), Malini Schueller discusses how Hong Kingston plays with gender and racial differences in *The Woman Warrior* and so subverts the "binary logic which hierarchically divides male and female, self and other, white and non white" (428). I quote Hong Kingston's own conclusion at the end of writing *China Men* that she didn't find "[men] that different" from women to Pfaff, in *Conversations* (17). This is an ironic vindication of the mixed-up narrator in *The Woman Warrior* who "can't tell the difference" (180). See also Ning Yu's discussion of "the rich intertextuality of *China Men*," in "A Strategy against Marginalization: The 'High' and 'Low' Cultures in Kingston's China," http://vweb.hwwilsonweb.com, p. 6.

7. See, for instance, Shirley Geok-lin Lim, "Growing with Stories" (279–280).

8. See Yuan Yuan, "The Semiotics of China Narratives in the Con/texts of Kingston and Tan," *Critique* 40 (1999), http://vweb.hwwilsonweb.com, p. 3; David Leiwei Li, "Re-presenting *The Woman Warrior*," in *Critical Essays*, 196; and Susan Brownmiller, "Susan Brownmiller Talks with Maxine Hong Kingston, Author of *The Woman Warrior*," in *Maxine Hong Kingston's* The Woman Warrior: A Casebook, edited by Sau-ling Cynthia Wong (New York: Oxford University Press, 1999), 178 (hereinafter *The Woman Warrior Casebook*).

9. See Virginia Woolf's *The Voyage Out* (London: Grafton, 1986), chap. 16, 220,

and Julia Kristeva's excerpt from "On Chinese Women," in *The Kristeva Reader*, edited by Toril Moi (Oxford: Blackwell, 1992), 156 (though I appreciate that Kristeva's psychoanalytical authority here is not matched by the same understanding of Chinese cultural or gender politics).

10. In *Reading Asian American Literature: From Necessity to Extravagance* (Princeton, N.J.: Princeton University Press, 1993), Sau-ling Wong argues that this field has only recently begun to be read with the same close attention to detail long established in the Anglo-American canon; my study aims to bring that attentiveness to Hong Kingston's two books (67).

11. Hong Kingston told Pfaff, in *Conversations*, that she thought, "*The Woman Warrior* was a selfish book. I was always imposing my viewpoint on the stories" (18).

12. See Hong Kingston's interviews with William Satake Blauvelt ("Talking with the Woman Warrior") and Marilyn Chin ("Writing the Other: A Conversation with Maxine Hong Kingston"), both in *Conversations* (81 and 91, respectively). Her remarks to Chin arise out of their discussion of *Tripmaster Monkey*.

13. See Malini Schueller, "Questioning Race and Gender Definitions," 422, and Sidonie Smith, "Filiality and Woman's Autobiographical Storytelling," in *The Woman Warrior Casebook* (59), on these points.

14. See Frederic Wakeman, "Chinese Ghost Story," and Mary Slowik, "When the Ghosts Speak: Oral and Written Narrative Forms in Maxine Hong Kingston's *China Men*," in *Critical Essays* (208 and 249–250, respectively), and E. D. Huntley, *Maxine Hong Kingston: A Critical Companion* (Westport, Conn.: Greenwood Press, 2001), who notes *China Men*'s narrative parallels where "past and present . . . mirror each other" (133).

15. I am quoting Huntley (72), but Rabinowitz makes a similar point to Hong Kingston in *Conversations* (69).

16. See Clara Claiborne Park, "Ghosts on a Gold Mountain," in *Critical Essays* (218).

17. J. E. Cirlot, *A Dictionary of Symbols*, trans. Jack Sage, 2nd ed. (London: Routledge, 1993), 380.

18. See the background provided by Huntley (8–10, 32) and Diane Simmons (*Maxine Hong Kingston*, 3–4, 46, 133–139).

19. Brave Orchid tells her husband that it is "the only thing we have left from China" (*CM*, 69). This linen relic of old China is still being used as "a white runner" in their Stockton home in *The Woman Warrior* (113).

20. See Huntley's comments (130, 144).

21. Hong Kingston elaborated on this point to Skenazy in "Kingston at the University" (139).

22. King-Kok Cheung makes this biblical passage the starting point of *Articulate Silences: Hisaye Yamamoto, Maxine Hong Kingston, Joy Kogawa* (Ithaca, N.Y.: Cornell University Press, 1993), 2.

23. Lovely Orchid is the Moll Flanders of *China Men*. She is a resilient figure who thrives on adventure and misadventure, and who survives dramatic spins of fortune's wheel. She tells her picaresque story in "The Making of More Americans,"

shortly before the retelling of Daniel Defoe's *Robinson Crusoe* in "The Adventures of Lo Bun Sun."

24. See Simmons' illuminating discussion of "The Ballad of Mulan" (*Maxine Hong Kingston*, 48–50, 59–61).

25. See her interviews with Bonetti (36–37), Hoy (48), and Skenazy ("Kingston at the University," 140), all in *Conversations*.

26. Sheryl A. Mylan notes the further resemblance of Brave Orchid's name and Fa Mu Lan's, which can be translated as "Sylvan" or "Wood Orchid," in "The Mother as Other: Orientalism in Maxine Hong Kingston's *The Woman Warrior*," in *Women of Color: Mother-Daughter Relationships in Twentieth-Century Literature*, edited by Elizabeth Brown-Guillory (Austin: University of Texas Press, 1996), 137. (See also chap. 1, note 39.)

27. See Hong Kingston's discussion with Skenazy ("Kingston at the University," 137) of the irrational forces that she confronted in her stories and Huntley's comments (23) on how the short-story form contains violence.

28. See Sau-ling Wong's discussion of "widows of the living," in *Reading Asian American Literature*, 198–199.

29. The tendency of parents who commit suicide in Hong Kong to take their young children with them to death rather than leave them behind has provoked a public debate about the selfish motives that lie behind family homicide-suicides. I agree with the narrator that parental murder of children is more often a despairing act of love, as in Toni Morrison's harrowing ghost story *Beloved*.

30. See Emily M. Ahern, "The Power and Pollution of Chinese Women," in *Women in Chinese Society*, edited by Margery Wolf and Roxane Witke (Stanford, Calif.: Stanford University Press, 1975), 214.

31. Joseph Campbell (with Bill Moyers), *The Power of Myth*, edited by Betty Sue Flowers (New York: Doubleday, 1988), 125.

32. David L. Eng, *Racial Castration: Managing Masculinity in Asian America* (Durham, N.C.: Duke University Press, 2001), 90. See the discussion of the love-hate relationship between Chin and Hong Kingston by Huntley (146–147) and by Garrett Hongo, "Introduction: Culture Wars in Asian America," in *Under Western Eyes: Personal Essays from Asian America*, edited by Hongo (New York: Doubleday Anchor, 1995), 14–18; also see Hong Kingston's discussions of this subject with Perry (183–184) and Seshachari (202–203), both in *Conversations*.

33. Hong Kingston commented to Arturo Islas and Marilyn Yalom that when she wrote *The Woman Warrior* "in 1975 there wouldn't have been a psychiatrist who could have looked at Moon Orchid and said, 'Oh she's going through refugee syndrome'" (*Conversations*, 30).

34. Donald C. Goellnicht argues in "Tang Ao in America: Male Subject Positions in *China Men*," in *Critical Essays*, that American racial discrimination against Chinese immigrant workers has "destroyed her father's ability to fabulate" (240).

35. Ursula Owen, "Introduction," in *Fathers: Reflections by Daughters*, edited by Ursula Owen (London: Virago, 1983), 10.

36. See Hong Kingston's remarks on the command of secrecy that opens Toni

Morrison and Alice Walker's novels and that suggests an intertextual connection with her own work, in her interviews with Donna Perry and Eric Schroeder, in *Conversations* (177 and 215, respectively).

37. Hong Kingston told Hoy that "there was a battle against silence in that story: my mother told me not to tell anybody. There was an artistic battle of what can be told and written and what is unwritable" (49). Leigh Gilmore calls Fa Mu Lan's scarified body "a living war monument," in "Violence and Self-Representation," *Autobiographics: A Feminist Theory of Women's Self-Representation* (Ithaca, N.Y.: Cornell University Press, 1994), 181.

38. Simmons provides a translation of the ballad (48–50).

39. Hong Kingston discussed her efforts to develop greater sympathy and understanding for *China Men* with Hoy (57).

40. She told Schroeder that "I thought if I began the book stating what that order was, I could confront it directly and disobey the order. And in that way I could free myself and my voice to be able to tell the story" (215).

41. Elaine Kim in *Asian American Literature* makes the point that the ghosts in *The Woman Warrior*'s subtitle "are not simply white people but 'shadowy figures from the past' or unanswered questions about unexplained actions of Chinese, whites, and Chinese in America" (200).

42. "Julia Kristeva in Conversation with Rosalind Coward," *ICA Documents* (1984), 22. See further her discussion of the imaginary father in "Freud and Love: Treatment and Its Discontents," *Tales of Love*, trans. Leon S. Roudiez (New York: Columbia University Press, 1987), 26–29, 41–48.

43. Sara Ruddick, "Thinking about Fathers," in *Conflicts in Feminism*, edited by Marianne Hirsch and Evelyn Fox Keller (New York: Routledge, 1990), 223.

44. Arguably Hong Kingston overcorrects this imbalance in *China Men* by representing the grandfathers as "mythical characters of the past golden age." See her remarks to Islas and Yalom in *Conversations* (27).

45. See Sau-ling Wong, "Autobiography as Guided Chinatown Tour?" in *The Woman Warrior Casebook* (35), and Amy Ling, "Maxine Hong Kingston and the Dialogic Dilemma of Asian American Writers," in *Critical Essays* (170).

46. Kristeva explained to Rosalind Coward that she conceived this imaginary metaphor as a third term intermediate between mother and father (23).

47. Hong Kingston repeatedly emphasized the freedom that both reader and writer have to change the story in her conversations with Islas and Yalom (31), Bonetti (38), and Skenazy ("Kingston at the University," 149). Huntley comments on the open-endedness of her writing (21, 66).

48. See Sharon Suzuki-Martinez's chapter "Trickster Strategies: Challenging American Identity, Community, and Art in Kingston's *Tripmaster Monkey*," in *Reviewing Asian America: Locating Diversity*, edited by Wendy L. Ng, Soo-Young Chin, James S. Moy, and Gary Y. Okihiro (Pullman: Washington State University Press, 1995), 162–163, for a discussion of Hong Kingston's "carnivalesque hybridization."

49. See Julia Kristeva's chapter on "Confucius—An Eater of Women," in *About*

Chinese Women, trans. Anita Barrows (London: Marion Boyars, 1977), 75, and Huntley's discussion of Kristeva's argument (108–109).

50. Walt Whitman, "Starting from Paumanok," *Leaves of Grass, The Complete Poems,* edited by Francis Murphy (London: Penguin Classics, 1996), 57. In an interview in *Conversations,* Hong Kingston told Fisher Fishkin, "I *love* that throughout *Leaves of Grass* he always says 'men and women,' 'male and female'" (161). She said much the same to Seshachari (212).

51. Lynda E. Boose coincidentally uses the term "temporary sojourner" in her discussion of "The Father's House and the Daughter in It: The Structures of Western Culture's Daughter-Father Relationship," in *Daughters and Fathers,* edited by Lynda E. Boose and Betty S. Flowers (Baltimore: Johns Hopkins University Press, 1989), 21.

52. Yuan Shu argues, in "Cultural Politics and Chinese-American Female Subjectivity: Rethinking Kingston's *Woman Warrior,*" *MELUS* 26 (2001), that the no name woman is a failure because "she steps out of the roles of a daughter and a wife defined by the Confucian tradition" (212).

53. See Sau-ling Wong's "Introduction" to *The Woman Warrior Casebook* (7–9).

54. See Gerald Prince's foreword to Genette's *Palimpsests: Literature in the Second Degree,* trans. Channa Newman and Claude Doubrinsky (Lincoln: University of Nebraska Press, 1997), ix–xi.

55. In her discussion with Skenazy, "Kingston at the University," Hong Kingston sees a resemblance between weak, pretty, and ultra-feminine characters like Moon Orchid and the village crazy woman, but contrasts them with "powerful peasant types like Brave Orchid" who adapt to hardship and survive. She overlooks the fact here that Brave Orchid once used her smart appearance to impress others (131–132). In *Reading Asian American Literature,* Sau-ling Wong probes the similarities hidden beneath the first impression that Moon Orchid and Brave Orchid are "diametric opposites" (196–197).

56. Goellnicht argues in "Tang Ao in America" that Ed desires to return to the mother (*Critical Essays,* 240), but Fichtelberg reads a more ambiguous narrative of escape to America (171–172), as indeed I do.

57. Hong Kingston told Marilyn Chin that she came to her "Chinese roots very tentatively" (94). She also remarked to Fisher Fishkin that her writing made some Chinese readers feel in touch with roots pulled up during the Cultural Revolution (166).

Chapter 3

---※---

"The Precious Only Daughter" and "the Never-Said"

Traces of Incest in "No Name Woman" and *The Woman Warrior*

Parents, Death, and a Sense of Mortality

What mortals haunt our lives more persistently than our parents—those giants who cast their long shadow over our childhood and who protect us with their apparent indestructibility from the terrifying reality of our closeness to death? Joan Riviere speculates that our profound horror of death stems from "the disappearance, so comparatively sudden, of a living existence, an entity, a person, a personality, a most complex and composite structure of attributes, tendencies, experiences, memories, idiosyncrasies good and bad, as well as the body they belong to."[1] If the creative impulse derives its power from the fear that we can suddenly disappear without trace, then the need of the daughter narrator to "remember Father's drowned-in-the-well sister" in "No Name Woman" (13) may have assumed a particular urgency. For when *The Woman Warrior: Memoirs of a Girlhood among Ghosts* debuted in 1976, Maxine Hong Kingston, born in 1940, was approaching middle age and would be on the threshold of her forties when *China Men* was published, in 1980. She was then old enough to be the mother of the young daughter who fabricates herself in *The Woman Warrior*, the girl who also "devote[s] pages of paper" (22) to the life story of her aunt. Moreover, in 1976 the writer's only child, Joseph Lawrence Chung Mei Kingston, was thirteen, or on the brink of puberty, like the narrator in "No Name Woman" (Huntley, 9).

It is not clear from either book just how old her parents might have been at the time she was writing. In *The Woman Warrior*, the narrator discloses that Brave Orchid gave birth to six children in America after the age of forty-five (98), which would make Hong Kingston's mother at least eighty-one at the time of publication. In fact daughter and mother squabble inconclusively over her age near the end of "Shaman." "'I'm almost eighty.' 'I thought you were only seventy-six.' 'My papers are wrong. I'm eighty . . . eighty-one in Chinese years. Seventy. Eighty. What do numbers matter? I'm dropping dead any day now'" (95). What they do agree on is the fact that they are both getting on in years. "'The last time I saw you, you were still young,' she said. 'Now you're old'" (95). In that no-man's-land between wakefulness and slumber, the daughter narrator can see her uncanny resemblance to her aging mother. "Eyes shut, I pictured my mother, her white hair frizzy in the dark-and-light doorway, my hair white now too, Mother" (93). Though the daughter reminds her mother of the children who surrounded her in middle age and invokes the image as a talisman against death— "wasn't it like prolonging youth?" (99)—and as a charm that assures long life—"but our family lives to be ninety-nine" (95)—her underlying narrative fear is that her parents had reached the age where they could die suddenly. In "White Tigers," she attends the funeral of the macho Great-Uncle who was a river pirate in China and recalls how she stood by his coffin and "secretly tested out feeling that he was dead—the six-foot bearish masculinity of him" (48). She returns intertextually to this passage in *China Men* and discloses the anxiety that prompted the morbid impulse to touch her Great-Uncle's corpse as it lay in the coffin. "I thought about myself dying and about parents dying" (185).

Her father's age was anyone's guess. In *China Men*, the reader is told that her "father was born in a year of the Rabbit, 1891 or 1903 or 1915" (15). As Frederic Wakeman has suggested, if the father from China took the "qualifying test for the last Imperial Examination ever given" (*CM*, 24), which was held in 1905, he would almost certainly have been born earlier than 1891 (*Critical Essays*, 209). This would make him old enough to be the narrator's grandfather.[2] Indeed, in both *The Woman Warrior* and *China Men*, grandfathers are more prominent characters than the diffident father figure. Even imagining that he could have sat for the imperial civil service exams as a teenage prodigy of fourteen, he would still have been nearly fifty when he began to father a family in America and, like other legendary China men, "almost a hundred years old" (*CM*, 185) when he died in 1991.[3] Even if this is another tall tale, there is a gap of almost two generations between the narrator and her parents. We can read the violent scene in *China Men* where BaBa snaps and beats his daughter(s) with a coat hanger (253) not simply as the abusive retaliation of the humiliated Chinese minority male (Goellnicht, "Tang Ao in America," 237; Perry, 184), but as the behavior of an elderly, sedate father who cannot cope with a large and noisy family or relate easily to his boisterous offspring.

It may have been equally hard for the daughter to relate to her parents and especially to connect the "menarche fable"[4] she is told in "No Name Woman" with the menopausal mother who recounts it. She may have perceived her father's pretty young sister, the subject of this talk-story, as a woman closer to her in age and experience, an imaginary relative who could close the considerable gap between herself and her parents. If it is hard for a child to accept that her parents will die, it can also be difficult for her to imagine that they ever had sex with one another. This "girl" devises a story in which she can relate to her aunt's longing for a sexual life; but she also depicts her as a dangerous ghost of the father's household, one of the *lares familiares* who must be propitiated, yet who mysteriously stands between her parents and death. In an interview with Eric Schroeder in 1996, Hong Kingston remarked that "we don't know exactly how old my grandmother is, my mother and my father are, because they have all these fake papers and stories, and so I just went ahead and gave them long lives and didn't worry about their ages" (219). Virginia Woolf's diachronic character *Orlando*, whose lifespan is four centuries, afforded Hong Kingston a creative means to cope with this nagging "worry" about her parents' advanced age by depicting the major players in her family chronicles as characters who are resilient in the face of death and who act as though they fully intend to live forever.

Alternative Representation and Reading of Chinese Immigrant Life Stories

When her adventurer Great-Uncle died at nearly a hundred, the narrator of *China Men* would proudly boast that "Chinese live a long time—to do many things and to make their ages span the legal immigration dates" (185–186). Yet the fact remains that Hong Kingston's parents were getting on in years; and her literary desire to record their story ran up against the social reality that they had spent a lifetime concealing their traces and papering over their tracks with aliases and diversionary accounts of their immigration to America. The daughter of such immigrant parents would complain to Brave Orchid: "You lie with stories. You won't tell me a story and then say, 'This is a true story,' or, 'This is just a story.' I can't tell the difference. I don't even know what your real names are" (*WW*, 180). Yet ironically, only by adopting her mother's strategy of blurring "what's real and what you make up" can the narrator honor the hidden truth of her mother and father's lives. Of necessity, illegal immigrant culture is intertextual in that it requires illegal immigrants to fabricate different versions of their passage into and through

America—variants that never read as wholly satisfactory because they leave the strong impression that the storyteller has deliberately withheld or left something obscure as a precautionary measure (Riffaterre, "The Intertextual Unconscious," 380; "Compulsory reader response," 58). Hong Kingston defended her own employment of devious narration "because I'm telling the story as these people give it, and some of the people have given their official version more often than they've give their secret version. They themselves can't afford to tell the truth. So they tell it the way I've told it. When I tell it with all these versions, I'm actually giving the culture of these people in a very accurate way."[5]

A prime example of this evasive exercise is her narration of the father's "multiple entry" into America in *China Men*. As discussed in chapter 2, Hong Kingston depicted this father coming into the country in a number of different ways (Bonetti, 38; Pfaff, 16–17). If the China father's complicated immigration story is hard to follow, it may be because it is a synthesis of the various attempts Hong Kingston's own mother and father made to get into America. Only after the publication of her two books did the author learn from her mother Ying Lan Hong that the father's illegal trip from Cuba to New York, with its hallucinogenic account of how his "thoughts reached out as if stretching in four directions—skyward, seaward, back toward land, and forward to the new country" (*CM*, 49), was closest to the truth—except that it left out the fact that he was caught and deported on three separate occasions. Indeed, her second and most compelling version of events, that he arrived in San Francisco and was detained on Angel Island, where he fraternized with the legendary Chinese immigrant poets who protested against their exile, imprisonment, or deportation (Kim, *Asian American Literature*, 258–259), actually tells the immigration story of her mother. Ying Lan Hong arrived in America via California, not Ellis Island, and traveled on the transcontinental railroad that her forefathers constructed, to join Tom Hong in Manhattan, thus reversing the parental journeys that are narrated in *China Men* (Huntley, 3). For Michael Riffaterre, intertextual reading is a pursuit of "the text as Sphinx and the intertext as Oedipus" ("Compulsory reader response," 77). Hong Kingston's two books are certainly riddled with questions about parentage—who are the mother and father, what life journeys did they make, and where are they to be found? Like Oedipus, the narrator seeks the answers to these questions at the intertextual crossroads where variant and illicit stories collide. *China Men* depicts the father as the embodiment of the enigma posed by the Sphinx. He is first shown as an infant crawling on all fours and finally as an old man leaning on his garden hoe for support (255).

The Father's Daughter, Sister, and the Three Fates

"No Name Woman," the story that formally begins Hong Kingston's family saga, depicts the aunt as an uncanny figure who violates the natural cycle of long life expectancy among the Chinese and, indeed, who ushers the reader from birth to death, and from the cradle to the grave, in the space of the two horrific pages that conclude the tale. In his brilliant psychoanalytic reading of "The Theme of the Three Caskets" in Shakespeare's *The Merchant of Venice*, Freud imagined the human life passage, so shockingly truncated in "No Name Woman," as an incestuous relationship with the mother figure in three fateful guises—"the woman who bears him, the woman who is his mate and the woman who destroys him."[6] He elaborated his theme with respect to *King Lear*, where an aging patriarch disowns his daughter Cordelia—as the narrator's father denies his sister—because she will say "nothing" when asked to profess her love for him. Freud argued that the daughter's dumb devotion prefigures what lay in store for this demanding old man—the embrace of "the third of the Fates alone, the silent Goddess of Death, [who] will take him into her arms" (247). As she prepares to go to war, Fa Mu Lan will remark that Chinese parents "do not like to talk out loud about dying" with their children (*WW*, 38). The narrator of *The Woman Warrior* transgresses this cultural taboo by stopping at the house of death in "No Name Woman." She depicts the aunt as a Goddess of Love, "unusually beloved, the precious only daughter, spoiled and mirror gazing because of the affection the family lavished on her" (17), but she goes on to show that she is the silent Goddess of Death in disguise. "The family broke their silence and cursed her. 'Aiaa, we're going to die. Death is coming. . . . You've killed us. Ghost! Dead ghost! Ghost! You've never been born'" (20). At the end of "No Name Woman," the narrator shudders with fear as she imagines that this Goddess of Death may be reaching out to enfold her from the grave. "The Chinese are always very frightened of the drowned one, whose weeping ghost, wet hair hanging and skin bloated, waits silently by the water to pull down a substitute" (22).

The narrator's mother, Brave Orchid, turns the aunt's brief tragedy of flesh into a dire warning against female curiosity, disobedience, and promiscuity; however, as Cordelia remains silent when asked to declare her love for her father, so too the no name woman will not name the father of her child. "She kept the man's name to herself throughout her labour and dying; she did not accuse him that he be punished with her. To save her inseminator's name she gave silent birth" (18). Freud saw that Cordelia is not only the fairest and most desirable of women but "the one loyal daughter" who is with her father at the end (237–238, 243). Indeed, Cordelia meets her own death because she leaves the protection of her new husband, the King of France, and returns to her homeland in order to be reunited with Lear. In a parallel movement in "No Name Woman," after her husband left, the aunt's parents "welcomed the chance to take her back from the in-laws; she could live like the little daughter for just a while longer" (17). In their possessive love, these doting parents are blind like Lear or Oedipus to the fateful irony they set in motion—that their "little daughter" will live only a little while longer.

A Secret Version of "No Name Woman": The Story of Father-Daughter Incest

At the heart of this story of adultery lies the age old question, "Who is the father?"[7] It is a question that preys on the mind of a young woman who also has a "private life, secret and apart" (19) from her family—not her unfortunate aunt's erotic life but an imaginary life every bit as wild and wayward. "Who is the father" is an especially charged question, one that reflects the daughter narrator's deep textual desire to go in search of her own father and discover his identity, though this desire must be deferred, in large part, until *China Men*. I propose now to suggest one answer to this question and to read the supposedly transgressive life of the aunt as the story of a daughter who is *too loyal and compliant*, who, to paraphrase Freud, is obedient to a compulsion (245), the compulsion of her own father. The "private life, secret and apart" she is punished for by the villagers (19), but can say "nothing" about, could be her father's incestuous love for her. Incest has been called "the best kept secret" in the family (Bell, 79). It is a secret that bears out the narrator's hunch that "sex was unspeakable and words so strong and fathers so frail that 'aunt' would do my father mysterious harm" (21–22). It is a secret that condemns the narrator's own father to say almost "nothing" in *The Woman Warrior* and to a life of self-imposed silence and aloofness for much of *China Men*. I will explore the possibility that incest is the strong "never-said" (17), the word that plunges down, when the aunt jumps to her death in the family well, into the textual unconscious of both books. Incest, with the fear of its transgenerational repetition, is a thematic connective that runs intertextually through the two books, raising questions, posing possible answers, creating dramatic tension between the mother and father text, and compelling the reader on a journey resembling that of Oedipus—of haunting déjà vu.

Lear's rash and angry response to Cordelia is "nothing will come of nothing" (I.i.90). The "dumb" and "silent" daughter of *The Woman Warrior* answers this nothing with "No Name Woman"—or literary creation ex nihilo. Hong Kingston spoke later of the act of narrating the aunt's life as the moment when she "retrieved her from the no-nameness, the nothing, and created her again." She remarked how she begins *The Woman Warrior* with the darkness of this first chapter, resembling the darkness over the deep and formless void in Genesis, and bursts from this darkness into the light and kinetic energy of "White Tigers." She "saw it as like the way creation works . . . first there was the darkness, and then the next day God did the light."[8] The creation of *China Men* would constitute a corresponding attempt to save her father from the chaos and nothingness where he is also mired; however, "in the beginning" writing is not "a pure gift" of love (Goellnicht, "Tang Ao in America," 240), but one drawn from the deep well of the daughter's inner life with its undercurrents of anger, aggression, and desire for revenge. Kristeva puts it another way, in *Tales of Love*, when she argues that from the very beginning eros is "permeated with thanatos,"[9] that is to say with the death drive that Freud examined in his "Theme of the Three Caskets."

The narrator will fill the echoing void in the aunt's and the father's lives with a love that sees and accepts the best and the worst in people and with writing that gives vent to the impulse to expose and punish and, at the same time, protect and save the family.[10] If incest is one of the most destructive and transgressive manifestations of love (Loewald, 393), Lynda Boose has suggested that the father who is anxious to avoid such attraction may "turn away from his daughter precisely at the moment in her psychological maturation when she will begin turning more actively towards him" (36). As "No Name Woman" illustrates, menstruation marks the moment when the daughter narrator takes a keen interest in her father's ancestral history. Yet her new sexual status as a potential object of incestuous desire makes it difficult for her to approach her father or ask him intimate questions, especially about his "drowned-in-the-well sister." "Don't let your father know that I told you. He denies her. Now that you have started to menstruate, what happened to her could happen to you. Don't humiliate us. You wouldn't like to be forgotten as if you had never been born" (13). Boose argues that "the resolution to the father's incestuous attraction may lie not in the seeming logic of distance but in the paradox of greater closeness" to his daughter (36). The father of *The Woman Warrior* and *China Men*, however, does not invite or appear to want this greater closeness and is characterized as having "lost his feelings" for others (*CM*, 248).

Searching for the Father

As a bolshie adolescent, the daughter's first inclination in both books is to provoke him into being more forthcoming (Skenazy, "Kingston at the University," 154). Indeed, the open challenge that the narrator issues to her father at the beginning of *China Men*—"You'll just have to speak up with the real stories if I've got you wrong" (15)—provides the latent textual pressure in "No Name Woman" as the narrator fabricates alternative versions of his sister's life which are an instigation for him to speak up. As it becomes apparent that her father—like most parents—does not respond well to provocation, however, she devises a more creative and humane means of rapprochement. As I suggested in chapter 2, the narrator pursues the "idea" of the imaginary father. She does so by listening intently for traces of a dialogue with him, in *The Woman Warrior*, and by retracing his footsteps and imagining what it might be like to be in his place, in *China Men* (Simmons, *Maxine Hong Kingston*, 110). Imagining this father allows her to adjust through writing the sense of emotional distance from her actual father who will say little or nothing about his life and overattachment to her mother on whom she depends as the main source of stories about the family. Hong Kingston would memorably describe *China Men* to Jody Hoy as "a search for my father, or all of us searching for our fathers," and she would cite the story of Defoe's character Friday who finds his father in *Robinson Crusoe* as a paradigm of emotional reunion with the "wonderful, loving, physical touching between the two of them" (56).

Hong Kingston's reconfiguration of *Robinson Crusoe* as "The Adventures of Lo Bun Sun" in *China Men* is the product of an intertextual dialogue between the mother, the father, and the daughter. The daughter narrator first heard this tale as her mother's talk-story but remembers how her "father came to listen to . . . part of the story, and he told it again" (*CM*, 227). In other words, her mother's talk-story made the usually withdrawn father draw near, take a closer interest, and fashion his own "retelling." Their daughter will, in turn, recount her own version of "The Adventures of Lo Bun Sun" and make this story the intertext that introduces her chapter on "The American Father." She thus expresses her hope that the intertextual dynamics of telling, listening, repeating, altering, reading, and writing narratives can gradually close the emotional gulf between herself and her father. Indeed, she will even recall the exact intertextual moment when her father stopped to listen and became engaged in the story—when her mother gave a detailed account of Lo Bun Sun planting rice. The narrative impetus

to imagine the father figure differently, to move from the nameless inseminator who opens *The Woman Warrior* to the closing image of the horticul-
turist in *China Men*,[11] derives from her own growing perception that her
own father could not be left out of the narrative, though it would first
appear that he was in "No Name Woman." Indeed, if intertextuality insists
that "the story changes as it is listened to and worked on" (Hand, 79), he
may have been there, silently attentive, all along.

Sister, Daughter, and Taboo Subjects in "No Name Woman"

In a revealing anecdote about the interest her own family began to take in
the fate of the "No Name Woman," Hong Kingston recounts how her sister,
a trained social worker, confronted her parents about the truth of the aunt's
life. "'Oh, wasn't there a sister in here somewhere?' And then my father, he
didn't say anything. My mother, at first, didn't say anything either, but then
she said, 'Oh, go ahead and tell her.' And then he said, yes, he had a sister.
. . . He did not say what became of her. And just by his silence, I assume
that what I surmised is so" (Skenazy, "Kingston at the University," 119). The
parents' dead silence, the encouragement the mother gives the father to let
down his habitual defenses of denial and repression, and the reluctant
"yes" that is finally dragged out of him parallel the stops and starts of "No
Name Woman" as taboo-transgressive material is painfully brought to the
surface of the text.

Although French feminists have valorized *écriture féminine*, writing
about or with consciousness of the body may be taboo for a young narrator who has just had her first period. If she was unprepared for the physio-
logical changes of adolescence, initial bleeding may have seemed like a
traumatic rupture. Hélène Cixous suggests that she may then feel that the
body familiar to her from childhood has been "replaced with a disturbing
stranger, sick or dead. . . . the cause and place of inhibitions."[12] Sudden and
unexpected bleeding can give rise not only to irrational fears of being
wounded but of having been violated like the aunt by some nameless force.
The physical pain of severe menstrual cramps can be a further shock, especially if she does not understand that her body is rehearsing the first stages
of labor. As the no name woman will so poignantly illustrate when she goes
into actual labor, even then a young woman may not fully comprehend
what is happening. "When she felt the birth coming, she thought that she
had been hurt. Her body seized together. 'They've hurt me too much,' she
thought. 'This is gall, and it will kill me'" (20). If she is a young woman
reared in a repressive Chinese culture where, as the narrator later complains,

"if we had to depend on being told, we'd have no religion, no babies, no menstruation (sex, of course, unspeakable), no death" (166), menstruation can become a deep and unmentionable source of shame, a monthly "curse" or recurrent stigma.

This daughter's protest is not a work of pure fiction. The Sinologist Arthur Wolf recounts the poignant story of his Chinese research assistant whose mother was too embarrassed to prepare her for menarche. When she had her first period, she thought she was bleeding to death and ran home crying (35). In view of the bloodshed involved, menstruation may even be perceived as an involuntary crime in which the young woman has the bewildering sensation that her body is attacking her. In the same way the aunt keenly feels how the body of villagers have turned against her during her labor pains. "The iron smell of blood" also fills Fa Mu Lan with foreboding in "White Tigers" as her parents are on the point of cutting their oaths of revenge into her back, but it already stains the pages of "No Name Woman," for blood is strongly associated with the female passages that are narrated in both the first and second story—"as when a woman gives birth . . . when I menstruated and dreamed red dreams" (38). Ironically, the stained undergarments of women will provide the narrator's father continual employment in America as he labors to wash away their "blood that stinks like brass" in his Chinese laundry (CM, 63).

Chinese Society, Female Pollution, and Social Abjection

In Chinese society, where, as Emily Ahern has shown, the bloody discharge is equivalent to a dead fetus, the menstruating woman is "regarded as both ritually unclean and dangerously powerful," and the unmarried daughter who undergoes menarche becomes that most dangerous of anomalies: a virgin who has reached sexual maturity (Ahern, 193, 199; Arthur P. Wolf, Sexual Attraction, 338). Indeed, the abject category into which female blood flow falls, given that it emanates within the body but is dispelled from it, uncannily mirrors the ambivalent, "no-win" status of women in Confucian society. They are nei ren, or humans for the inside who are paradoxically doomed to be outsiders, who are told, as is the daughter narrator in The Woman Warrior, that "there is an outward tendency in females" (49), who learn to their bitter cost that they can never fully belong either to the household into which they are born or the one into which they marry, and who are regarded as the proverbial cuckoos in the nest—migratory interlopers, encroachers, and strangers in the family's midst (Huntley, 109; Ahern 199, 210, 213).

Catherine Clément has argued that "at puberty, during menstruation, pregnancy and childbirth, and after menopause, . . . the magical virtues of women reach their greatest intensity."[13] Because Chinese reproductive culture endowed menstrual blood with a "very substantial" capacity to build the body of the child (Ahern, 196), it may therefore have been more in awe of the magical virtues of women than Western patriarchy, where the prime life-giving properties were attributed to semen. In fact, "No Name Woman" concentrates these magical virtues by bringing together women characters who represent the key stages of the female life cycle—the pubescent narrator who has begun menstruation, the aunt who becomes pregnant and gives birth, and the menopausal mother in her late fifties.[14] Traditional Chinese mothers left it to the local shaman to tell their daughters the facts of life (Wolf, *Sexual Attraction*, 35). While still living in China, Brave Orchid was trained in both shamanism and gynecology and would seem eminently well suited for this social task. Yet, when raising a family in neon-lit America, she dodges this responsibility. Rather than explain that bleeding is a natural monthly occurrence, Brave Orchid shrouds the whole subject in the frightening taboos of the afterlife and afterbirth. She warns her daughter of the sexual risks facing a nubile young woman by telling a savage tale of the aunt who jumps to her death with her newborn child and whose ghoulish punishment, according to popular belief, will be to drown in the bloody pool of the underworld "filled with birth fluids."[15]

Puberty, Liminality, and Adolescent Rite of Passage

The cultural anthropologist Victor Turner has studied the initiation rites that have traditionally been devised to channel the chaotic, psychosexual energies of puberty and empower the young to negotiate the testing transition between childhood and adulthood. Hong Kingston's narrator demonstrates a number of the liminal, or "threshold," characteristics that Turner identified in the neophyte undergoing adolescent rite of passage. Her ordeal involves feelings of social invisibility, anonymity, and humiliation and features isolation, silence, and disregard for personal appearance.[16] She confronts physical scarification in recounting how the parents of Fa Mu Lan carve and tattoo their daughter's back ceremonially in "White Tigers." With a mother who "marked [her] growing with stories" (13), however, the narrator is also acutely conscious of the psychological scars that individuals acquire over the course of their childhood, the hidden wounds from which people bleed inside, and the suffering that leaves a deep textual imprint on the body.

Looking back at the fledgling storyteller who begins writing in earnest with "No Name Woman," Hong Kingston described her as "just some dumb kid" (Marilyn Chin, 88). By her own rueful admission, this "dumb kid" had no better sex education in modern-day America than her aunt thirty years before in rural China. "No one talked sex, ever" (WW, 14). This means that the unexpected onset of menstruation and the synonymous discovery that she had a renegade aunt who became pregnant out of wedlock and committed suicide with her newborn child could have come as a double shock. The woman warrior's "red dreams" suggest that her first period may have begun while she slept and traces of this blood seeped through into her unconscious and stained her dreamscape. Hong Kingston's young woman narrator may have woken to the disturbing sensation that she had little understanding of how her body (and her mind) really worked. Her mother's cautionary tale would not have allayed this anxiety but exacerbated it by bringing home the fact that she did not really understand her own family either. "Now that you have started to menstruate, what happened to her could happen to you" (13). She is suddenly told that she is not to be trusted because she has grown to resemble an aunt of whose existence she has been oblivious. The narrator must now imagine the facts of life for herself. She must recognize not only how the female body changes during puberty, but also how the fertile body suddenly acquires the volatile sexual power to change everything. "But women at sex hazarded birth and hence lifetimes" (14). She cannot bury her head in the sand like her mother, who shared a bedroom with the aunt but denied the sight of her own eyes. "She could not have been pregnant, you see, because her husband had been gone for years" (11). She must try and work out how her aunt fell pregnant; but to do so is speculate about the identity of the father and to begin to think about her own father, a man who has lived the majority of his life as though his sister's blood did not flow in his veins and her tragedy had nothing to do with him.

Menstruation and Marriage

Like the aunt whose "protruding melon of a stomach" paradoxically symbolizes to her neighbors "the break she has made in the 'roundness'" (11, 19), so the daughter who menstruates becomes "a full blood member" of the family and at the same time signals that there is a dangerous "breach in the wall" of her womb. As Lynda Boose perceptively remarks, the bodily margins of the menstruating woman are regarded as especially dangerous to society "because they mirror the points of vulnerability to the body politic."[17] This breach is plugged up by the practice of exogamy or marriage out of the patriarchal household. Yet arranged marriage also gives her the opportunity to become a mother and build the defensive nucleus of a uterine family around her, to becomes the focus of her children's affections— and, she hopes, the center of attention for her son—and thus to create another breach in the multigenerational family structure of the Confucian and patrilineal tradition.[18] Her mother teaches the pubescent narrator that blood has powerful mana and that its escape from a living body can have terrible and unforeseen consequences (Ahern, 198–199). Brave Orchid recounts how the family "stood together in the middle of our house" and tried to defend its bloodline before the "the pictures and tables of the ancestors" while the villagers rampaged through the interior and "smeared blood on the doors and walls. One woman swung a chicken, whose throat she had slit, splattering blood in red arcs about her" (12). As she imagines how the ancestral home is violated and its occupants cursed—"'Pig.' 'Ghost.' 'Pig,' they sobbed and scolded while they ruined our house" (12)—the daughter is drawn by her mother's parable of blood pollution toward the darkest fantasy of taboo-transgression within the family—incest.

The Curse of Incest

The taboo against incest is regarded as a cultural universal, yet the strength of this taboo does not prove, as has been argued, that it works or that incest is a rare occurrence in the family.[19] What the prohibition suggests is the daughter narrator's dilemma as a writer: the victims have difficulty in reporting incest and regard it as a crime against the family to do so. The idea of incest is socially anathema—a "curse" like menstruation or the curse that the Sphinx put on Thebes because of Oedipus' incest. In the tragedy of Oedipus, parricide and incest express the son's secret and unconscious attraction and aggression toward his parents, but in reality it is the father or mother who has the power to act on these feelings for their child, not the other way round. Incest is an even more heinous act than parricide or matricide, because it murders the impressionable young son or daughter twice over in body and mind. Entrusted with the welfare of the son or daughter, the incestuous parent instead takes advantage of the child's innocence and vulnerability, sexually exploiting and perverting the intimate bond of emotional identification that already exists between them (Loewald, 396–397).

The word *incest* is explicitly mentioned only once in "No Name Woman." The daughter narrator first hints at "the never-said" in "the crowded house" (17), where the attractive aunt turned young and old male heads. Even as the narrator works up the courage to say the word *incest,* which is taboo, she begins to retreat from the suggestion that the father of the aunt's child could be someone within her own family. "He may have been somebody in her own household, but intercourse with a man outside the family would have been no less abhorrent." She describes China as an inbred, clannish society where "all the village were kinsmen" and "everybody has eight million relatives" and where "parents researched birth charts . . . to circumvent incest in a population that has but one hundred surnames" (18). To stand out as an individual and resist the herd instinct, to think of oneself as "unusually beloved" or sexually attractive or free spirited like the aunt, and to be treated as a "precious only daughter" (17) who courts special attention when a grown woman—such actions flout the unwritten rule for social survival that "children and lovers have no singularity here" (18).

Chinese Family Space and Lack of Privacy

When Hong Kingston journeyed to China for the first time, in 1984, and visited her ancestral village and inspected the family quarters detailed in "No Name Woman" (Huntley, 11), she was "shocked at what close quarters the people lived in, how small the rooms are" and realized that she "didn't describe the village right in 'No Name Woman.' I was imagining an American farm with land, a farmhouse with a barn, and outhouses [where] people would come across the field from one farmhouse to another." What she found was a cramped, crowded, jostling environment where "houses have common walls," and collective ears and eyes, and families live on top of one another (Skenazy, "Kingston at the University," 134–135). The American myth of wide-open spaces exerted its romantic influence over the writer so that she underestimated how little privacy there was in her ancestral village and how unlikely it was that her aunt could have had sex in a field or an outhouse without being observed. "The villagers punished her for acting as if she could have a private life, secret and apart from them" (19). Indeed having seen the village for herself, she began to appreciate that free love could be as explosive as the dynamite that the Grandfather of the Sierra Nevada Mountains uses to blast the tunnels for the transcontinental railroad. "When there is a huge family that lives in one room and . . . the cousins and uncle and aunt live in the next room, . . . anything you do changes the whole village" (Skenazy, "Kingston at the University," 135; see also Hoy, 51; Rabinowitz, 71).

Incest and *Sim-pua* Marriage in Chinese Society

The temptation that faces the American or first-world reader may be to regard incest as a remote danger that can be banished to distant regions of China, not a problem close to home that is symptomatic of a community turned in on itself (Wong, *Reading Asian American Literature*, 43). Yet even if "No Name Woman" facilitates displacement and removes the problem geographically to China, the intolerable thought of incest does not go away. Nor can it be repressed for long. It returns with the narrator's wistful longing to enjoy her aunt's special place as a daughter at the heart of the family. "She may have been unusually beloved, the precious only daughter, spoiled and mirror gazing because of the affection the family lavished on her. When her husband left, they welcomed the chance to take her back from the in-laws; she could live like the little daughter for just a while longer" (17). Sidonie Smith rightly wonders in a footnote to this story why "this married aunt [was] living with her own parents rather than with her in-laws. And who had been the stranger, or was he a stranger, who had entered her house/womb?" (*Woman Warrior Casebook*, 84). One possible explanation is furnished by the narrator herself, when she alludes to the widespread practice of *sim-pua* marriage. "Among the very poor and the wealthy, brothers married their adopted sisters, like doves"; however, the custom of adopting and training up a "little daughter-in-law"[20] was not as common in the rural Canton delta as in other parts of China[21] and the narrator quickly discounts it. "Our family allowed some romance, . . . providing dowries so that their sons and daughters could marry strangers" (19).

Yet, as Marjorie Topley has pointed out in "Marriage Resistance in Rural Kwangtung," it was virtually unheard of for a grown up woman to return to her natal home and be supported and "spoiled" by her parents after her marriage (80). As the narrator herself remarks, "daughters-in-law lived with their husbands' parents, not their own" (15). If the aunt was not a natural but adopted daughter who was reared from infancy as foster sister and future wife to one of the four Hong sons, however, there would be no need "to take her back from the in-laws" (17). Moreover, because it was customary for the *sim-pua* to live in her future husband's household from early childhood, it would not be strange for Brave Orchid to find herself living under the same roof as the aunt after she herself married into the Hong household (15). The *sim-pua*, or little daughter-in-law, was reared to a blind love for her husband's parents and was frequently adopted before being weaned so that she would form a strong and exclusive bond with them. In many instances, the *sim-pua* felt inseparable from her foster mother. Her crippling emotionally dependency on her mother-in-law was calculated to inhibit the development of romantic love for her foster brother (Johnson, *Women, the Family, and Peasant Revolution in China*, 19). While for all intents and purposes, the *sim-pua*'s future-in-laws became her real parents, her marital ties to the son they had selected as her husband in early childhood often came to seem unnatural. When she reached puberty, she could find that the prospect of a conjugal relationship with her foster brother gave rise to feelings of incestuous repugnance and sexual aversion.

In his study of the Taiwanese practice of *sim-pua* marriage, Wolf collected compelling evidence that the strength of the incest taboo worked to the advantage of the controlling matriarch in suppressing later erotic attraction between her precious son and his foster sister. He noted the reluctance of these partners to consummate their union, the relatively low levels of fertility and the higher rate of adultery and divorce that occurred in *sim-pua* marriages. In fact, he argued that despite the strong emotional ties that *sim-pua* formed with their husband's family, many women preferred to leave and support themselves as prostitutes rather than continue in a sexually intolerable relationship with their adopted sibling.[22] Although "No Name Woman" conveys a palpable sense of "the affection the family lavished on" the aunt and the sexual attraction that she inspired in the male sojourner relatives "home between journeys" (17), what is missing from the narrative is any sense of real feeling for her wronged husband. The mechanical recitation of the bare facts of their life together—"the night she first saw him, he had sex with her. Then he left for America. She had almost forgotten what he looked like" (14)—suggest that this marriage was dead even before it began. The promiscuous behavior of the aunt makes her come alive again in the story but the out-migration of her husband may not have been the only cause of her infidelity or the disintegration of their marriage. *Sim-pua* were more likely than grass widows (like Brave Orchid) to engage in adulterous affairs, largely because of the sexual disgust, embarrassment, or disinterest felt in "incestuous" marriage to a foster brother.[23]

Father, Son, and Daughter Rivalries

To some extent, a *sim-pua* reading of the "No Name Woman" neutralizes the fears of incest in the narrative. This is because the high failure rate of the *sim-pua* marriage points to the success of the cultural taboo against incest. According to the so-called Westermarck effect, early familiarity among family siblings effectively prohibits incest and even discourages later sexual intimacy between persons who are not blood relatives but who were raised together as brother and sister.[24] Although a *sim-pua* marriage would suggest that the aunt might have felt sexual indifference or even aversion to her husband, it does not explain the emotional antipathy the narrator's own father seems to feel for his little sister—in such marked contrast to the affection in which she was held by the other members of the family. "They must have all loved her, except perhaps my father, the only brother who never went back to China having once been traded for a girl" (17). Readers have seen that this passage could reflect sibling rivalry and fraternal jealousy of the spoilt only daughter who usurped the father's place as the baby of the family and who stole the heart of his "crazy" and besotted old father. "One day he brought home a baby girl, wrapped up inside his brown western-style greatcoat. He had traded one of his sons, probably my father, the youngest, for her. My grandmother made him trade back. When he finally got a daughter of his own, he doted on her" (17). Though it was a common practice for parents to trade a natural daughter for an adopted daughter in the superstitious belief that they were thus more likely to conceive or "lead in" a son for the *sim-pua* marriage (Arthur P. Wolf, "The Women of Haishan," 95–96; Topley, 77), the grandfather's impulse to swap his youngest son for a little wife turns the male's privileged place in Confucian society upside down. In light of the fact that girls were dirt cheap, especially in poor families with more than one daughter (Wolf, "The Women of Haishan," 98), it is possible that the grandfather brokered a deal that allowed him to keep the "baby girl" even after his wife made him hand her back and reclaim his son.

As Leigh Gilmore senses, however, the father's "animosity" runs very deep in this story (178). In probing it further, the narrator confronts the unedifying spectacle of a paternal grandfather who was a dirty old man—"different from other people, 'crazy ever since the little Jap bayoneted him in the head.' He used to put his naked penis on the dinner table, laughing" (17). And then suddenly, out of the blue, instead of playing with his penis beneath his overcoat, he brought home a fetishistic substitute in the form of a baby girl. "And one day he brought home a baby girl, wrapped up inside his brown western-style greatcoat" (17). When Neila Seshachari tactfully asked Hong Kingston how she found the courage to "grapple so brilliantly with psychic realities" and write "in such surprisingly uninhibited ways" about her grandfather as an exhibitionist here in "No Name Woman" and masturbator later in "The Grandfather of the Sierra Nevada Mountains," she gave an evasive autobiographical answer. "I feel that writing is also a very secretive act" (198).

Incest, the Extended Chinese Family, and Autobiographical Writing

I propose here that autobiographical writing becomes an incestuous narrative activity when it risks such indiscretion; transgresses the socially sanctioned boundaries that make the private, sexual life of the parent off limits to the child or that protect the child from the unsolicited advances of the parent; and explores the intergenerational love, jealousy, and hate that the members of the family may refuse to acknowledge or name. The daughter narrator of *The Woman Warrior* is careful to protect the father's good name by beginning "No Name Woman" with the official story her mother circulated—that the aunt became pregnant "years" after her husband sailed for America with the other Hong family men and that their sojourners' journey in 1924 was the "grandfather's last trip" out on the road (11). In her mother's account of the raid on the Hong house, the rampaging villagers break into "your grandparents' rooms, to find your aunt's, which was also mine until the men returned" (12). The daughter narrator does not comment on the physical proximity of these rooms or pursue the Confucian idea of the unbroken home that suggests they might be interconnected. Later in the story, however, she stresses the social necessity of personal effacement, studied avoidance of eye and bodily contact, and emotional impassivity in the "crowded house" of an extended and close-knit Chinese patrilineal family. "Brothers and sisters, newly men and women, had to efface their sexual colour and present plain miens. Disturbing hair and eyes, a smile like no other threatened the ideal of five generations living under one roof" (17–18).

In the course of explaining the unwritten code for sexual survival in this extended household, she begins to comprehend the severe social training that may have instilled her parents' cultural habits of coldness and detachment. Hong Kingston later complained that Western critics fell back on "the stereotype of the exotic, inscrutable, mysterious oriental" Other to analyze such social behavior.[25] The narrator will condemn her mother's emotional cruelty in continually reminding her that she is "ugly" and be exasperated by Brave Orchid's reluctant reply near the end of *The Woman Warrior*: "That's what Chinese say. We like to say the opposite" (181). As an intertextual "interlocutor,"[26] rereading what she first wrote in "No Name Woman," however, she can see her parents may have been motivated by the perverse fear that she resembled her aunt and was susceptible in puberty to the same "heart-catching tangles" (16) of fate. Of course the parents' fear that the history of the aunt will be repeated in the life of their daughter may also be a fear of transgenerational incest. A daughter who menstruates become that most intimate and surprising of strangers—a nubile young woman whom the family looks on with new eyes, who threatens sexual arousal and pollution of the whole household (Boose, 35), and who may awaken in her own father memories of past sexual trauma.

The story of a weeping woman ghost is an evocative way for Hong Kingston to begin the writing of her girlhood memoirs, for a common folk-lore belief was that drowning persons see their lives flash before their eyes as they go down to their death.[27] In other words, these last terrifying moments may have been a possible revelation for the aunt, offering her one and only chance to read her abridged and anonymous life as an intelligible biography waiting to be told. It is a narrative catharsis for her Chinese American niece to retrieve "No Name Woman" from the family pool of stories and claim this female relative from the mainland as a "forerunner" (15), for, as Kay Ann Johnson so succinctly observed, "Chinese women were embedded in perhaps the oldest, most highly developed, male-dominated kinship system in history" (24), yet daughters had no recognizable place in a male descent line.

Birth Order and the Fate of Daughters in the Chinese Family

What compounds the young narrator's sense of displacement is her uncertainly as to her own birth order in the family. Is she the "oldest" or the "biggest" daughter, firstborn or middle child after the "Oldest Daughter and Oldest Son" who may have been first born to her parents and died in China (*WW*, 96)? With the odds heavily stacked against them in the traditional Chinese family, girls quickly discovered that birth order was a crucial factor in calculating their diminished chances of survival and contentment. Girl children born to childless couples had the highest probability of remaining in their natal families, but those unfortunates born into a family with two or more children were often given away as *sim-pua* or servants and, in either role, treated like slaves.[28] In America, the narrator is the firstborn, but had her older brother and sister survived in China, she would have been third in line and imagines the likelihood of being sold into lifelong servitude. "In China my parents would sell my sisters and me" (*WW*, 93). In "Shaman," she describes her mother, Brave Orchid, walking past "the sellers of little girls," noting the fathers who were occasionally forced to sell their precious only daughters and looking down with pity and contempt at the "miserable families who did not have the sense to leave the favoured brothers and sisters home" (75–76). After puberty, in "A Song for a Barbarian Reed Pipe," the daughter narrator tries to make herself "unsellable" by picking her nose and affecting a limp. Yet she realizes that it is not simply "American-pretty" (19) looks but the female reproductive capacity over which she has no control that puts her in danger, as it did her aunt. She thus fearfully concludes that her sojourner "parents need only wait until China, and there, where anything happens, they would be able to unload us, even me—sellable, marriageable" (170).

Intertextuality and the Writer's Discovery of a Female Descent Line

As an intertextual reader and writer, Hong Kingston herself felt she was "descended from Walt Whitman and Nathaniel Hawthorne and Virginia Woolf" (Fisher Fishkin, 167). The author has repeatedly alluded to the literary importance that Virginia Woolf's *Orlando* had in her writing of *China Men*, with its diachronic character who can travel across time, history, and gender and "live many connecting experiences" (Schroeder, 219). Woolf's *A Room of One's Own* has been no less important in helping her to imagine a female descent line that will enable the narrator of *The Woman Warrior* to "see her [aunt's] life branching into mine" and find the "ancestral help" she needs (16). In *A Room of One's Own,* Woolf cast her mind back in time to the nameless women of the past who left no entry or testimonial in the book of life. Like the no name woman, they looked for love but instead encountered seduction, rape, and unwanted pregnancy. At the end of lives that had hardly begun, they found madness, suicide, or a death sentence. They brought shame to their family when they may have hoped to contribute a personal chapter to its collective history.

Hong Kingston's Sense of Kinship with Virginia Woolf

Lauren Rusk has recently reminded readers how Virginia Woolf created a literary sense of kinship with these lost women. In *A Room of One's Own,* Woolf imagined that Shakespeare had a gifted sister who met ruin yet whose poetic spirit lives on in women writers. She also alluded to the eighteenth-century legend of the wronged Mary Hamilton who was hanged after drowning her baby yet whose memory is orally preserved in a haunting ballad.[29] As Woolf conjured up the doomed talents of Shakespeare's sister Judith, likewise the narrator of *The Woman Warrior* will bring the tragic sister of her own father back to life, and this aunt meets Mary Hamilton's fate twice over when she drowns herself and her newborn daughter in the family well. Though it is never clear whether the no name woman is a fictitious or real relative, her story resonates with the heteroglossia of Brave Orchid's oral storytelling, with the dialogue between the mother raconteur and her quiet but observant daughter scribe, and with the whispered gossip and scandal that gave Chinese women a secret sense of social power over men (Ahern, 201). Apropos of "No Name Woman"—a tragic heroine who is ostracized by her kith and kin and who gives birth with "a fence enclosing her, a tribal person alone" (*WW*, 21)—the French feminist Hélène Cixous conceived this heteroglossia as the outpouring of a female outcast who "has never ceased to hear the resonance of fore-language. She lets the other language speak—the language of a 1,000 tongues which knows neither enclosure nor death."[30]

The Narrator's Recovery of Her Suicide Aunt from the Family Well

The first task of the narrator is to recover the aunt and her child from the dark waters of the past and make their bodies the wellspring of a writing or *écriture féminine* that "bridges . . . the spaces of silence created by people whose stories have remained untold" and that throws lifelines to "persons floundering in deep waters."[31] Many poor rural women, weighed down by hardship and suffering, sunk without trace in early twentieth-century China, and the cruel practice of drowning female infants was so common (Johnson, *Women, the Family, and Peasant Revolution in China*, 33) that the narrator is safe to assume that the aunt's newborn was "probably a girl" (21). She may even imagine herself as the daughter that her aunt could not afford to have. "To be a woman, to have a daughter in starvation time was a waste enough" (14). For Chinese peasant women with no social control over their own lives, suicide was their last resort, affording them a powerful if deadly weapon of destruction against their family oppressors.[32] The aunt dramatically publicizes her thirst for revenge when she pollutes the local drinking water with her drowned and bloated body and with the "dirty blood" of its postpartum discharge (Ahern, 194). A glancing intertextual reference to a feminine social custom in *China Men* enables the reader to appreciate how exquisite is the revenge the aunt exacts on the whole village by her drowning. "The women went to the well to catch the first water of dawn, the Glory of the Well, good for the skin" (*CM*, 34). As they drew the pure water for their daily skin care, they would also have caught their first glimpse of the disfigured face of the aunt, once so lovely, so particular about "a smooth brow" and clear complexion, and fastidious about her beauty routine (*WW*,

16–17).[33] From her mother, Hong Kingston later learned that the well where the aunt drowned herself and the adjacent Hong family temple were the village space for courting. "My mother said that the guys used to hang around on the steps of the temple and make remarks at the girls to try to get them to drop . . . their water jars. . . . You know, guys whistling at girls, . . . it's so sexy" (Rabinowitz, 71). A "spite suicide" who haunts the main source of drinking water and who "waits silently by the water to pull down a substitute" (22) would have subsequently made this light-hearted flirtation seem accursed and taboo.

Brave Orchid gives a brutal account of finding the aunt "and the baby plugging up the family well" (12) when she went to collect water to wash away the foul taste and waste of the village raid the night before. Her daughter narrator picks up the story and tries to redeem the final, desolate moments of the aunt's life. "Carrying the baby to the well shows loving. . . . Mothers who love their children take them along" (21). Yet she has so thoroughly internalized the negating voice of her mother and the forbidding silence of her father that she ends by repeating the parental commandment she has just broken. "Don't tell anyone you had an aunt. Your father does not want to hear her name. She has never been born" (21). It is, however, not only a spiteful but a childish ruse to pretend that a family member has never been born, as Freud has shown in his study of the family romance, and the narrator must finally reject such a mean fiction if she is to become a more mature storyteller.

In effect she must unplug the mother and child from the family well —a symbolic ordeal that requires her to confront not only the horror of death, but also that lesser terror of writer's block. The recovery of their dead bodies is an affect-charged act of de-repression that unblocks her hidden declamatory power, power that helpless Chinese women once felt they could articulate only through suicide (Margery Wolf, 114). The young mother was not given a place of honor in the traditional Confucian family and was often subject to hostility and abuse in her husband's household. As the narrator remarks, her fertile body introduced "foreign growth" into the patrilineal family and so "threatened the ideal of five generations [of males] living under one roof," while obviously being indispensable to its continuance (*WW*, 18, 21; Johnson, *Women, the Family, and Peasant Revolution in China*, 9–10, 18; Ahern, 200, 210, 213). Because Chinese patriliny accorded the new mother no formal or benevolent status, the family well can also be read as an evocative symbol of the male unconscious that keeps women down and represses recognition of their reproductive and nurturant powers. This male unconscious becomes the textual unconscious of *The Woman*

Warrior, it mobilizes its defensive energy from the father's denial of his sister and refusal to honor her memory, and it will find release in *China Men.*

The Fallen Woman at the Well of Life

The aunt's drowned body is a grotesque mockery of the archaic belief that the mother, not the father, is the fountainhead of life, and her swollen corpse has the hideous "power to remind" (26) the narrator that the maternal figure is the original source of language and culture. Unlike the father, her influence over the child begins prenatally and flows from the unconscious fetal state into the semiotic body language and mother tongue learned in early infancy, through into the imaginary realm of later juvenile development, before trickling off in the symbolic and social order of patriarchy.[34] It is interesting that Hong Kingston likened her own method of writing to a depth charge that locates "the sources of creativity, in order to get down to the id of the self or the subconscious."[35] As we have already seen, Nathaniel Hawthorne's *Scarlet Letter* was an important intertextual source of creativity when she began the writing of "No Name Woman." Hawthorne depicts his adulterous heroine Hester Prynne as a tragic daughter trapped in an incestuous marriage with an impotent, unfeeling, and sexually repulsive father figure aptly named Chillingworth. In the Christian iconography of his novel, her fall is ultimately fortunate, leading to her growth in grace and dignity as a woman artist. A skilled seamstress, Hester learns to work with the raw material closest at hand—her own passionate and wounded heart. As she allows her heart to become a wellspring of creative sympathy and solace with others, Hester assumes the character of a Madonna. Her apotheosis both critiques and subverts the misogyny of Puritan American patriarchy. Patricia Chu argues that nineteenth-century bildungsromans such as *The Scarlet Letter* "were more sympathetic to fallen women than Brave Orchid's story."[36] By reading Hawthorne into her writing of "No Name Woman," however, Hong Kingston signals the daughter's intertextual sympathy with a long tradition of fallen women from the weeping Magdalene to the Samaritan woman at the well in the Gospel of John (4:6–26). Like Hester Prynne, their adulterous eyes, mouths, breasts, vulvas, and wombs are life-giving sources, their impure bodies are pregnant with pure possibility, and their sexual "extravagance" (*WW,* 13) reflects what Luce Irigaray calls "the maternal body's gifts of generosity, abundance, and plenitude."[37] Their divine reward was a well of water springing up to everlasting life; the patrifamilial punishment meted out to the no name woman is a well of eternal oblivion.

Drowning in Male Culture: The Identity Crisis of Adolescent Girls

The brutal dispatch of the aunt to the waters of oblivion paints a black and depressing picture of woman's sexual objectification for the adolescent narrator of *The Woman Warrior*. In her account *Reviving Ophelia*, Mary Pipher argues that American "adolescent girls today also face a problem with no name."[38] They may live in a democratic society predicated on consent, not coercion and control, but when they enter puberty they become aware that power still descends primarily to men and that women are expected to consent to this arrangement.[39] They begin to feel the social pressure to win male approval, as the narrator does when she dreams of making herself "American-pretty" so that the Chinese, Caucasian, Negro, and Japanese boys in her class will all fall in love with her (19). Indeed, the straight-A student and cheerleader—whom the narrator both aspires and refuses to become (49, 162)—is the American paradigm of female acquiescence. As childhood comes to an end, girls grieve at the impending loss of their scope for free and spontaneous expression of themselves and, like the aunt, may fear that they will "drown" in the alien waters of a sexist, racist, and image-conscious culture. Such girls may resort to the narrator's imaginary means of expressing her adolescent pain and confusion: the self-mutilation graphically illustrated in the story of Fa Mu Lan; the dramatic mood swing from aggression to weakness that is chronicled in the narrator's account of bullying a Chinese schoolmate before her psychosomatic collapse "with a mysterious illness" (163); the fragmentation of identity that is associated not only with the turmoil of adolescence, but also with her dual cultural heritage, and that is mirrored in her narrative collage of literary fragments; and finally the eating disorder that articulates the social perception that model women need male protection—"no one supports me; I am not loved enough to be supported" (49)—and must literally shrink in size because, as the narrator reasons, "no one hurts the cute and small" (153).[40]

Yet "No Name Woman" depicts the sadistic pleasure that the village vigilantes derive precisely from their social power to hurt the cute and small. The bucolic nursing interlude that follows the illegitimate birth and precedes the murder-suicide of mother and child underlines the cute characteristics that protect the young from being killed or devoured. The aunt's newborn "made little snuffling noises" when she first offered the breast. She "clenched her teeth at its preciousness, lovely as a young calf, a piglet, a little dog" (21), knowing that she must harden "her breasts against the milk that crying loosens" and harden her heart so that the nursing bond would be tough enough to keep them joined in death. "Carrying the baby to the well shows loving. . . . Mothers who love their children take them along" (21).

The Family Politics of Father-Daughter Incest

Cute and adorable child-women who are sexually used by all-powerful men and whose wasted lives are then symbolically poured down the well constitute the prime victims of patriarchal incest in the family. Indeed, as Vikki Bell points out, the child-women is most at risk of incest in the male-dominated household where the father is an absolute ruler who expects to have all his needs met, who regards his wife and children as his personal possessions, and who demands their unquestioning obedience to his will. The father's presumption that the family is his disposable property can lead to the pathological targeting of the powerless young daughter as the object of sexual abuse. In the traditional Chinese household, where close feelings were deliberately withheld or repressed, the father was a figure of remote authority revered by his sons. A certain degree of familiarity, however, was allowed between the father and daughter.[41] For women starved of affection, the role of the cherished daughter brought pronounced emotional satisfaction, but it may also have intensified the risks of incestuous intimacy. Father-daughter incest may be tacitly tolerated as long as no other man's goods are coveted (Bell, 60–62, 67, 77–78, 111). When the villagers pillage the Hong family house, they forcibly signify their disapproval of the fact that their neighbor's wife has been stolen. "They ripped up her clothes and shoes . . . tore her work from the loom. . . . They overturned the great waist-high earthenware jugs; duck eggs, pickled fruits, vegetables burst out and mixed in acrid torrents" (12).

Abuse of the *Sim-pua* in the Family

It remains an open question whether the village would have reacted with such ferocity had they discovered family secrets about the aunt's sexual activities before she married, particularly if she was raised as a little daughter-in-law. For though the *sim-pua* was reserved as future wife for her foster brother, in reality she was often treated as a domestic slave to the entire household. Perhaps because she bore the brunt of servitude and oppression in the family, the *sim-pua* was contemptuously mocked in playground games as "swollen like a snail." In many ways, as Arthur Wolf has observed, "the *sim-pua* was like an abused child or a prisoner in a concentration camp" (*Sexual Attraction*, 369, 268). The narrator turns a taunt used by schoolgirls into a wondering description of the "women [who] looked like great sea snails—the corded wood, babies, and laundry they carried were the whorls on their backs" (17). Beast of burden in her adopted family, she was subjected to institutionalized maltreatment that may have made it socially acceptable for her to provide occasional sexual service to the paterfamilias. Wolf poignantly foretells the fate of the aunt when he concludes that "the typical *sim-pua* lived on the edge of an emotional abyss" (*Sexual Attraction*, 277).[42]

Father-Daughter Incest and the Taboo against Exposure

Father-daughter incest has been called the family's "best kept secret." It is often guarded by a "conspiracy of silence" (Bell, 79), and its force is such that the narrator can never bring herself to ask her own father about his "drowned-in-the-well sister" (13). Anthropologists have represented the taboo against incest as a defining moment of human culture. Indeed, "incest" and "taboo" are "words so strong" (*WW*, 21) and so off-limits to discussion that cultural critics long recoiled from questioning to what extent the taboo effectively prohibited the occurrence of incest within the universal family (Arens 44; Bell, 2, 111; Boose, 30). Arthur Wolf's study of *sim-pua* unhappily married to foster brothers seems to support the Westermarck hypothesis: that the incest taboo expresses a natural sexual aversion between conjugal partners who have been reared intimately together since early childhood (*Sexual Attraction*, 2–19). In contrast, father-daughter incest appears to make the Freudian argument for a naturally occurring attraction —an attraction so strong that it overrides the social taboo and punctures the myth that it ever constituted a real sexual deterrent. Yet feminists have perceived a complicated pattern of *both* attraction and dislike at work in father-daughter incest. They have concluded that, above and beyond desire, it is the patriarchal expression sine qua non of social and sexual power over women in the family, for the father who "breaks in" his young daughter sexually is domesticating her to a life of servicing men and habituating her to femininity in a male supremacist society (Bell, 68, 87). This is why the narrator depicts her aunt as dumbly resigned to her sexual assault. "The other man was not, after all, much different from her husband. They both gave orders: she followed. 'If you tell your family, I'll beat you. I'll kill you. Be here again next week'" (14).

Incest is a crime that fathers commit in the name of love and that daughters can confuse with parental care and attention (Bell, 120). Because incest is committed in stealth and difficult to detect, and because it requires such a comprehensive denial of sexual predation and its emotional after-effects, members of the family who "name the unspeakable" (*WW,* 13) often struggle with strong feelings of guilt, betrayal, and disloyalty.[43] In other words, although the incest taboo is not always strong enough to prevent the act, it does exert an insidious pressure on the family to keep quiet. "Don't tell. 'Never tell'" (*WW,* 165). At the close of "No Name Woman," the narrator admits that it took her two decades before she could breathe a word about her aunt or bring herself to contemplate her sexual fate. "In the twenty years since I heard this story I have not asked for details nor said my aunt's name" (22). Giving a name and face to their traumatic sexualization is an important step forward out of oppressive silence and denial for the daughter victims of incest; however, the narrator of *The Woman Warrior* never does name the aunt or her sexual victimizer. In fact, the taboo prohibiting identification is so far-reaching that she never divulges her own father's name or the first name she is called as a daughter. As Hong Kingston pointed out, "nobody calls her anything. . . . She is still in search of her name, she's still trying to find her powers, she's still trying to find out who she is" (Skenazy, "Kingston at the University," 133). Nor can she find "vengeance" (*WW,* 53) in reporting the sexual crime committed against the aunt when she never knows for sure what "secret evil" (*WW,* 14) took place. Indeed, the author herself famously "regretted calling the book *The Woman Warrior*" because she could not identify with the role of "a female avenger" (*WW,* 45) and was uncomfortable with the metaphor of words as a weapon of aggression, retribution, or malice (Skenazy, "Kingston at the University," 132; see also Bonetti, 36–37).

Repairing the Damage of Incest through Creative Writing and Intertextuality

In her study of father-daughter incest, Janet Liebman Jacobs argues that the victim's acknowledgement of her sexual abuse triggers the slow and painful journey from repression to consciousness of trauma (137–138). The daughter, however, is also embarking on a turbulent and dangerous psychological passage in which her false sense of intersubjectivity, constructed through what happens in incest, is now shattered. Jacobs concludes that it is not the factual reporting of the father's incestuous crime but the creative reassembly of the broken pieces of her life, through such therapeutic activities as art, writing, and spirituality, that is crucial for the incest victim's ultimate recovery (157–163). Kristeva had argued, as we will recall, that "the notion of *intertextuality* replaces that of intersubjectivity" (*Desire in Language,* 66).

Hong Kingston's two books suggest that intertextuality can correct the incestuous distortions of intersubjectivity by writing both the victimized daughter and the abusive father with his own history of suffering and victimization back into being.

Incest Victims and Posttraumatic Stress Disorders

Feminists have complained that, while the male trauma of war veterans is recognized, the suffering of less powerful groups in ordinary circumstances is overlooked or considered unremarkable—that of battered wives and children; the downtrodden, disabled, or disenfranchised in the workforce; the scapegoats in the playground; and daughter victims of rape and molestation in the home. Over the course of *The Woman Warrior,* the girl narrator either presents the symptoms of posttraumatic stress disorder or, as we saw in chapter 2, shows other characters close to her who are similarly afflicted. In "No Name Woman," she demonstrates a compulsive need to replay the traumatic events leading up to the aunt's death, yet can only imagine the aunt's assailant as a "masked" figure, a blank, or "black and white face in the group photograph the men had had taken before leaving" (14)—in other words, as a generic male, not a recognizable character. This dim figure reflects the psychological need of the abused young woman to erase the perpetrator from her mind and his return with sinister force from repression as "a faceless intruder, a malevolent presence that the child fears but cannot name" (Jacobs, 36).

In "Shaman" he rises from the shadowlands of the unconscious as a "Sitting Ghost" and enacts the twin evils of repression and rape by climbing onto Brave Orchid's bed, landing heavily on her chest, and pressing her down so that she lies powerless beneath him (67). Like the aunt's attacker, he has "no eyes, no face," no true human identity. He is a creature who rolls into one the terrors of the child's night—the ghoul and goblin, ogre, bogyman and even yeti—with "mounds of hair . . . bigger than a wolf, bigger than an ape, and growing" (70). He haunts the female dormitory where Brave Orchid's medical classmates, "some of these girls . . . young enough to be her daughters" (62), study and sleep. Just as the sexual predator often strikes when his young victim enters that liminal state between slumber and fitful awareness (Jacobs, 36), "where the stories left off and the dreams began" (*WW,* 25), so the Sitting Ghost steals in and out of the dormant minds of the women boarders, amassing his energy from their nightmares and fears, deepest hopes and dreams. "Like Frankenstein's monster, like the mummy dragging its foot" (*WW,* 174), or like Freddy from Elm Street, he makes a repeated comeback from the unquiet grave where he lies in the terrified mind of the child. In "A Song for a Barbarian Reed Pipe," he is reincarnated as the lumbering "hulk," "gorilla ape," "freak," and pervert who may actually stalk the narrator and her sister (179) or who may, on the other hand, be a figment of her wild imagination.[44]

Incest as a Violation of Home

Simmons observes that these homesick "young medical students" so far from their families were "particularly vulnerable to psychic trauma, to ghost sickness" (77). Incest, however, documents the vulnerability of young women to sexual, as well as psychic, trauma in their own homes. Indeed, home is a far more problematic and painful concept for incest victims than for the pioneer women of To Keung Medical School who "pieced together new directions" (73).[45] Incest teaches them that they are not safe at home, especially at night. As Brave Orchid demonstrates, women who can sleep safe in their beds are the lucky ones. One coping strategy of defenseless young victims is to project the private horror of incest onto a cruel outside world where they can "hear babies crying" and "tortured people screaming, and the cries of their relatives who had to watch" (WW, 71). The Sitting Ghost not only feeds on the suffering of the helpless but mocks and mimics their secret pain. This is why Brave Orchid fears that the phantom will assume her "dead relatives' shapes" and appear as "a beautiful sad lady" with a haunting likeness to the "drowned" aunt (69), or metamorphosize into the sexy "Fox Spirit," like the one who keeps the sojourner from returning to his family in the China Men intertext "The Ghostmate" (CM, 75), or take the form of the "pillow ghost," the alluring young woman who used her bedroom skills to seduce husbands away from their mothers and sisterly sim-pua wives.[46]

Psychological Distancing from Incest

Brave Orchid undergoes a shamanistic soul journey after "a full-grown Sitting Ghost loomed up to the ceiling and pounced on top of [her]." "At about three A.M. I died for a while. I was wandering. . . . For ten years I lost my way" (70). Her out-of-the-body experience is similar to Fa Mu Lan's ecstatic ascent in "White Tigers" beyond the tree line of the mountains, "inside the clouds—inside the dragon's breath—[where she] would not know how many hours or days passed" (26). As Janet Jacobs points out, incest victims can go to great lengths to distance themselves from their sexual violation and may resort to such psychological mechanisms of dissociation from the body as numbing, trance, or other altered states of consciousness (129–131). Indeed, the suffocating fear of the Sitting Ghost is uncannily consistent with the symptoms of sleep paralysis common among medical workers on night shifts or among trauma victims. As one sufferer reported, "A black shape gathers in the corner of the room. . . . It comes closer and eventually . . . I feel its pressure and it's holding me and then, under its weight and power, I feel I'm being dragged down."[47] A child who lies rigid with fear in the night anticipating sexual assault by a dark and menacing male force may be especially susceptible to the irrational superstition and hallucinations often associated with acute sleep paralysis (Jacobs, 40–41). The imaginary reconstruction of Brave Orchid as a ghostbuster with supernatural powers can be a cry for nocturnal help to the good-enough mother. She will lead her daughter "out of nightmares and horror movies" and make her feel "loved" and "safe" again by crooning her name back into harmony with "my father's, my brothers' and sisters'" (73).

The Profile of Incest Victims

Daughters with a history of abuse characteristically suffer from fragmented recall, intrusive flashbacks to their victimization, and split consciousness (Jacobs, 10–12). In "A Song for a Barbarian Reed Pipe," the narrator wonders fearfully whether the abusive history of her aunt may be hereditary. "I wanted to ask again why the women in our family have a split nail on our left little toe." Her embarrassed parents will only whisper anxiously to each other, "She didn't get away," leading their bewildered daughter to conclude that her family was "descended from an ancestress who stubbed her toe and fell when running from a rapist" (177). In *The Woman Warrior*, truth can certainly be stranger than fiction, and the reality is that both sexual abuse and the posttraumatic stress disorders it triggers can be passed on from one generation to the next. Incest survivors are prone to a split consciousness in which they are attracted to relationships that replay their traumatic history of violation and where they alternate between their original role of victim and the internalized identity of their assailant.[48] Characteristically, young incest victims may develop a colorful fantasy life in order to escape the holding pattern of violence they are locked into at home. Here they may endlessly reinvent, but not necessarily integrate, their trauma consciously into their lives. As the narrator vividly illustrates, escapism also has its risks for an introverted and bemused Chinese American daughter who is unsure "what is Chinese tradition and what is the movies" (13) and who cannot always tell the difference between the imaginary world both she and her mother make up and the ghetto world of "poverty" and "insanities" where her family lives.

> There were adventurous people inside my head to whom I talked. With them I was frivolous and violent, orphaned. I was white and had red hair, and I rode a white horse. Once when I realized how often I went away to see these free movies, I asked my sister, just checking to see if hearing voices in motors and seeing cowboy movies on blank walls was normal, I asked, 'Uh,' trying to be casual, 'do you talk to people that aren't real inside your mind?' 'Do I *what?*' she said. (170)

Fantasies of Male Freedom and Valor

Envious and competitive fantasies of male heroism in which the girl behaves as a tomboy, aspires to be the idealized son and heir, plays the cowboy riding to the rescue, or mounts a magical white charger that carries her into battle or flies her to freedom recur in the developmental profile of incest victims. This is consistent with Janice Haaken's observation that "the trauma story anoints the survivor with a heroic status—as the bearer of unspeakable truths."[49] In "A Song for a Barbarian Reed Pipe," the narrator confesses that as a young girl she, too, "prayed for a white horse of my own" that would "start the movies in my mind coming true" (176). In *China Men,* the intertextual reader discovers that this romance with the horse is not simply a childish projection of the movies where the Lone Ranger calls "Hi ho, Silver" and where the narrator imagines herself—or her namesake, a blonde saloon gambler—dressed as a cross between a cheerleader and a "cowgirl in white boots with baton-twirler tassels and spurs" (243). Her magical view of the horse was also shaped by an early childhood memory of literary *jouissance.* There one of her grandfathers showed her how to take pleasure in words and taught her that they sometimes have the power to control and dispel nameless fears. "Say Goong pointed up at a wide brown eye as high as the roof. I was ready to be terrified but for his delight. 'Horse,' he said. 'Horse.' He contained the thing in a word—*horse,* magical and earthly sound" (*CM*, 167).

In the controlling fantasy of *The Woman Warrior,* the romance is replayed when "a kingly white horse" appears out of nowhere to Fa Mu Lan on the eve of battle. This magical steed personifies the psyche of the woman warrior and enacts the ancient myth that horse and rider are one. Though kingly, it does not terrify the girl because it has retained the familiar charm of the child's rocking horse or the brightly painted charger of a carousel. "It wore a saddle and bridle with red, gold, and black tassels dancing" that is a perfect fit for a small frame. It invites Fa Mu Lan to leap on its back and "marvel at the power and height it gave to [her]" (39). It does not make a sound when it "stepped into the courtyard," but it can "talk" through sign language. A creature as "strange" as the woman warrior with "words carved on [her] back" (42), its hooves bear the ideographic character "to fly" in place of horseshoes. The warhorse paws the ground, signaling to the female avenger that it is high time to lead an army against the male plunderers and rapists of China. "My army did not rape, only taking food where there was an abundance" (40).

The Woman Warrior as Honorary Male Savior and Female Avenger

Janet Jacobs cites this myth of the woman warrior as a vivid example of "the fantasies of maleness that pervade the imaginary world of incest survivors."[50] In these fantasies, the daughter creates a heroic but fundamentally masculine alter ego gravitating around patriarchy. These inventive fantasies accommodate her conflicting needs to be safe from an abusive father, to be saved by a father who in make-believe is no longer a violent but an idealized figure, to be the savior who will rescue the loving father who is "a missing person" from her childhood or who is held captive to suffering, and to be the cross-dressing avenger who will "take [his] place" (WW, 37) and, at the same time, punish him for his sexual transgressions against women (Jacobs, 33–34, 71–82). Whereas Hong Kingston's vision of Fa Mu Lan has captivated feminists who read there woman's bid for freedom from patriarchy, Louise Edwards reminds us that in Confucian typology the woman warrior is a "'hero among women' in her adoption of masculine traits." Although she temporarily crosses gender boundaries, she poses no fundamental threat to a male social order but ultimately serves and perpetuates it.[51] "'Now my public duties are finished,' I said. 'I will stay with you, doing farmwork and housework, and giving you more sons'" (47). Jacobs shrewdly observes that the girl's "fantasy of aggressive retribution" is often shot through with a deep and unconscious masochism because it "is embraced by those who in reality must submit to the oppressors they have idealized" (80, 94). The woman warrior's fiercest anger is reserved for the "fat men [who] sat on naked little girls" (34). These are patriarchs like the pig-faced baron with "fat ringed fingers" whom she beheads and symbolically castrates. She condemns him to death with words that articulate the tragedy of all young victims of sexual abuse. "You took away my childhood" (45–46).

The scars of childhood give the narrator pain throughout *The Woman War-rior*: "'You've done this,' I said, and ripped off my shirt to show him my back. 'You are responsible for this'" (46).

These scars have not healed completely when *China Men* opens. Indeed, the revenge of the woman warrior carries over into the first intertext, "On Discovery." The narrator still fantasizes about acts of ritual humiliation and emasculation that will pay male pillagers back for their rape of "little girls." The adventurer Tang Ao comes to "the Land of Women" expecting that he can loot and ravage a new world as fellow male conquerors have seized the unspoiled bodies of young women, or, as the baron says matter-of-factly to Fa Mu Lan, "Everyone takes the girls when he can. The families are glad to be rid of them" (45). Indeed, the presumption of a colonizing patriarchy is that women are fertile lands that males can plunder and then discard at will. "When [the women] asked Tang Ao to come along, he fol-lowed; if he had had male companions, he would've winked over his shoul-der" (*CM*, 3).[52] The narrator's female revenge is also highly personal in this disturbing intertext that has provoked so much critical and gender contro-versy. Tang Ao gets the treatment meted out to a *mei-tsai*, a *sim-pua*, and countless no name women like the aunt. He is trained for domestic and sexual servitude by the court ladies in the Land of Women.

Incest, Male Approval, and Emotional Numbing

Incest can sometimes be a pathological expression of the daughter's hero worship of male virility and valor—as in the fantasy of the woman warrior —and her vicarious access to masculine social drive through sexual submis-sion to a powerful father figure. Paradoxically though, she seeks affectionate validation of her own needs and identity, what she experiences in incest is emotional manipulation and sexual exploitation. The gender lesson she learns is that "masculine sexual behaviour . . . is devoid of tenderness" and "concerned with conquering: 'getting a woman'" (Bell, 76). This lesson also prompts the narrator's morbid impulse to touch her Great Uncle's corpse at his funeral and "secretly test out feeling that he was dead—the six-foot bearish masculinity of him" (*WW*, 48). It will lead her to wonder whether "males feel no pain; males don't feel" in *China Men* and to test out her the-ory by giving a schoolboy a good kick in the playground (251). As we have already seen, it is her own father's unresponsive and numb behavior in the home that makes her doubt whether "men had feelings" and resolve that "girls and women of all races . . . had to toughen up. We had to be as tough as boys, tougher because we only pretended not to feel pain" (*CM*, 186, 252).

Incest and Eating Disorders

This determination to toughen up may be a psychological means for "girls and women of all races" to dull the pain of incest. It can also, however, reflect a daughter's efforts to transform herself from vulnerable victim of sexual predation into a favored son like the father, or a tomboy that the father will genuinely *like* and not abuse. Victims of incest often seek control over their violated bodies through a pathological fixation with slimming and regulation of their daily food intake. Girls suffering from the eating disorder anorexia may see in the mirror a body that is acquiring the sculpted perfection of a male *kouros*. Their extreme dieting can further ape male youthfulness by causing amenorrhea. The woman warrior mistakenly hopes that her martial arts training will produce this cessation of menstrual bleeding. "Then can I use the control you taught me and stop this bleeding?" she asks her sages, only to be told, "Let it run" (35). If menstruation is a perplexing time for the narrator of *The Woman Warrior*, in which she is presented with the jigsaw pieces of the aunt's life, it can be particularly upsetting for incest survivors, who see their defensive tomboy image threatened by puberty (Jacobs, 86). The narrator refuses to be co-opted into the traditional role of food production prescribed for women and gloats at her mother's reprimand: "Isn't a bad girl almost a boy?" (49). Her distaste for food is understandable, given the animal menagerie that swims in her thrifty Chinese mother's cooking pot. Like Alice in Wonderland, she is not only looking to shrink her body,[53] but also gain some semblance of control over the Carroll-like pandemonium in an immigrant household overrun by "racoons, skunks, hawks, city pigeons, wild ducks, wild geese, black-skinned bantams, snakes, garden snails, turtles that crawled about the pantry floor and sometimes escaped under refrigerator or stove, catfish that swam in the bathtub" (85–86). Her decision not to eat contradicts the Chinese lore she has imbibed at the breast that "all heroes are bold towards food" (84). Her oral complex against food (and speech), however, is a passive-aggressive defense against a mother who can swallow anything and devour everyone. "If I could not-eat, perhaps I could make myself a warrior like the swordswoman who drives me" (49). The hero she sees herself becoming resembles her mother less than the lean and mean male ego ideal fantasized by daughter victims of incest.

Incest and Mood Swings

Incest victims are prone to the narrator's volatile mood swings from "bad girl" to "good girl" behavior. This points to their incestuous double bind:

what sexually pleases their father causes them shame and self-loathing. The narrator's rough appearance—her tangled hair, dirty hands, messy habits, and wrinkled clothes (170)—is obviously a crude attempt to prevent the development of an attractive female body and repulse sexual or marital interest. Her repugnant personal habits, however, also suggest that she has internalized her paternal relatives' visceral disgust for girls as vermin, dirt, or "maggots" that lay their eggs and worm their slimy path through the rice (45). Yet dirt will become a mark of honor for the *China Men* who build the transcontinental railroad, clear the Hawaiian wilderness for sugar cane plantations, launder the menstrual-soiled undergarments of "marriageable" (*WW,* 170) women and the semen-stained clothes of unmarried men, dig cellars, and plant gardens. Indeed, the narrator who "callused [her] hands" and "scratched dirt to blacken the nails, which cut straight across to make stubby fingers" (*WW,* 158) is not simply adopting a tough tomcat persona in the playground or unconsciously simulating callous male behavior. She is indicating her identification with the work ethic of her immigrant parents and the fathers who were the making of the Hong family and of America. In other words, the bad girl will also go to extreme measures to prove that she is a good girl who "know[s] how to get As" and can excel in male intellectual domains such as science and mathematics (*WW,* 179; Jacobs, 52, 83). In the closing moments of *The Woman Warrior,* the daughter narrator finally snaps from pent-up resentment. "My throat hurt constantly, vocal chords taut to snapping." In exploding with anger against her parents, she at last bursts out of silence and boils over with words of furious decrial. "My throat burst open. . . . I looked directly at my mother and at my father and screamed, 'I want you to tell that hulk, that gorilla-ape, to go away and never bother us again. . . . You think we're odd and not pretty and we're not bright. You think you can give us away to freaks. . . . Do you know what the Teacher Ghosts say about me? They tell me I'm smart, and I can win scholarships. I can get into colleges. . . . I can do all kinds of things'" (179).

The Divided Consciousness and Conflicted Feelings of Incest Victims

Abused daughters are of two minds, not only as to whether they are good or bad girls, but also whether they should condemn their fathers as perpetrators of incest or condone them as victims who cannot help themselves. In "White Tigers," the daughter narrator is faced with a related contradiction as she tries to work out why her mainland relatives were persecuted by the Communists. If they are "not the poor to be championed," why were they "executed like the barons in the stories, when they were not barons"

(52), not the sort presumably who "sat on naked little girls" (34) and stole the woman warrior's childhood (46)? The divided consciousness of incest survivors makes it difficult for them to decide whether their fathers are persecutors or the oppressed. The more forcibly their "confusing" feelings of anger, outrage, and pity are repressed, the more likely they are to take a terrible "revenge." Indeed, the notorious episode in "A Song for a Barbarian Reed Pipe," where the narrator bullies a quiet Chinese classmate in the school lavatory, is an excellent illustration of how internalized aggression and maltreatment can build up enormous emotional pressure that suddenly erupts without warning and finds violent externalization in scapegoating and psychosomatic illness. Sau-ling Wong, who discusses this disturbing passage at length, sees the narrator's victim as the double who represents the hidden or disavowed aspects of the personality. She notes that, unusually, it is the protagonist who shows "criminal tendencies" and not that uncannily reserved "Other" self whose only antisocial offense is to have no friends outside of her close-knit and overly protective Chinese family.[54] As I have already indicated, however, it is common for victimized daughters to have the irrational conviction that incest is their fault and that their reporting of abuse *is* the real crime. Indeed, the perpetrator often strikes when the child is drifting off to sleep and in a susceptible state where they are liable to be confused about what is happening to them. The resulting self-blame, in concert with the experience of repeated sexual penetration, can leave daughter victims with a deep sense of inner evil and secret culpability (Jacobs, 51).

Incest, Scapegoating, and Self-Hatred

Hong Kingston sets her passage at dusk, another intermediate realm where the child's defenses are likely to be lowered (Wong, *Reading Asian American Literature*, 81, 86–87). During this liminal period between naked day and shadowy night, and in the playground, which is another transitional space, the narrator reverts to the magical and omnipotent thinking of early childhood and imagines herself slipping the boundaries between reality and illusion. "I could disappear with the sun; I could turn quickly sideways and slip into a different world. It seemed I could run faster at this time, and by evening I would be able to fly" (157). The quiet and deserted school grounds are ideal for playing hide-and-seek. "In this growing twilight, a child could hide and never be found" (158). They are a perfect cover for the bully—or the child molester—who wants to harass and victimize without fear of detection. These conditions allow the narrator to engage in the slow torment of a classmate. The five or more harrowing pages that she devotes to recalling the incident in excruciating but intimate detail suggest the sadistic pleasure derived from scapegoating someone more powerless than herself. Sau-ling Wong suggests that the bullied schoolgirl represents the hated racial Other who "does not have power because she is female and, ultimately, because she is Chinese in a white society" (89, 91); however, this "sissy-girl" with her "baby soft" face, "tiny white teeth, baby teeth" and "China doll hair cut" (WW, 158, 160, 156) also reminds the narrator of the "fragile" and unprotected daughter victims eaten alive by patriarchy. As she takes "the fatty part of her [schoolmate's] cheek" between her dirty thumb and finger and "work[s] her face around like dough" (158), she is unconsciously miming the misogynistic slur of her own father in China Men that "eating pastries is eating dirt from women's fingernails and from between their fingers" (CM, 14).

A depressing characteristic of girls who have been scarred by incest is their dual identification with both the male aggressor and his sexual prey (Jacobs, 92) and their volatile switch between the role of the helpless victim who must "hide" and the stalker who "seeks" out his young female target. By the narrator's own admission, she and her intended victim appear almost identical. They come from the same Chinese immigrant background and are similarly quiet, withdrawn, and defensive in white American society. They both cling to the company of a sister who is close to them in age and whom they regard as an "almost-twin, the person most like [them] in all the world" (170). In one arresting particular, however, they are different. The narrator is the older sister, whereas the look-alike she bullies is the younger. Indeed, the very fact that this double is treated like the baby of the family in need of constant care and protection may provoke the emotional hatred and cruelty of the narrator, as it may also have provoked the hostility of her own father toward his younger sister. "I looked into her face so I could hate it close up. She wore black bangs, and her cheeks were pink and white. She was baby soft. I thought that I could put my thumb on her nose and push it bonelessly in, indent her face" (158). In the blink of an eye, the quiet classmate has been transformed from a feeling person into a "China doll" that can be disfigured and abused.

One psychological response to incest is for girl victims to engage in self-destructive behavior where they turn the aggression they have experienced against themselves. Another is for them to project their sadistic treatment onto other perceived victims or onto transitional objects such as dolls (Jacobs, 96). In a hard-up Chinese immigrant family that is especially stingy toward girls and where daughters do not have a room of their own, however, the narrator vainly wishes for "a doll of [her] own." She eventually shames a more affluent white classmate into giving her the broken pieces of a discarded doll with "a head and body to glue together" (178). With no doll of her own to replay the roles of the violator and violated, and to enact her contrary urge to harm and safeguard another helpless victim like herself, the narrator alternatively turns against the "China doll" and becomes pathologically protective of her own younger sister. "I kept my sister with me, protecting her without telling her why" (175). The empty schoolyard where she tortures the "China doll" must thus be seen as a dream screen where she projects an abusive history with its dim and confused feelings, nameless and misshapen fears onto the outer world. In this eerie setting, the shadowy and hulking figure who haunted Brave Orchid's dormitory, who waylaid her on her doctor's calls as "a fantastic creature, half man and half ape" (80), and who looms in the terror-filled reality of incest victims (Jacobs, 36), again returns to threaten the daughter narrator as a "giant thing covered with canvas and tied down with ropes . . . a gorilla in captivity" (157).

Incest, Repeated Trauma, and Psychosomatic Illness

There are striking points of correspondence between the case histories of daughters who have been sexually abused by their fathers and the behavioral pattern that unfolds in the stories told by the young narrator of *The Woman Warrior*. This is not to infer that Hong Kingston's protagonist is herself a victim of incest. What her narratives suggest is that an abusive history can be compulsively replayed and the damage inflicted can cause a chain reaction of pain and suffering across generations. Once the daughter narrator has found a scapegoat and given vent to her repressed rage, she promptly turns her aggression back against herself. "The world is sometimes just, and I spent the next eighteen months sick in bed with a mysterious illness." Though she says that "there was no pain and no symptoms," her body externalizes its somatic history of past pain and suffering when "the middle line in my left palm broke in two" (163). The body is also rewriting intertextual history and the decision Hong Kingston took to break the lifeline of the Hong family saga in two and separate the narratives of *The Woman Warrior* and *China Men*. "Instead of starting junior high school," the narrator goes on to say, "I lived like the Victorian recluses I read about" (163). Her traumatic treatment of a Chinese classmate triggers a breakdown but also coincides with the approach of puberty and menstruation, those unsettling bodily changes that prompted the first story "No Name Woman." As an intertextual reader, the narrator is canny enough to see her likeness to the nineteenth-century women hysterics who suffered from reminiscences and who also "had to figure out again how to talk" (*WW*, 163) with the help of Freud and his famous "talking cure."[55]

Elizabeth Barrett, Paternal Tyranny, and Incestuous Desire

A Victorian recluse with whom the book-loving daughter narrator could readily identify is the invalid Elizabeth Barrett. As Cora Kaplan notes, Barrett was struck down by a "severe and mysterious illness" at fifteen that "kept her bedridden for almost eighteen months."[56] The popular play *The Barretts of Wimpole Street* dramatizes her psychosomatic illness as a form of passive-aggressive resistance to her father's overbearing and incestuous interest.[57] This daughter evades her father's possessive grasp through the writing of poetry and correspondence and through the intertextual relationship that she creates with another writer who reads poetry, Robert Browning. Indeed, Browning's and Barrett's love poetry represented men and women in "living conversation" (Bakhtin, 280) that fostered mutual regard. Like Hong Kingston's two books, Browning's dramatic monologues accentuated the connection between colloquial speech and writing and demonstrated the heteroglossic vitality of words that are, in the words of Bakhtin, "already populated with the social intentions of others" (300). Browning fell in love with Barrett intertextually—through his love for reading her poetry and writing of it to her in letter form. Barrett responded to his romantic declaration: "I love your verses with all my heart, dear Miss Barrett, . . . and I love you too."[58] Through this love she eventually finds the will—not to talk but to walk—and so escape her father's incestuous web. An important object lesson that Barrett exemplifies for the narrator of *The Woman Warrior*, and for the frightened girl who first heard of the traps into which women can fall in "No Name Woman," is that daughters do not want a love affair with the father. What they want is access to his "love affair with the world." Jessica Benjamin therefore concludes that "the key to the missing desire in women is in one sense the missing father" who can say to his daughter without social or sexual coercion, "Yes, you are like me" (79, 88–89); however, even this short statement is problematic for the silent father of *China Men*, who is not a powerful agent, as Benjamin's feminist theory assumes, and who cannot open official doors for his daughter. In the next and final chapter, I will consider some of the back doors that he opens, leading his daughter to another world or community, often hidden from view, where he can say "you are like me." What was perhaps more important—given the author's perception that she was "living the life that [her father] wanted to live" (Perry, 188)—was to find a way for him to tell his daughter in return "I am like you."

Notes

1. "The unconscious phantasy of an inner world reflected in examples from literature" (1952), *The Inner World and Joan Riviere: Collected Papers, 1920–1958*, edited by Athol Hughes (London: Karnac Books, 1991), 316.

2. Kay Bonetti ("An Interview with Maxine Hong Kingston" [1986], in *Conversations with Maxine Hong Kingston*, edited by Paul Skenazy and Tera Martin [Jackson: University of Mississippi Press, 1998]), asked Hong Kingston whether "the fact that your parents were really old enough to be your grandparents when you were born" was significant (46). (Hereinafter, I shall refer to this volume as *Conversations*.)

3. Hong Kingston's father died in 1991 and her mother in 1997 as Diane Simmons (*Maxine Hong Kingston* [New York: Twayne Publishers, 1999], 42) and E. D. Huntley (*Maxine Hong Kingston: A Critical Companion* [Westport, Conn.: Greenwood Press, 2001], 22) note.

4. The phrase is used by Paul Outka, "Publish or Perish: Food, Hunger, and Self Construction in Maxine Hong Kingston's *The Woman Warrior*," *Contemporary Literature*, 38 (1997): 447–482 (reprinted at http://vweb.hwwilsonweb.com, pp. 1–3, esp. 3). The phrase was suggested by Leigh Gilmore, *Autobiographics: A Feminist Theory of Women's Self-Representation* (Ithaca, N.Y.: Cornell University Press, 1994), 177.

5. Phyllis Hoge Thompson, "This Is the Story I Heard: A Conversation with Maxine Hong Kingston and Earll Kingston," *Biography—Hawaii*, 6 (1983), 12.

6. Sigmund Freud, "The Theme of the Three Caskets," *Art and Literature*, vol. 14, edited by Albert Dickson, translated by James Strachey (London: Penguin Books, 1990), 247. See David Willbern's analysis in *"Filia Oedipi:* Father and Daughter in Freudian Theory," in *Daughters and Fathers*, edited by Lynda E. Boose and Betty S. Flowers (Baltimore: Johns Hopkins University Press, 1989), 91.

7. As A. S. Byatt writes in her grand narrative of adultery, *Possession: A Romance* (London: Vintage, 1991), "The classic detective story arose with the classic adultery novel—everyone wanted to know who was the Father, what was the origin, what is the secret?" (238).

8. See her remarks to Skenazy ("Kingston at the University" [1989], in *Conversations*), and Gilmore's chapter on violence and self-representation in "No Name Woman" and *The Woman Warrior* more generally ("Violence and Self-Representation, *Autobiographics*, 163–184), which begins with an account of the creation story in Genesis.

9. Julia Kristeva, *Tales of Love*, translated by Leon S. Roudiez (New York: Columbia University Press, 1987), 31.

10. While at the University of California, Santa Cruz, Hong Kingston remarked

that she did not think her parents had any idea of "the amount of anger and passion that I put into the book [The Woman Warrior], the vehemence with which I write." See Skenazy ("Kingston at the University," 120).

11. Gérard Genette cites the many retellings of Robinson Crusoe inspired by Defoe's original novel as a prime example of the fertile transplantation and colonization of narrative from one cultural context to another that takes place in hyper- (or inter-) textuality. See Palimpsests: Literature in the Second Degree, translated by Channa Newman and Claude Doubrinsky, foreword by Gerald Prince (Lincoln: University of Nebraska Press, 1997), 368–375.

12. Hélène Cixous and Catherine Clément, "Sorties: Out and Out: Attacks/ Ways Out/Forays," The Newly Born Woman, introduction by Sandra M. Gilbert, translated by Betsy Wing. Vol. 24 of Theory and History of Literature, edited by Wlad Godzich and Jochen Schulte-Sasse, 4th ed. (Minneapolis: University of Minnesota Press, 1991), pt. 2, 97.

13. "The Guilty One," The Newly Born Woman, pt. 1, 8.

14. If the daughter is around thirteen, Brave Orchid must be at least fifty-eight, assuming that she gave birth to her American born family after the age of forty-five.

15. See Marjorie Topley's description in "Marriage Resistance in Rural Kwang-tung" and Emily Ahern's account of this blood pit, "The Power and Pollution of Chinese Women," both in Women in Chinese Society, edited by Margery Wolf and Roxane Witke (Stanford, Calif.: Stanford University Press, 1975), 75 and 214, respectively.

16. Compare the behavior of Hong Kingston's adolescent narrator in The Woman Warrior with Victor W. Turner's enumeration of the characteristics of young men and women undergoing tribal initiation rites in The Ritual Process: Structure and Anti-Structure (London: Routledge and Kegan Paul, 1969), 94–106.

17. The quotes are taken from Boose's discussion of menstruation in "The Father's House and the Daughter in It: The Structures of Western Culture's Daughter-Father Relationship," in Daughters and Fathers, 34–35.

18. See Margery Wolf, who devised the term "uterine family" in her essay "Women and Suicide in China," in Women in Chinese Society, 125, 132, and Kay Ann Johnson, Women, the Family, and Peasant Revolution in China (Chicago: University of Chicago Press, 1983), 10–23. Johnson describes the woman's uterine family as existing "within her husband's family but . . . centered around herself as mother and . . . based primarily on her affective relationship with her children" (18).

19. See Boose's discussion of the incest taboo (30) and David Eng's Freudian and racial contextualization of the issue in Racial Castration: Managing Masculinity in Asian America (Durham, N.C.: Duke University Press, 2001), 7–9.

20. Arthur P. Wolf, in his magisterial study of sim-pua marriages in Sexual Attraction and Childhood Association: A Chinese Brief for Edward Westermarck (Stanford, Calif.: Stanford University Press, 1995), notes that sim-pua is a Hokkien term for the "little daughter-in-law," but that the Mandarin term for the females who entered into this "minor marriage" is "t'ung-yang-hsi" (24).

21. Whereas Topley argues thus for rural Kwangtung (77), Arthur Wolf notes that "in South China more people have married in the minor fashion than have married in any fashion in the United States" (*Sexual Attraction,* 23). The major form of marriage was the traditional "sight-unseen" marriage that Brave Orchid makes with the narrator's father.

22. In addition to Wolf's full-length study of the subject in *Sexual Attraction and Childhood Association,* see his essay "The Women of Hai-shan: A Demographic Portrait" in *Women in Chinese Society* (92–106) and Margery Wolf, "Women and Suicide in China" (127–128), both in Wolf and Ritke, eds., *Women in Chinese Society.*

23. See W. Arens' discussion of the incestuous nature of the *sim-pua* marriage, *The Original Sin: Incest and Its Meaning* (New York: Oxford University Press, 1986), 75–78.

24. See Mark A. Schneider and Lewellyn Hendrix's discussion of Westermarck's hypothesis of incest and sexual avoidance as it is set out in Arthur Wolf's study of *sim-pua* marriages, "Olfactory Sexual Inhibition and the Westermarck Effect," *Human Nature* 11:1 (2000). Reprinted at http://www.siu.edu~socio/olfactory.htm, pp. 1–15.

25. Maxine Hong Kingston, "Cultural Mis-readings by American Reviewers," in *Critical Essays on Maxine Hong Kingston,* edited by Laura E. Skandera-Trombley (New York: G. K. Hall, 1998), 95.

26. I am paraphrasing Kristeva in "Word, Dialogue, and Novel," in *Desire in Language: A Semiotic Approach to Literature and Art,* edited by Leon S. Roudiez, translated by Thomas Gora, Alice Jardine, and Leon S. Roudiez (New York: Columbia University Press, 1980), who theorized that "the writer's interlocutor . . . is the writer himself, but as reader of another text" (86).

27. Herbert Blau, "The Makeup of Memory in the Winter of Our Discontent," *Memory and Desire: Aging-Literature-Psychoanalysis,* edited by Kathleen Woodward and Murray M. Schwartz (Bloomington: Indiana University Press, 1986), 31.

28. See Arthur Wolf's comments in "The Women of Hai-shan" (93, 98–99) and *Sexual Attraction and Childhood Association* (29–31, 184).

29. Lauren Rusk, "The Collective Self: Maxine Hong Kingston and Virginia Woolf," in *Virginia Woolf and Her Influences: Selected Papers from the Seventh Annual Conference on Virginia Woolf,* edited by Laura Davis, Jeanette McVicker, and Jeanne Dubino (New York: Pace University Press, 1998), 182.

30. Hélène Cixous, "The Laugh of the Medusa," translated by Keith Cohen and Paula Cohen, in *New French Feminisms,* edited by Elaine Marks and Isabelle de Courtivron (Hemel Hempstead, Herts.: Harvester Wheatsheaf, 1981), 260. See Donald Goellnicht's discussion of *écriture féminine,* with its stress on "glossolalia/polyphony/heteroglossia," in "Father Land and/or Mother Tongue: The Divided Female Subject in Kogawa's *Obasan* and Hong Kingston's *The Woman Warrior.*" In *Redefining Autobiography in Twentieth-Century Women's Fiction: An Essay Collection,* edited by Janice Morgan, Colette T. Hall, and Carol L. Snyder (New York: Garland, 1991), 120.

31. See Angelika Bammer, "Mother Tongues and Other Strangers: Writing 'Family' across Cultural Divides," in *Displacements: Cultural Identities in Question,*

edited by Angelika Bammer (Bloomington: Indiana University Press, 1994), 93; Germaine Bree's foreword to *Life/Lines: Theorizing Women's Autobiography*, edited by Bella Brodzki and Celeste Schenck (Ithaca, N.Y.: Cornell University Press, 1988), ix; and King-Kok Cheung's reminder in *Articulate Silences: Hisaye Yamamoto, Maxine Hong Kingston, Joy Kogawa* (Ithaca, N.Y.: Cornell University Press, 1993) that "historical silences, for the most part, cannot be retrieved" (75).

32. Margery Wolf notes in "Women and Suicide in China" that the female suicide's parents and brothers sometimes exacted retribution by "destroying part of her husband's house" (113). This raises the intriguing possibility that the Hong family house might have been destroyed to avenge the aunt's death, and not to precipitate it as "No Name Woman" suggests.

33. See Sau-ling Wong's discussion of the no name woman's beauty routine as extravagance in *Reading Asian American Literature: From Necessity to Extravagance* (Princeton, N.J.: Princeton University Press, 1993), 193–194.

34. Jane Silverman Van Buren summarizes in *The Modernist Madonna: Semiotics of the Maternal Metaphor* (London: Karnac Books, 1989), 15–19.

35. See Elise Miller, "Kingston's *The Woman Warrior:* The Object of Autobiographical Relations," in *Compromise Formations: Current Directions in Psychoanalytic Literature*, edited by Vera J. Camden (Kent, Ohio: Kent State University Press, 1989), n. 4, 152; and Hong Kingston's comments to Arturo Islas and Marilyn Yalom, "Interview with Maxine Hong Kingston," in *Conversations* (26).

36. Patricia Chu, "'The Invisible World the Emigrants Built': Cultural Self-Inscription and the Antiromantic Plots of *The Woman Warrior*," *Diaspora* 2:1 (1992), 102.

37. Luce Irigaray, "On the Maternal Order," in *je, tu, nous: Toward a Culture of Difference*, translated by Alison Martin (New York: Routledge, 1993), 43.

38. Mary Pipher, *Reviving Ophelia: Saving the Selves of Adolescent Girls* (New York: Ballantine Books, 1994), 12.

39. See Pipher (21) and Sau-ling Wong's discussion of the American ideology of consent in *Reading Asian American Literature* (41, 44).

40. See Pipher's remarks on 20–22, 150, 158, 170, and esp. 175, where she argues that anorexia epitomizes the "American-feminine" qualities of weakness, dependency, and acquiescence. "Anorexia signifies that a young woman is so delicate that, like the women of China with their tiny broken feet, she needs a man to shelter and protect her from a world she cannot handle."

41. Kristeva argues, for what it is worth, in "Confucius—An Eater of Women," *About Chinese Women*, translated by Anita Barrows (London: Marion Boyars, 1977), that women were sometimes able to actualize themselves in the role of "cherished daughters of their fathers" and not only tyrant mothers of sons (73–75, 96).

42. See also the comments of Topley (77, 85) and Arthur Wolf (93, 99), both in *Women and Chinese Society*, and Johnson (*Women, the Family, and Peasant Revolution in China*, 12–13), which suggest that the *sim-pua* may have sometimes been regarded as little different from the *mei-tsai*, or bonded servant, who was purchased to become a concubine.

43. See Michèle Roberts' essay "Outside My Father's House," in *Fathers: Reflections by Daughters*, edited by Ursula Owen (London: Virago, 1983). She begins with the same psychological struggle as the daughter narrator of "No Name Woman." "Break the silence, I tell myself, break the taboo. I'm struggling against feelings of betrayal and disloyalty" (103).

44. His other incarnations are as the giant Fa Mu Lan battles in "White Tigers" (41), the "half man and half ape" that stalks Brave Orchid on her nightly house calls as a doctor in "Shaman" (80), and the "gorilla in captivity" fantasized in the school playground in "A Song for a Barbarian Reed Pipe" (157).

45. See Simmons' discussion of how problematic the concept of home was for them (79).

46. Arthur Wolf observes in *Sexual Attraction* that "the pillow ghost was exorcised by substituting for the threatening daughter-in-law/wife a woman who was in many respects a daughter/sister" (103–104), namely, the *sim-pua*.

47. Barbara Rowlands, "Terrors of the Night," *South China Morning Post* (December 3, 2001).

48. Both Janet Liebman Jacobs, *Victimized Daughters: Incest and the Development of the Female Self* (New York: Routledge, 1994), 29, 112, and Jill L. Matus, *Toni Morrison* (Manchester: Manchester University Press, 1998), 47, comment on the depressing "frequency with which incest is repeated across generations."

49. Janice Haaken, "The Recovery of Memory, Fantasy, and Desire in Women's Trauma Stories: Feminist Approaches to Sexual Abuse and Psychotherapy," in *Women, Autobiography, Theory: A Reader*, edited by Sidonie Smith and Julia Watson (Madison: University of Wisconsin Press), (356). See also Linda Morante, "From Silence to Song: The Triumph of Maxine Hong Kingston," *Frontiers: A Journal of Women's Studies* 9:2 (1987), who notes the narrator's adolescent "longing for the imaginary steed that will carry her into the never-never land of adventure" (79).

50. I consulted Jacobs' work on the subject of father-daughter incest, not knowing that she cited Hong Kingston's myth of the woman warrior Fa Mu Lan as an illustration of daughter victims' identification with a glorified male persona. Her reading of the woman warrior bears out my own intuition of an incestuous subtext to the narrative.

51. Louise P. Edwards, *Men and Women in Qing China: Gender in the Red Chamber Dream* (Leiden: E. J. Brill, 1994), 92, 102.

52. Edwards (95) discusses the interaction of the woman warrior and Tang Ao in *Jinghua yuan* texts of the mid-Qing period, and, in a parallel with Hong Kingston's "White Tigers," she notes how one woman warrior tells Tang Ao she has vowed to kill every tiger on the mountain (99).

53. The corresponding fantasy was elongating her body through "the power and height" she gained as Fa Mu Lan on her magical white charger (39).

54. See Wong, *Reading Asian American Literature* (82–83, 88), and Morante, who argued in her 1987 article that the bullied Chinese classmate was a doppelganger (78–79).

55. This history is discussed by Christine Froula, "The Daughter's Seduction:

Sexual Violence and Literary History" and Dianne F. Sadoff, "The Clergyman's Daughters: Anne Bronte, Elizabeth Gaskell, and George Eliot," both in *Daughters and Fathers* (117–122 and 303–307, respectively), and Naomi R. Goldenberg, *Resurrecting the Body: Feminism, Religion, and Psychoanalysis* (New York: Crossroad, 1993), 177–179. Lee Quinby remarks ("The Subject of Memoirs: *The Woman Warrior*'s Technology of Ideographic Selfhood," in *Critical Essays on Maxine Hong Kingston,* edited by Skandera-Trombley) that "the combined dread of and longing for insanity that Kingston expresses throughout *The Woman Warrior* results from the deployment of sexuality's process of hysterization of women" (138).

56. Cora Kaplan, "Wicked Fathers: A Family Romance," in *Fathers: Reflections by Daughters,* edited by Owen, 142.

57. In *Daughters and Fathers* Boose notes that the paternal preference is usually for the oldest daughter (38).

58. See Kaplan (148) and my article on the Browning-Barrett relationship that is replayed in A. S. Byatt's *Possession,* "'Thou art the best of mee': A. S. Byatt's *Possession* and the Literary Possession of Donne," *John Donne Journal* 14 (1995), 132–133.

Chapter 4

"I'll Tell You What I Suppose from Your Silences and Few Words"
The Search for the Father in *China Men*

The Daughter's Family Romance

The daughter narrator of *The Woman Warrior* often appeared more at home with the "adventurous people inside [her] head to whom [she] talked" and with whom she was free to be "frivolous and violent, orphaned" than with her own family (170). Freud described these wild and wishful fantasies in which the child takes revenge on her parents by replacing them with their betters as "the neurotic's family romance."[1] Yet he recognizes that, although this violent daydreaming may be a sign of pathology, it is also a common activity of "all comparatively highly gifted people" and, in fact, is an extension of the make-believe of the playground.[2] Patricia Chu argues that "a powerful subtext of [*The Woman Warrior*] is Maxine's desire to rise above her parents' low status in America" and that the narrator tries to gloss over her ignoble feelings as a daughter (101). Freud came to the defense of the child who showed such apparent hardness or "depravity" of heart and argued with considerable tenderness that the family romance "preserve[s], under a slight disguise, the child's original affection for [her] parents" (224). In short, the narrator of *The Woman Warrior* and *China Men* is not rejecting her parents per se but showing her aversion for the diminished and disappointed figures that they have become with age and adversity in America. "You have no idea how much I have fallen coming to America," Brave Orchid poignantly exclaims to her daughter. In fact, her daughter knows only too well, and the heroic romance that she relates in "Shaman" exalts the "intelligent, alert, pretty" young woman her mother once was and who vanished with old China (*WW,* 74, 58).

The Recovery of the Father in the Family Romance

Freud argued that in the family romance the child was "turning away from the father whom [she] knows today to the father in whom [she] believed in the earlier years of [her] childhood" (225). Similarly, the narrator of

China Men tells tall stories that attempt to recuperate the father after he has all but disappeared from the feminist plot of *The Woman Warrior*.[3] Her imaginary interlocutors are "beautiful cowgirls, and also men, cowboys who could talk to me in conversations: I named this activity Talking Men" (*CM,* 181). The "Talking Men" of the daughter storyteller's second book will be equipped with attributes that her taciturn and strangulated father tragically lacks or refuses to share with his family. "Worse than the swearing and the nightly screams were your silences when you punished us by not talking. You rendered us invisible, gone" (*CM,* 14). Did his daughter retaliate earlier by disregarding her father and leaving him out of the main action of *The Woman Warrior?* In fact, Freud surmised that it was neurotic children "punished by their parents" for sexual misdemeanors who were most likely to "revenge themselves on their parents" in fantasy (224). The intertextual reference in *China Men* to the daughter's imaginary conversations with "Talking Men," however, shows that she never lost interest in her father. Even during the long periods of her childhood when he was unresponsive, she carried on an inner dialogue with her father and the "talking men" who represent lost parts of himself or are his past relations and likenesses. She imagines what might have been, before she was born and before her father resolved on "never slipping into the past," and indeed before he was born, in the time of his forefathers. "I want to hear the stories about the rest of your life, the Chinese stories. I want to know what makes you scream and curse, and what you're thinking when you say nothing, and why when you do talk, you talk differently from Mother" (*CM,* 15). The men to whom she talks inside her head restore the father to his place in the family romance. This figure is not "the noblest and strongest of men," as Freud poignantly hoped the father would be remembered when he got older (225). Nonetheless, he is a character whom the daughter will rescue from the crude role of a cursing Caliban muttering semi-illiterate obscenities like "your mother's smelly cunt" (12). She will reconfigure him in such a way that the reader is given a further glimpse of the man who once was "the ideal in masculine beauty, the thin scholar with the hollow cheeks and the long fingers" (*WW,* 110).

The Magnification of the Father

Freud argued that the supernatural beings that are given divine credence and powers by organized religion actually derive from the magic reality of early childhood and are an exaltation of "those incredible beings called parents" (Rizzuto, 7). In her pseudo-Catholic "confession" to Brave Orchid as mother superior near the end of *The Woman Warrior*, the daughter narrator struggles to express this psychological process of projection and elevation. "What's it called, Mother . . . when a person whispers to the head of the sages—no, not the sages, more like the buddhas but not real people like the buddhas. . . . They're like magicians? What do you call it when you talk to the boss magician?" She admits to her mother that she "talked-to-the-top-magician and asked for a white horse" (178), like the magical steed that comes to the aid of Fa Mu Lan and carries her to war in place of her father. When she rehabilitates the image of her father as "The American Father" in *China Men*, she will allude intertextually to this confessional passage in *The Woman Warrior* and introduce him as "a silent magician" who could not only delight his children with party tricks and sleight of hand but who, more significantly, "had the power of going places where nobody else went, and making places belong to him" (*CM*, 238). In short, her father was magnified as the top magician, the god, the Prospero figure to whom she prayed in childhood—or prayed would make a place for her in his life.

The Father Places of *China Men*

The narrator's recollections of "the father places" (*CM*, 240) that she secretly explored as a child are so important because they make her feel—or allow her to make believe—that she belonged to him. The father places of *China Men* are also described as sites of hide-and-seek, and they follow the inner law of the playground so evident in the scapegoating episode of "A Song for a Barbarian Reed Pipe." This does not mean, however, as Leslie Rabine suggests, that "in the father's house" the daughters stay "hidden from the fathers, unseen and unrecognized by them" (481). Rather the daughters inhabit that transitional space intermediate between fantasy and reality, where the child is free to play, explore, imagine, and create alone but conscious of the presence of the absent parent (91) and where both intersubjectivity and intertextuality first arise.[4]

Down the Rabbit Hole

The daughter narrator honors the memory of her father by recalling "the dirt cellar" that was "one of his places" in "The American Father" (*CM*, 238). During the long stretches of *The Woman Warrior* and *China Men* when the father appears absent from the family romance, this place is maintained by the mother on behalf of the father and bears her distinct traces. "My mother swung her broom at [the rats in the cellar], the straw swooping through the air in yellow arcs," like a witch using her magic broomstick to cast out the evil rodents that infest their tenement house in America. The dirt floor is reminiscent of the primitive conditions in which both the no name woman and the poet Ts'ai Yen gave birth in *The Woman Warrior* and suggests that the daughter may regard the father's dirt cellar as her own creative birth-place. "That was the house where the bunny lived in a hole in the kitchen." The bunny hole will lead the daughter underground, like Alice in Wonder-land, to the father who "was born in a year of the Rabbit" (*CM*, 15)[5] and to a first generation of Chinese immigrant parents who made great sacri-fices for their American-born children (Marilyn Chin, 98; Hongo, 9–10) as the rabbit does in "White Tigers" when it jumps into the fire to feed Fa Mu Lan (31). The daughter also recalls how her "mother had carried [the bunny] home from the fields in her apron" (238) as she "carries" the American father when he is too tired and disheartened to go on in *China Men*.

The Search Underground for the Father

When the daughter plays her symbolic game of hide-and-seek in "The American Father," she follows her father down into the dirt cellar and dis-covers him lifting "the lid that covered the bottomless well." She "burst out of hiding and saw it—a hole full of shining, bulging, black water, alive, alive, like an eye, deep and alive" (*CM*, 238). The bulging eye of the well mirrors her child's sense of wonder and recalls her earlier visual astonish-ment in "The Making of More Americans" after entering Fourth Grand-father's stable for the first time. There she was blinded by the sudden move-ment from dazzling sun to sudden darkness and dumbfounded by the sight of a dark mass "solid and alive, heavy, moving, breathing" that would take mysterious shape when Say Goong invoked the symbolic language and authority of the father and spoke the magical word "Horse" (166–167). "A horse was a black creature so immense I could not see the outlines"—a crea-ture that heightens the little child's fear that she can never measure up to her parents or achieve their adult stature. As we saw in the last chapter, the daughter narrator is also awestruck by the power of language to tame and control living things when she hears this grandfather "contain the thing in a word—*horse*, magical and earthly sound." Like Alice in Wonderland, she ponders the puzzling correspondence between physical realities and the names that are given to them.[6] As she "stood on the brink of a well," she too is poised for an adventure underground. Indeed, she imagined the mouth of the well "opening to the inside of the world" and fancies that she has found a portal that will take her all the way through "to the other side of the world. If I fall in, I will come out in China" (*CM*, 238–239). The older storyteller recalls the child's fiction with intertextual awareness of a tradition of reading children's literature seriously (Gardner, *The Annotated Alice,* 28). The "bottomless well" in which the girl "saw silver stars" and "the black sparkling eye of the planet" (239) can take adults down into the child's imaginary world and into the Freudian interior of the unconscious. It can act as an intertextual companionway between *China Men* and *The Woman Warrior* leading back to China and specifically to "the black well of sky and stars" that the no name woman gazed up at as she went into labor, before throwing herself down the village well to her death and into the underworld (20).[7]

An Intertextual Correspondence to Alice's Adventures Underground

Readers of the Alice books and the many intertexts that have come after may glimpse a more disturbing story in the "shining, bulging, black water" of the well or the "heavy, moving, breathing" atmosphere of the horse stable. The child, "ready to be terrified but for [her Fourth Grandfather's] delight," experiences this oppressive interior as "waves of dark skin over a hot and massive something" that sounds suspiciously phallic until the "snorting and stomping" assures her—and us—that "the living night" is not human (166–167). Modern Alice revisions have violated the taboos in the original books and narrated a hidden subtext of girl children sexualized by lecherous father figures or prurient old bachelors and of the Victorian poor who, like the destitute Chinese families Brave Orchid observed, were forced to sell their "precious" daughters (and sons) into prostitution. They have suggested that one of the chief dangers facing Alice was that of falling down the hole into adult sexual pathology, paternal incest, or familial abuse. Modern and postmodern Alices have also been prone to the mysterious illnesses and eating disorders suffered by the narrator of *The Woman Warrior* and have compulsively replayed the original Alice's bodily fluctuation between bigness and littleness. In a sexually deviant rewriting of her adventures underground, menarche is an even greater shock for Alice than for the daughter narrator of "No Name Woman." Indeed, her hysterical reaction to her first period provokes her murder. But, as Kali Israel insightfully remarks, however twisted or perverted these later intertexts of Alice may seem, they reaffirm the power of storytelling and show that an abusive history "can generate many kinds of stories, many kinds of containments, and representations that should not be reduced to their traumatic origins."[8]

The Well as a Symbol of Creative Life

Thus, the black, glittering water of the underground well in the father's dirt cellar is indeed "alive, alive, like an eye, deep and alive" and, more to the point, like the eye of the daughter storyteller, wide open in wonder—or terror—as she peers over the edge. With artistic maturity she will regard this well as her passage back in time to the inexhaustible springs of cosmic life, to the exhausted bodies of the mother and father who are the source of her life, and to the bottomless depths of the human psyche where creative inspiration is drawn and meaning is poured continually into the world. In an interview with the poet Marilyn Chin, Hong Kingston calls to mind the young girl looking intently into the well when she describes her feeling as a creative writer that she is "at the source of life and words. I feel that I'm sort of standing over this hole in the universe, and it's all pouring in" (92). Indeed, the shining black water of the well can be seen as a magnification of the ink well that both father and daughter use as writers. It will appear especially "black and full of possibilities" for the narrator of *The Woman Warrior*, who "had an American name that sound like 'Ink' in Chinese" and who, like the aspiring writer Jo March in the children's book *Little Women*, was often "smeared with ink" (149, 120).

The Intertextual Influence of Louisa May Alcott

Like other American women growing up in the 1940s and 1950s, Hong Kingston read Louisa May Alcott. She recalls coming across a white girl character who marries a "funny-looking little Chinaman." Her reader response to this crude racial stereotype was twofold: to feel that she was being excluded from imaginative identification with *Little Women*—"I'd been pushed into my place. I was him, I wasn't those March girls"—and to see that Chinese men and women had been misrepresented, minimized, or "left out" altogether in the books she grew up reading. Her intertextual response as a writer who reads is "that kind of reading made me create my new place in literature" (Hoy, 62; see also Blauvelt, 83).

Alcott's *Little Women* as Unconscious Intertext

Hong Kingston is insistent that she wrote against the white American grain of Alcott and remembers the March family saga as a negative intertext. In actuality, she created a "new place in literature" by unconsciously appropriating Jo March's characteristics for her own narrator—her tomboy behavior, sexual immaturity, anger, rebelliousness, and absorption in writing to the exclusion of all else. Indeed, it was not *Little Women* (1868–1869), or its sequel *Little Men* (1871) for that matter, that made her feel "ejected . . . out of literature" (Blauvelt, 83), but one of Alcott's lesser known works that has not stood the test of time, *Rose in Bloom* (1876).[9] In that book "the fair Annabella" becomes fascinated with "little Fun See" Tokio, an Orientalist caricature with a mishmash of a name and motley manners that combine "Chinese courtesy and American awkwardness." By the close of the novel, Annabella has become "perfectly absorbed in her dear little Chinaman." The romance plot embedded in Alcott's female bildungsroman ends on an uncertain note, with its implicit questioning of miscegenation—"Do you see how she ever could like him?" Nonetheless the besotted Annabella who could love a "funny-looking little Chinaman"[10] was ahead of her times and would, perhaps unknowingly, inspire Hong Kingston when she became absorbed in the rewriting of *China Men*.[11]

In her sociohistorical survey of the many lives of *Little Women*, Barbara Sicherman examines the intertextual longevity of the book. She suggests that the text showed a remarkable mobility and inspired women readers from heterogeneous immigrant, racial, economic, and class backgrounds to interpret the American dream differently. She concludes that the enduring popularity of this novel from the late nineteenth and throughout the twentieth century attests to the fact that this is "a text that opens up possibilities rather than foreclosing them."[12] The spirited dialogue and free translation that *Little Women* has provoked among women readers who may otherwise seem worlds apart is famously illustrated by the French feminist Simone de Beauvoir. In her *Memoirs of a Dutiful Daughter*, an intertext that resonates in Hong Kingston's subtitle to *The Woman Warrior: Memoirs of a Girlhood among Ghosts*—this formidable and seemingly unromantic intellectual declared her passionate identification with Jo March and conviction that she was meant to marry Laurie (Sicherman, 249, 252–253). As both Sicherman and Showalter implicitly recognize, it is Alcott's respect for the different personalities, speech mannerisms, and social aspirations of the four March sisters that gives *Little Women* its heteroglossic vitality and that has generated living conversation among an extended, multivocal, and intertextual network of women readers. The free and easy way in which Jo traversed the divide between high and low culture by liberally peppering her speech with the popular slang of the streets while studying Shakespeare, Plato, Homer, Milton, Kant, Hegel, and Schiller for more noble thought and expression (*Little Women*, 343, 352–353) has been a source of special delight to young readers.

Growing up female is problematized in *Little Women*, with the development of the four close-knit sisters neither uniform nor unbroken. Whereas the "big sister" Meg and the precocious "little sister" Amy mature early and quickly, the tomboy Jo puts off full passage from childhood to adulthood until her thirties (Showalter, xx) and the shy Beth "leaves off" altogether, fulfilling the death wish of Humpty Dumpty to Alice (*The Annotated Alice*, 266). Despite her professed sense of alienation from Alcott's writing, Hong Kingston acknowledged that *The Woman Warrior* is also "a story of adolescent growth. It tells the journey from being a girl to a woman and so there's just that rite of passage of a young person" (Seshachari, 193); however, just as *Little Women* shows marked resistance to the social idea of forcing girls to grow up before they are ready and expecting them, when they do, to conform to a standard gender role or rate of psychosexual development, so too *The Woman Warrior* projects a daughter narrator who is in two minds as to whether she is young or old. When she returns to the family home in "Shaman," she curls up into a mattress shaped by the child bodies of her brothers and sisters (93), but her hair has grown white and her face has aged into resemblance to her mother (95). Indeed, as I have already mentioned, Hong Kingston would publish *The Woman Warrior* with its Chinese American revision of a girl's uneven journey to adulthood relatively late in life at thirty-six. It is interesting to note that Alcott published *Little Women* at the identical age and Jo March is almost this age when her journey to maturity comes to an end in the novel.

THE INTERTEXTUAL ACTIVITIES IN *LITTLE WOMEN*

A writer who read "all of Louisa May Alcott," as Hong Kingston did at the formative age of eleven or twelve, on the cusp of puberty, cannot altogether escape *Little Women's* textual influence, if only at an unconscious level (Blauvelt, 83). Apart from Jade Snow Wong's *Fifth Chinese Daughter*, there was a shortage of cogent literary models for young women of Chinese descent growing up in America after the Second World War (Hoy, 62). Although *Fifth Chinese Daughter* made Hong Kingston realize that Chinese American girls had not been represented in mainstream American literature, *Little Women* was a chameleon work that invited women readers to imagine what had been left out and rewrite the text according to their own "castles in the air." Like the narrator of *The Woman Warrior*, Jo has an active fantasy life and dreams of having "a stable full of Arabian steeds, rooms piled with books, and . . . a magic inkstand" as a bottomless well of inspiration for her writing (*Little Women*, 143); however, though Jo is remembered as the aspiring author, all of the sisters are depicted as active readers and literary contributors to the Pickwick Club and all learn the hard way the need for constant revision of their life story. As Showalter notes, Alcott herself led a "double life as dutiful daughter and rebellious fantasist," and her secret publications included sensational stories of seduction, incest, adultery, and revenge that explore the dark world of "No Name Woman" (*Little Women*, xiv). When Hong Kingston came to write her Chinese American version of memoirs of a dutiful daughter, she would depict the narrator caught up, as was Alcott and her literary alter ego Jo, in a "vortex" of violent emotions (*Little Women*, xiii, 266) and giving vent to her "bad girl" image in *The Woman Warrior*'s stories of anger, disobedience, and defiance. Alcott's parents were well connected to the intertextual network that would influence Hong Kingston's narrative writing, with her mother a descendent of the Salem community dramatized in *The Scarlet Letter* and her father a friend of Hawthorne and the American transcendentalists who were interested in the culture of the East.[13]

ALCOTT AND THE GENDER DIVISION OF THE FAMILY STORIES

Alcott's *Little Women* and *Little Men* may have first given Hong Kingston the idea of organizing her family history into the gender divisions of *The Woman Warrior* and *China Men*. Though *Little Men*, Alcott's sequel to *Little Women*, depicts an adopted boys' home/school that still revolves very much around Jo, now the matriarch of the family, and is nothing like the mature father narratives in *China Men*, it is nonetheless interesting that Hong Kingston should have also devised a male sequel to *The Woman Warrior*. Furthermore, her *China Men* intertext, "The Wild Man of the Green Swamp," shows faint traces of resemblance to Alcott's "Wild Boy" Dan, who "liked to rove about in the woods" in *Little Men*.[14] *China Men* traces the fortunes of the Chinese forefathers who came to America during the Civil War, the historical event that would have a profound effect on Alcott's own life and narrative. The daughter narrator of *China Men* remembers the family attic as a "father place" (239), but intertextually it was first a small daughter space, for it was famously in the garret of the March house that Jo did her scribbling and became rapt "in an imaginary world, full of friends almost as real and dear to her as any in the flesh" (*Little Women*, 266, 147). Maxine Hong Kingston herself recollects writing like Jo March "oblivious to everything" in the family basement, in an impromptu tree house, in a hidden corner of the pantry, and finally in a low-ceilinged attic (Huntley, 26; Skenazy, "Kingston at the University," 124). Her desk and writing file was sometimes "a little cigar box," while "Jo's desk up here [in the garret] was an old tin kitchen, which hung against the wall" (*Little Women*, 147).

Jo March and a Daughter's Devotion to her Father

Alcott's Jo March and Hong Kingston's daughter narrator are the second daughters to be born in the family, but both come "first" as far as readers are concerned. Alcott's daughter longs to be the "son Jo" her father never had and to fight alongside him in the Civil War. Indeed, the Reverend March is depicted as a Lincoln figure who inspires that "perfect filiality" that another devoted daughter, Fa Mu Lan, shows to both her mother and father (*Little Women*, 3–4, 223, 203; *WW*, 47). As we have already seen, Jo's wishful, tomboy fantasy of being a surrogate son and "man of the family now papa is away" (5) is replayed in Hong Kingston's version of the Mu Lan legend; like Fa Mu Lan, Jo is essentially a "hero among women" in her adoption of masculine traits that mirror the patriarchal moral code of her father (Edwards, 102, 111). Furthermore just as *Little Women* opens with the four sisters' aching sense of their father's absence in the War, so too *China Men* begins, in the intertext "On Fathers," with the strong impression that the Chinese immigrant father is missing, admittedly in a different kind of war that is being waged on the American battlefield of work. "Waiting at the gate for our father to come home from work, my brothers and sisters and I saw a man come hastening around the corner. Father! 'BaBa!' 'BaBa!' We flew off the gate; we jumped off the fence." They run to welcome, nuzzle, and clasp a stranger who disappoints them with the news: "I'm not your father. You've made a mistake." The expectant children who watch out for—and reach out to—their father see him greet them "a moment later, from the other direction" (6–7).

The Father as Missing Person

This intertext is a metaphor for a father who is "missing in action" for most of *The Woman Warrior* and much of *China Men* and whom the daughter narrator is often at a loss to identify, even when near at hand in the text. As in *Alice through the Looking Glass*, she will have to find him in the present by "walking in the opposite direction" (*The Annotated Alice*, 205), back into his past. In so doing, she will begin to counter the sense that the publication of *The Woman Warrior* and *China Men* separately can give—that "men and women will continue to work in opposing directions" (Cheung, "*The Woman Warrior* versus *The Chinaman Pacific*," 245). Jo March misses her father but is comforted to be told that she has her grandfather's brave and honest spirit (*Little Women*, 53). The daughter narrator of *China Men* will depict paternal ancestors who had a liking for women and children and who will stop feminist readers of *The Woman Warrior*, in particular, from writing Chinese patriarchs off as misogynistic and abusive. She will reconstruct the resilient and sometimes benign spirit of the Great Grandfather of the Sandalwood Mountains, the Grandfather of the Sierra Nevada Mountains, and the Third and Fourth Grandfathers who settled in America, and so set the scene for her withdrawn and moody father to make a comeback in the text.

THE POWER OF ANGER IN ALCOTT'S AND HONG KINGSTON'S NARRATIVES

Lynda Zwinger calls *Little Women* "an allegory about the power of a writer's anger,"[15] which means that the text is driven by the same inner dynamics as *The Woman Warrior* or, indeed, *China Men*, where the father's smoldering anger leaves his children scared and habitually on edge (12). In all three books, the principal family characters have problems coping with strong and socially unacceptable emotions. Marmee and Jo engage in a frank dialogue about female gendered anger and frustration, with Marmee making an astonishing admission to her daughter, and one that is a reversal of the daughter's confession to Brave Orchid in *The Woman Warrior*. "I am angry nearly every day of my life, Jo; but I have learned not to show it; and I still hope to learn not to feel it, though it may take me another forty years to do so" (*Little Women*, 79). Marmee is unconsciously acknowledging that feelings cannot be repressed as long as individuals are alive and may return to haunt the next generation after they are dead. These subversive emotions continually puncture the surface of not only *Little Women* and *The Woman Warrior*, but *China Men* as well. Like the March family, whose name, derived from the German Marchen, alludes to their fairy tale origins in the daughter's family romance (Zwinger, 74; *Little Women*, 342), the Hongs are also a family of storytellers who have fallen on hard times and relive/relieve them in talk-story.

THE ROLE OF THE MATRIARCH IN ALCOTT'S AND
HONG KINGSTON'S FAMILY NARRATIVES

Both matriarchs of the family, Marmee and Brave Orchid, are sensitive to the social comedown they have suffered as a result of their husband's financial incompetence and gullibility. "You have no idea how much I have fallen coming to America" (*WW*, 74). Both fathers are bankrupted by close friends. The saintly Marmee never breathes a word of reproach, but the eldest daughter Meg "remember[s] better times" and articulates her mother's suppressed wish that "we had the money papa lost when we were little" (*Little Women*, 2, 36). The less-than-perfect Brave Orchid reproaches her husband years after he lost his share in a New York business. "You let your so-called friends steal your laundry. You let your brothers and the Communists take your land. You have no head for business" (*CM*, 247–248). Jo's elder sister Meg wistfully recalls a former life of affluence where she dressed in fine silk dresses and had servants like Brave Orchid in China. "I should like a lovely house full of all sorts of luxurious things; nice food, pretty clothes, handsome furniture, pleasant people, and heaps of money. I am to be mistress of it . . . with plenty of servants, so I never need work a bit" (*Little Women*, 142; *WW*, 61). She will suffer the humiliation of having to tutor a neighboring family with more money than education or class (*Little Woman*, 37) as BaBa will be forced to teach illiterate farm boys in China and Brave Orchid will complain in America, "We're the slaves of these villagers who were nothing when they were in China. I've turned into the servant of a woman who can't read" (*CM*, 245).

The Marriage Plot in *Little Women* and *The Woman Warrior*

Both Jo and the narrator of *The Woman Warrior* will resist the marriage plot that brings traditional closure to the female bildungsroman (Chu, 100). Jo's refusal to marry Laurie has continued to greatly disappoint and frustrate the young women readers of *Little Women* (Sicherman, 248–249; Showalter, xix). When read intertextually through Hong Kingston's "No Name Woman," however, a romance between Jo and her adopted "brother" Laurie—only too happy to live forever in the March "Land of Women" like Tang Ao—does appear incestuous and bears some resemblance to the *simpua* marriage. Alcott's Jo and Hong Kingston's daughter narrator will refuse to follow the marriage route tread by siblings like Meg or dictated by parents like Brave Orchid. They will obstinately reject the compliant behavior that was still deemed "American-feminine" in the twentieth and not simply the nineteenth century, when *Little Women* was written. They will dispute the truth of Amy March's remark that "women should learn to be agreeable, particularly poor ones" (*Little Women*, 295). They will also fight the childish regression, dependency, and eventual death to which the stay-at-home Beth succumbs when her scarlet fever precipitates an incurable "mysterious illness" very like that of Victorian recluses and the hysterical narrator of *The Woman Warrior*. Instead, they will chose the road less traveled and work hard to make a living as storytellers. As Hong Kingston's daughter narrator proudly reassures her mother in *The Woman Warrior*, "I work all the time. . . . I know how to work when things get bad" (99). In *China Men*, she will go "out on the road" in sympathetic identification with her hard-working and flamboyant predecessors—the "Cantonese who have always been revolutionaries, nonconformists, people with fabulous imaginations, people who invented the Gold Mountain" (*CM*, 87). She will depict her father's father, Ah Goong, as an eccentric pilgrim wandering across America after "The Driving Out" of the *China Men* who built the transcontinental railroad.

THE INTERTEXTUAL JOURNEY OF THE READER IN ALCOTT'S AND HONG KINGSTON'S WRITING

The March daughters keenly feel the restrictions on travel resulting from gender, family poverty, and the Civil War. At the beginning of *Little Women*, Marmee directs them to follow the only road that is open to them —that as readers of Bunyan's *Pilgrim's Progress*. "Our road is before us, and the longing for goodness and happiness is the guide that leads us through many troubles and mistakes to the peace which is a true Celestial City." Jo vows to "do my duty here instead of wanting to be somewhere else" (*Little Women*, 9–10). Their spiritual and literary aspirations are not all that different from the secular pacifism and perseverance of the Brother in Vietnam. Marmee encourages her daughters to transform the reading of *Pilgrim's Progress* into an inner journey and to "see how far on you can get before father comes home" (10). Hong Kingston's daughter narrator follows what Eng astutely calls "the errancies of personal memory" (91)—and the vagaries of an imagination as restless, romantic, and eager for vicarious adventure as that of Jo March. In *China Men* she rewrites her male sojourner relatives as eccentric knight-errants. The Great Grandfather of the Sandalwood Mountains, for instance, furiously hacks away the Hawaiian undergrowth with his machete "like a knight rescuing a princess" (103). The March girls read to close the physical distance that separates them from their father and to commune with him in spirit. *China Men*'s opening intertexts, "On Fathers" and "The Ghostmate," suggest that Hong Kingston's daughter fears a more ominous metaphysical separation from a father who has lost his sense of direction and purpose as a China man in America (Eng, 37). He has succumbed to the danger that Brave Orchid foresaw during her own out-of-the-body experience in "Shaman (69, 73). His mind and soul have gone wandering and he cannot find his way home without help. The writing of *China Men* enables the daughter to both trace and create for her father a male descent line. The intertextual act of writing a past that he can read and identify with is motivated by the daughter's desire to bring her father to his senses and make him come back in spirit to his family.

The Female Creation of a Male Descent Line in *China Men*

In discussing her restoration of a male descent line in *China Men*, Hong Kingston said that she "wanted to write about my grandfather, whom I never met" and that her mother, not her father, was the crucial link to the paternal grandfather (Thompson, 4; Perry, 178). Her father's strenuous psychic effort to deny his sister in *The Woman Warrior* seems to have required him to detach himself from the rest of his birth family as well. He never mentions the names of his three brothers in *China Men*,[16] and the only allusion to their fate occurs early in the daughter narrator's account of "The Father from China," when she records that BaBa's oldest brother Dai Bak decided to go out on the road to San Francisco while second brother Ngee Bak headed for Chicago and third brother Sahm Bak went north to Canada (*CM*, 48). As Rabinowitz remarked in a discussion with Hong Kingston on the intertextuality of her two books, though *China Men* is a collection of the men's stories, "These are narratives that have been retold through women" (70). What the daughter makes clear later in her narrative of "The Grandfather of the Sierra Nevada Mountains" is that Brave Orchid was not only the champion talker and impatient listener characterized in *The Woman Warrior*, but a long-suffering auditor of the paternal grandfather's stories. As we have seen in chapter 1, a key feature of Hong Kingston's intertextual writing practice was her respect for the art of careful listening to others. Indeed, were it not for the mother, the old man's sojourner tales would have been lost because "MaMa was the only person to listen to him, and so he followed her everywhere, and talked and talked. What he liked telling was his journeys to the Gold Mountain" (127). Here readers also learn that Grandfather Ah Goong liked to sit outside Brave Orchid's open door and reminisce about his sojourner journeys to the Gold Mountain while she worked like Penelope at her loom. She not only passed on his stories to her daughter but wove into them vivid, firsthand details of her own. Their joint gender recollections are, in turn, intertextually rewritten and reconfigured in *China Men*.

Mother and Daughter as Intertextual Collaborators in Narration

When she recounts the genesis of the poet Ts'ai Yen's song for a barbarian reed pipe, the daughter narrator of *The Woman Warrior* realizes that she has inherited her mother's dual talent as a listener and raconteur. Her own reading and writing of family events are a creative translation of her mother's dialogic skills, and the dynamic interplay of the conversational and literary voice in intertextuality connects mother and daughter as surely as the ties of blood. "The beginning is hers, the ending, mine" (*WW*, 184). If the men's stories were orally transmitted by the women in the Hong family (Pfaff, 18), Ah Goong provided an important "beginning" for her mother. Indeed, his tales of the Gold Mountain were a crucial source for Brave Orchid as a storyteller and, in turn, for the daughter who would translate the grandfather's his-story in *China Men*. Ts'ai Yen would leave behind "Eighteen Stanzas for a Barbarian Reed Pipe," and though the words that she sang were incomprehensible to her foreign-born children and captors, her voice conveyed the "sadness and anger" of a Chinese woman in exile (186). The daughter narrator faces a more difficult act of translation as she begins the corresponding eighteen sections of *China Men*, for, although she understands the scant words that her father speaks, she does not comprehend the paternal history of sadness and anger that lies behind them.

Learning to Live Backwards and Remember Forward

Hong Kingston emphasized the family resemblance in the stories of *The Woman Warrior* and *China Men*. As they are passed on from one generation and gender to another, they also preserve distinctive traces of each teller so the reader has the impression of proceeding down a long gallery of mirrors in which s/he is "looking through me looking through my mom looking at my grandfather" (Thompson, 4). Here again the parallel is with *Alice through the Looking Glass* and the discovery of infinite regress, where the girl child dreams of the Red King who is dreaming of Alice who is dreaming of the Red King, and so on (*The Annotated Alice*, 238–239, 293, 344). Eng argues that Hong Kingston "resolutely work[s] against notions of mimetic realism so as to look awry at what the visible image would have us most readily apprehend" and focus instead "on personal memories and the dreamwork—on the *unconscious* aspects of looking" (37). This apprehension of the "errant and unpredictable quality of personal memories" (Eng, 55) lies at the heart of not only the romance quest on which sojourners like Ah Goong embark, but also the surreal journey of Alice through a looking glass world in which she must learn, like the narrator of *China Men*, to walk in the opposite direction, live backwards, and recognize how memory can work both ways (*The Annotated Alice*, 205, 247). The White Queen would chide Alice that "it's a poor sort of memory that only works backwards" (248). Hong Kingston would confide similarly that, "if there is such a thing as reverse memory, maybe that's what I am getting into; because it seems to me, I'm writing the memory of the future rather than a memory of the past"

(Rabinowitz, 76). Skenazy later deconstructed this paradox of a memory that "works both ways" by suggesting that, in changing the past of the no name woman and reevaluating her relationship to her mother, the daughter narrator created a new vision of the future in *The Woman Warrior* ("Coming Home," 110). I would add that, by remembering her father's fathers in *China Men*, she not only changed her relationship to her father in the present, but also conceived a past and a future for him where before there was none. She remarks on the fact that her father phoned "the Time Lady" on New Year's Eve to hear her "distinctly name the present moment, never slipping into the past or sliding into the future" (*CM*, 15).

Ah Goong—The Maddest of All Her Forefathers [17]

Her father's father is crucial to the family saga that begins to unfold in *The Woman Warrior* and is played out in *China Men*. He is mentioned on the opening page of "No Name Woman." Later in this first story, he achieves notoriety when the daughter narrator gives prominence to the salacious family gossip that circulated about him. "There are stories that my grandfather was different from other people, 'crazy ever since the little Jap bayoneted him in the head.' He used to put his naked penis on the dinner table, laughing" (*WW*, 17). The indirect quotation alluding to the brutal Japanese invasion of China is almost certain to have come from Brave Orchid, who tended refugees wounded by the enemy forces before her narrow escape out of Canton harbor in 1939 (*WW*, 87–88; *CM*, 68–69), and it is the first indication in the narrative that she is a major source of anecdotes relating to Ah Goong. The graphic description of the grandfather as a brain-damaged or dirty old man who plays practical jokes on his startled family by banging his penis down on the dinner table like a large sausage on a plate is a deeply disconcerting interpolation in "No Name Woman." It destroys the opening mood of the passage where the aunt is tenderly remembered as "unusually beloved, the precious only daughter, spoiled and mirror gazing because of the affection the family lavished on her" (17). I have argued at length in the two previous chapters that this lurid passage generates undercurrents that disturb the whole of *The Woman Warrior* and that carry on into *China Men* like a bad, recurrent, and intrusive memory.

The Grandfather as Dirty Old Man

If readers of *The Woman Warrior* concluded that the grandfather only exposed himself in senility, *China Men* leaves them with no such illusions. In "The Father from China," the first major story of *China Men* and the textual counterpart of *Woman Warrior's* "No Name Woman," the daughter narrator not only reiterates but crucially revises the mother's story of the grandfather exposing himself at the family table. She shifts its date from 1939 back to the year of her father's birth, sometime between 1891 and 1903 when Ah Goong thoughtlessly traded him for a girl (*CM*, 15).[18] "Perhaps it was that very evening and not after the Japanese bayoneted him that he began taking his penis out at the dinner table, worrying it, wondering at it, asking why it had given him four sons and no daughter, chastising it, asking it whether it were yet capable of producing the daughter of his dreams" (21). As Eng observes, "Conscious memories . . . do not develop in any strict linear or chronological fashion. Instead they are continually subjected to a fresh rearrangement of meaning in accordance with new psychic and material circumstances" (79), as individuals revisit the original home that is lodged in their childhood imaginary and reconsider their complex feelings about the people who inhabit it.

The Grandfather's Fetishism

Chronologically reshuffled, the grandfather's exposure of his penis cannot simply be dismissed as a crude joke that brings pathetic pleasure to an old man at the end of a hard and joyless sojourner existence. Now it begins to manifest the inner thrust of his dreamwork. Now it suggests that his exhibitionism may be a chronic compulsion—a fetish with longevity—expressing the desire for a daughter that is prohibited in a Chinese male kinship system and that is reasserted through the unconscious ruses of displacement and substitution. Now Ah Goong lectures his penis like a ventriloquist speaking through his finger puppet or a girl admonishing her doll in the tone of an anxious mother. "Left to himself," we later learn in "The Grandfather of the Sierra Nevada Mountains," "he would have stayed in China to play with babies" (127). This is a strong indication that playing with his penis is a fetishistic substitute for rearing a girl child. It complicates the critical assumption that what we see reflected in Ah Goong's interrogation and belittling of his own penis is simply the questionable authority of patriarchy or the immigrant's crisis of masculinity in which sojourners who enjoyed phallocentric power in China felt impotent and feminized as expendable "coolie" labor in America (Eng, 98–100; Goellnicht, "Tang Ao in America," 230–232).

In fact, in feeling the lack of a daughter so keenly and in berating his penis for its failure to produce a female, Ah Goong unknowingly challenges Freud's patriarchal concepts of gender and sexuality. He subverts the Freudian theory of femininity that a baby is a substitute for the penis a woman lacks by openly showing his family that his penis is a poor piece of meat in comparison with "the loveliest dainty of a baby girl" (18). Furthermore, he contradicts Freud's view that the fixation with a sexualized object, such as a Chinese woman's bound foot, shows that a fetish is a surrogate penis projected like a prosthesis on the deficient female body.[19] Ah Goong does not idealize the phallus that is so central to the hold the father traditionally has over his family and that men, in general, have had over women. He concludes that his penis is no use because it cannot provide him with what he wants so viscerally that he can taste it—a daughter. When he looks enviously at his poor neighbor's newborn daughter, he sees a plump and pink little morsel who is good enough to eat and "love filled his heart and his liver" (18). The mealtime drama that is played out at the dinner table as the family eats in silence and watches in distaste as Ah Goong pulls out his penis reflects a pathologized hunger for a baby girl.

Ah Po—the "Father's Tyrant Mother with the Bound Feet"

In Freud's early theory of female sexual development, the sexuality of little girls is masculine in character and is eventually directed toward securing the father as a love object and obtaining the penis she lacks/wants through the fantasy of having a child by her father.[20] As I have suggested at length, however, the incestuous subtext in *The Woman Warrior* can be read to suggest that Ah Goong desires not only to have a daughter as a love object but to possess her entirely by fathering her child. In the critical appraisal of Ah Goong's pathology, the role of his wife Ah Po, the matriarch of the Hong family, is often overlooked. In *The Woman Warrior*, she is briefly mentioned as the "father's tyrant mother with the bound feet" who treats her daughter-in-law Brave Orchid like an errand girl and who forced Ah Goong to trade his youngest son back (61). Ah Po is depicted unsympathetically in *China Men*. Her granddaughter notes that "there is a Cantonese word that sounds almost like 'grandmother,' *po*, and means a female monster that looms and sags" (13). In other words, she appears to be mom the monster or the mother-in-law from hell. Both books, however, also resist the "blame the mother" mentality[21] and suggest that there are gender socialized causes that may account for her callous behavior to her family. In "No Name Woman," Brave Orchid tells her daughter to thank her lucky stars that she was not born in Ah Po's day, when girls had their feet bound at seven and when "sisters used to sit on their beds and cry together . . . as their mothers or their slaves removed the bandages for a few minutes each night and let the blood gush back into their veins" (16). One could say, to paraphrase Humpty

Dumpty's death threat to Alice, that with proper assistance Ah Po's life as a carefree girl left off at seven (*The Annotated Alice*, 266). The nightly pain that she endured through the remainder of her childhood was to serve the future fetishistic pleasure of men and to bind her to the ideology of the traditional patriarchal family. She would grow up to become, as Kay Ann Johnson sadly observed, an older woman who would "continue to strangle the hopes of [other] daughters and daughters-in-law" (26) and whose stunted and twisted feet produced a stunted and twisted personality exacting its tyrannical revenge in the home.

Ah Po also represents the much derided and burlesqued figure of the shrew whose domineering and mercenary behavior contrasts so dramatically with the loyalty and service of the woman warrior to patriarchal rule. She forces Grandfather Ah Goong to leave his home in China, where he would have preferred to play happily with a precious baby girl, and orders him to "make money" in the Gold Mountain (*CM*, 127). When he settles down in America, she instructs him to return with luxury goods from the West: "Dunhill lighters, Rolex wristwatches, Seth Thomas clocks, Parker pens, Singer sewing machines" (46)—like a Hong Kong shopper with a wish list of brand names. Housebound by her gender and footbound by custom, Ah Po has little alternative but to capitalize on her life of idleness, inactivity, and useless consumption. Unable to walk even a short distance without physical support, she is inevitably ignorant of the physical suffering and spiritual anguish that her husband endured when he went out on the road. "The Gold Mountain is lonely. You could get sick and almost die, and nobody come to visit" and dismisses his poignant complaint. "'Idiot,' shouted Grandmother. 'What do you know? Don't listen to the idiot. Crazy man'" (42).

The Henpecked Husband

Yet her daughter-in-law listens and indeed may have been the only person ever to take the stereotyped slow wit of the family seriously. When Brave Orchid emigrates to America, she relates to her husband how "your father followed me and wept on the road when I left" (*CM*, 69). In "The Grandfather of the Sierra Nevada Mountains," her granddaughter locates the source of these tears and imagines what Ah Po refuses to hear—the economic deprivation, racial humiliation, and sexual frustration that Ah Goong experienced as a laborer on the Central Pacific Railroad. While "he felt his heart breaking of loneliness"—as it did after he tearfully walked away from his dream of possessing a baby girl—and while he laments the fact that "the railroad he was building would not lead him to his family" (129), his wife hectored him incessantly with covetous demands. "Are you wasting the money? Are you spending it on girls and gambling and whiskey? Here's my advice to you: Be a little more frugal. Remember how it felt to go hungry. Work hard. . . . I need a new dress to wear to weddings. . . . If you weren't such a spendthrift, we could be building the new courtyard" (143). Were it not for the terrible judgment that is exacted on Ah Po's daughter in "No Name Woman," it would be tempting to conclude that the villagers avenged her long-suffering husband when they vandalized her family house and destroyed the possessions that she valued so much more than him.

The Shrew and the Woman Warrior

Ah Po is also imagined in the revenge that Fa Mu Lan takes on the "cowering, whimpering women" who "could not escape on their little bound feet" from their inbred and pampered lives in the baron's household. Some crawl away in ignominy, shunned by their natal families as ghosts. Others, however, form a "band of swordswomen who were a mercenary army" (*WW*, 46–47). They illustrate the fact that the shrew and the woman warrior are symbolically related. Indeed, the daughter narrator underlines this connection in "A Song for a Barbarian Reed Pipe." The captive soldier poet Ts'ai Yen has a singing voice that rings out like "an icicle in the desert" (186), but the narrator heard the sound of this "woman's voice high and clear as ice" once before at a Chinese opera. The female vocalist was playing the part of the shrewish new daughter-in-law, and the high note that she sang was her desire to be beaten and tamed (172–173).[22] Whether their words threaten or defend male power, these outspoken women who take control—sometimes in revenge for being controlled through footbinding—demonstrate by their actions that Confucian patriarchy is fatally weakened.[23]

Headstrong Wives and Insecure Husbands

The decline of the domestic economy and the collapse of the Ch'ing dynasty, under pressure from Western capitalist imperialism, led to increasing male out-migration and left Chinese women with little choice other than to take charge of the household during the prolonged periods that their husbands labored abroad (Topley, 72, 86–87). Male emigration, however, tore the family apart and, in the words of Kay Ann Johnson, caused "profound personal and spiritual tragedies" (30), as "No Name Woman" shows. In *China Men*, Hong Kingston tersely summarizes the infamous "Laws" of Chinese exclusion, disenfranchisement, and antimiscegenation that stripped sojourners of their human rights and dignity and spawned the Chinese bachelor communities in America "unable to father a subsequent generation" (Cheung, *"The Woman Warrior* versus *The Chinaman Pacific,"* 108) as though neutered and left wondering like Ah Goong "what a man was for, what he had to have a penis for" (*CM*, 144).

The Chinese Matriarch and Her Uterine Family

Ah Po further exemplifies the domineering and manipulative hold the Chinese matriarch exercised over the uterine family, a close-knit social unit that she organized for her own personal security and aimed to strengthen with a plentiful supply of dutiful sons (Johnson, 9–10, 18–21; Margery Wolf, 125; Ahern, 199). Indeed, as Mad Sao's mother shows later in "The Making of More Americans," the matriarch tried to keep her sons tied to the umbilical cord for life and even beyond, from the grave! Both before and after her death, she haunts Mad Sao with her insatiable needs. She writes him letters of emotional blackmail: "I remember you, my baby. . . . Do you remember your mother's face? . . . Sail back to me. . . . Sell everything. Sell the girls, and mail the profits to Mother" (*CM*, 171–172). She appears to him as a "hungry ghost" in America, chastising him for having allowed his own family to supplant her: "You fed your wife and useless daughters, who are not even family, and you left me to starve" (176). Kay Ann Johnson elegantly balances the contradictions when she observes that, "in order to ward off threats to the solidarity of their uterine families, older women usually had to become the most stalwart defenders of the patrilineal family structures within which their own uterine families necessarily resided" (21). As for Ah Po, she is still alive and demanding money of her son at the age of ninety-nine and remains a force to be reckoned with up until the end of *China Men* (248–249).

The Father's Exclusion from the Uterine Family

The rural families sojourner fathers and sons left behind were "demographically distorted and highly vulnerable to stress,"[24] and Ah Po shows the needy face of such families. She also demonstrates that both women and men were becoming a new kind of "slave"—slave to the industrial and consumer capitalism that would eventually undermine Chinese patrilineage and break ancestral lines (Kay Ann Johnson, 27–30). With their husbands away for long periods, it is understandable that women should cling for dear life to their sons and defend their uterine families with ferocity. Ah Goong's personal tragedy was that he wanted to participate in this uterine family but Ah Po would not allow it. "He would have stayed in China to play with babies or stayed in the United States once he got there, but Grandmother forced him to leave both places" (*CM*, 127). In "The Grandfather of the Sierra Nevada Mountains," he works on the railroad all the livelong day, and indeed labors continuously from 1863 until the transcontinental track is completed in 1869. On the dangerous and circuitous road that he takes home after "The Driving Out," he comes across a toddler who climbs into his arms. "'I wish you were my baby,' he told it. 'My baby.' . . . 'My daughter,' he said. 'My son'" (147). Ah Goong eventually returns to China to father sons, but it is his wife who will bask in her uterine family while he is pressured to go back to work in America.

"Grandmother . . . quickly spent the railroad money, and Ah Goong said he would go to America again" (150). Ah Goong's relatives view his fondness for babies, for daughters, and for the domestic life as a sure sign that he is soft in the head—not the heart. Even traditional elders who upheld the patriarchal family system, however, might be driven by the loneliness of old age to turn to their wives' uterine family, particularly after the death of their own mothers, only to find themselves left out in the cold like the eccentric Ah Goong. Indeed, as Margery Wolf suggests (129–132), the aging patriarch could feel as isolated in his wife's familial power base as the new daughter-in-law, which may partially account for Ah Goong's later kinship with Brave Orchid.

Ah Po's Greed and Ah Goong's Alienation

Ah Po's greed traps Ah Goong in a perpetual cycle of deferral of and, ultimately, alienation from desire. "'Make money,' she said. 'Don't stay here eating.' 'Come home,' she said" (127). Her cupidity, however, also gives his journey as a "homeless wanderer" (150–151) a mythic dimension. As he tramps cross-country, this Chinese Everyman reiterates the lament of the mysterious old man who also wanders "without a sense of direction" (*CM*, 126) in Chaucer's *Pardoner's Tale* warning of the evils of avarice. "Leeve mooder, leet me in! . . . Allas! whan shul my bones been at reste?"[25] Ah Goong's "trickster" father, Bak Goong, would devise his own ingenious solution to the homesickness that the exile felt deep in his bones. With his team of Hawaiian sugarcane workers, he "dug a wide hole" and shouted, "Hello, Mother. . . . I miss you. . . . I want home. Home. Home. Home" (*CM*, 113, 117). These *China Men* of the Sandalwood Mountains bear out Freud's theory that homesickness reflects the desire to return to the mother's body "where each one of us lived once upon a time and in the beginning."[26] As we have seen, the "mooder" from which Ah Goong feels most estranged is not the motherland where he was born but the uterine family that is an extension of his wife's body. "The Grandfather of the Sierra Nevada Mountains" concludes with three alternative endings to Ah Goong's rocky life as a sojourner. In the first, he goes down in flames, perishing in the San Francisco earthquake and fire and perhaps fulfilling his wife's wish that he would disappear without trace once his money-earning days were over.[27] In the second, his family bails him out after he deteriorates into a "dirty, jobless man with matted hair, ragged clothes, and fleas all over his body" who eats out of garbage cans (150–151); and so Ah Goong is reborn as the dirty old man of "No Name Woman." In the third and final fairy-tale ending to his story, his wish is finally granted. Like a phoenix, he rises out of the ashes of the San Francisco fire and earthquake and is "seen carrying a child out of the fire, a child of his own in spite of the laws against marrying" (151).

Ah Po's BiBi

"Allas," however, Ah Goong did not remain in America to discover the human warmth of another wife and family in his old age. He returned to Ah Po and fathers the four sons that she craves, only to find that he had been shut out of her emotional life. The person who takes this father's place in Ah Po's heart is the narrator's own father, who remained in the emotional background of *The Woman Warrior* but emerges from the shadows in *China Men* as BiBi, "the *dim sum*, the little heart" of the family (15), petted and feted youngest son. In her analysis of the gender politics of the nuclear family in Western capitalist society, Nancy Chodorow argued that, whereas the male breadwinner can afford to be romantic, women's socioeconomic dependence on men has acculturated them to make rational calculations in their choice of a mate. To offset the sense of dependence that also underlies their sexual and marital relations, they may turn to close female friends and kin or rely on their own children for emotional intimacy (197–201).

In two crucial respects, the values of the uterine family BiBi was raised in converge with those in Chodorow's nuclear model. It was in the interests of both Confucian ideology and the controlling Chinese matriarch to discourage the development of romantic love and intimate sexual bonding between husband and wife (Kay Ann Johnson, 18–19, 27). Moreover, the Chinese emigrant family was especially reliant for its economic welfare on the male sojourner's income. At the same time, the long absences from home of migrant husbands not only distorted family relationships, but also impelled women to satisfy their emotional needs through their children. The aunt is a reminder of how dangerous it could be for the childless woman to look for love outside the home or to be looked at by besotted eyes inside it.[28] Although Chodorow concludes that men can feel threatened when they become fathers and fear jealously that the child will supplant them in their wives' affections, Hong Kingston represents Ah Goong as a father who envies a mother's emotional closeness to her children, who, contrary to Chinese patriarchal norms, is partial to daughters, and who longs for "feminine" attachments and sense of connection to others.

Emotional Tensions in the Emigrant Family

Angelika Bammer astutely suggests that cultural displacement can make it especially difficult for migrant fathers and the families they leave behind to work through the Oedipal conflict and achieve a mature psychological balance between separation and attachment. This is because "the family is virtually the only remaining link to the home they have lost," making it "as difficult for children to distance themselves from their parents as for parents to let go of their children."[29] Both Ah Po's besotted love for "her BiBi, her lap baby" (17)—MaMa's proverbial beautiful baby boy—and Ah Goong's passionate and possibly pathological desire for a daughter reflect the incestuous undercurrents of Freud's family romance. Freud focuses on the child and argues that "the most intense impulses of sexual rivalry" can make a child feel slighted by his or her parents ("Family Romances," 221–222); however, just as children can regard a new brother or sister as a usurper of the parents' love, so, too, parents can resent having to share their partner's affections with a child or, vice versa, jealously scheme to have the child all to themselves. Parental body language can betray the desire to ingest, incorporate, or absorb offspring. Ah Po loved her BiBi so much that "she licked the snot from his nose" as if she was licking a plate clean, while Ah Goong's mouth and throat "puckered all over with envy" when he saw his neighbor's delicious baby girl lying "ignored in a yam basket" (*CM*, 17–18).

Ah Po the Doting Mother

In the dysfunctional family at risk of disintegration through out-migration or incest, the child can become a substitute for the absent or sexually absenting partner. I have tried to show how Ah Goong's emotional rejection by his wife, sexual starvation in America, and hunger for affection from the remaining women in his family may have set the scene for the tragedy of the "No Name Woman," even if he was not the "father" who caused his daughter's downfall.[30] Ah Po's smothering mother-love, however, may have given rise to the lesser tragedy of BaBa's disappointment with life. At his birth, she declared him destined for greatness. "Your little brother is different from any of you. Your generation has no boy like this one. . . . This is the boy we'll prepare for the Imperial Examinations" (16). Yet her sensitive, intelligent, cultivated youngest son with graceful hands and long fingers "made for holding pens" (16) would be classified in America as an illiterate "coolie" (45). Her fond maternal dream that he would elevate her agrarian family in social status by becoming a mandarin scholar would alienate him from his farmhand brothers and make him singularly unfit to cope with the pedestrian life of a rural schoolmaster in China or an unskilled manual worker in America.

The Symbolic Sacrifice of the Father

The clever BaBa's chief distinction would be self-sacrifice in which he resembled his slow-witted father Ah Goong. In *China Men*, his daughter narrator commemorates the burnt offering that he made of his life in order to feed his family. In *The Woman Warrior*, she alludes intertextually to the sacrifices he made when she describes the rabbit that appeared when Fa Mu Lan had eaten the last of her food while testing her survival skills on the mountain of the white tigers. The rabbit studies her intently, as if reading her innermost need, before jumping with conscious premeditation into her campsite fire. "I saw the rabbit had turned into meat, browned just right. I ate it, knowing the rabbit had sacrificed itself for me. It had made me a gift of meat" (31). Though the aggrieved daughter narrator of this fantasy will churlishly complain later in "White Tigers" that "no rabbit . . . will jump in the fire when I'm hungry" (51), she thinks back over this incident near the beginning of *China Men*. Not only does she specifically connect it now with her "Father from China," but she deliberately invests it with a sacred significance. "My father was born in a year of the Rabbit. . . . In one of his incarnations, one of the Buddhas was a rabbit; he jumped alive into a fire to feed the hungry" (15).

The oblation of both the Buddha and Christ resonates in this passage, redeeming the apparent waste of her father's life, and denoting that "The Father from China" is not writing with a vengeance but a sacred act of remembrance. The daughter's retrospective view of her father as a good provider who gave his own flesh and blood the gift that was taken away from him—that of a head start in life—is tinged with the guilty recognition psychoanalyzed by Hans Loewald that, "in our role as children of our parents, by genuine emancipation we do kill something vital in them—not all in one blow and not in all respects, but contributing to their dying" (395). Acknowledging her own "burden of guilt," Marilyn Chin remarked to Hong Kingston, "It's a generation that did everything for their children. They pretty much sacrificed their lives so their children could have an education, so that the children could go on" (Chin, 98; see also Hongo, 10).

Struggle to the Death in the Family

In psychic reality, it is kill or be killed. If the parent grows weak, as happens to BaBa in "The American Father," when he loses his job at the Stockton gambling house and sinks into deep despondency, the child will be more keenly conscious of consuming the diminishing reserves of the father. If the parent is indomitable and, like Brave Orchid, does "not understand how some of us run down and stop. Some of us use up all our life force getting out of bed in the morning" (*CM*, 248), the child may have to resort to violent behavior to break free. The Hong children play "in earnest"—not at being good little pilgrims like the March girls (*LW*, 10)—but at murder and mayhem. "They fought with knives, the cleaver and a boning knife; they circled the dining room table and sliced one another's arms . . . cutting bloody slits, an earnest fight to the death." The appalled neighbors conclude that the "kids turned into killers" (252). When the daughter narrator tries to imagine why BaBa screams in his sleep, she similarly concludes that "what he dreamed must have been ax murders. The family man kills his entire family" (251). BaBa does not go berserk, as the narrator feared, in her fantasy expressing the forbidden impulse that parents sometimes have to "murder" their children. He does snap, however, chasing one daughter with a coat hanger, beating another with his shoe, and finding unexpectedly that their roughhouse triggers the cure of his long apathy and depression.

The Role of Guilt in the Family Narrative

What this shows is that guilt can be motivational for the father who contemplates harming his children, or even inspirational for the daughter who narrates the pain that the Hong children cause their parents and the harm parents can do in return. In the memorable words of Loewald, "Guilt then is not a troublesome affect that we might hope to eliminate in some fashion, but one of the driving forces in the organization of the self. The self, in its autonomy, is an atonement structure, a structure of reconciliation, and as such a supreme achievement" (394). An intertextual reading of *The Woman*

Warrior and *China Men* brings together seemingly irreconcilable images of fathers as weedy scholars or "muscular railroad men" (*CM*, 142), dirty old men or pure of heart like the Buddha, perpetrators of crimes against women or victims of their wiles, but also men who "valued girls" and taught daughters the intertextual skills of reading and writing (*CM*, 30, 208). For the daughter narrator who makes a long list of her guilts at the end of *The Woman Warrior* (182), narration is the atonement structure in which she seeks revenge and makes restitution, alternatively "murdering" and redeeming the loved and hated figures in her family saga.

Ah Goong and the Role of Shame in Narration

In her review of *China Men*, Mary Gordon argued that Hong Kingston's victory is not only to show understanding of men and to convey a daughter's struggles to comprehend the contrariness of the fathers in her family, but finally to show them forgiveness.[31] Yet forgiveness can come across as condescending, and even the Buddha's message of compassion can sound smug and glib in translation—"I feel your pain"—especially if it does not involve any corresponding sense of personal culpability or the occasional pang of shame, the kind that still cracks the daughter narrator's voice in two (*WW*, 148). The critical valorization of terms such as "transgression," however, has made it hard to accept that guilt and shame might have a role to play in bringing about greater understanding and rapprochement between the men and women in Hong Kingston's two books. Adam and Eve, the mythic father and mother of the human race, covered their genitals when they first knew shame.[32] Grandfather Ah Goong became the subject of family derision by constantly and unashamedly exposing his. "When we children talked about overcoat men, exhibitionists, we meant Grandfather, Ah Goong, who must have yanked open that greatcoat—no pants" (*CM*, 127). While working on a railroad demolition team in the Sierra Nevada mountains, he developed a related habit, first of urinating like a waterfall and then masturbating like a charge of dynamite out over the cliffs he was blasting.

> One beautiful day, dangling in the sun above a new valley, not the desire to urinate but sexual desire clutched him so hard he bent over in the basket. He curled up, overcome by beauty and fear, which shot to his penis. He tried to rub himself calm. Suddenly he stood up tall and squirted out into space. "I am fucking the world," he said. The world's vagina was big, big as the sky, big as a valley. He grew a habit: whenever he was lowered in the basket, his blood rushed to his penis, and he fucked the world. (133)

Reading Ah Goong's Masturbation

Critics have been divided as to whether they should read his sexual act as liberating, playful, shocking, defiant, or just plain indecent. Tomo Hattori sees it as a cock-a-hoop gesture and redefines masturbation as *jouissance* that "activates a full and successful autoerotic homosexuality" in which "Ah Goong ennobles himself in the joy of open-ended dissemination."[33] He means, I think, that onanism is enjoyable or as the metaphysical poet Andrew Marvell exclaimed tongue-in-cheek: "Such was that happy Garden-state, / While Man there walked without a Mate. . . . Two Paradises 'twere in one, / To live in Paradise alone" ("The Garden," stanza 8), except that his lyrical vision was addressed to those who had lost all "Passion's heat" (stanza 4), to those who were old or defeated or had retired from the contest of life. Ah Goong's play with his penis—whether as the exhibitionist, the fetishist, or the masturbator—is caused, as we have seen, by loneliness, a state—as opposed to a sexual act—that is unnatural and that can give rise to pathology. Even in the Hong photo album, he stands alone and isolated. "Grandfather always appears alone with white stubble on his chin," "a thin man," like his son, "with big eyes that looked straight ahead" (*CM*, 127). His exasperated family, wary that he will not be able to resist exposing himself to the camera's eye, exclude him from their group photo. Only Brave Orchid tries to make him presentable. "My mother, indignant that nobody had readied Grandfather, threw his greatcoat over his nightclothes, shouted, 'Wait! Wait!' and encouraged him into the sunlight" (127). Her decency to the old man is the more exceptional for his family's collective sense of shame. This is not to say that Brave Orchid condoned Ah Goong's indecent behavior; it is only to suggest that she wishes to give him his rightful place in the sun. Her attitude is one of acceptance, rather than forgiveness, and it is an exemplary stance for the intertextual readers of *The Woman Warrior* and *China Men*.

Eng sees Ah Goong's sexual act as a political statement, the explosive statement of a China Man who has been fucked by racist immigration laws and who says fuck to the world in return (Eng, 100–101; Hattori, 8). But he also sees that Ah Goong's waste of his seed is a metaphor for the wasted lives of the fathers in *China Men* whose sexual energy went into the digging of holes in the ground or in the side of cliff faces (*CM*, 131; *WW*, 83). Ah Goong, we will remember, does not father children until his old age (*CM*, 16). Cheung acknowledges that Ah Goong's masturbation is a pathetic and debasing activity that he performs as he is "being lowered in a wicker basket" but sees it "countered by an uplifting sense of cosmic potency" (*Articulate Silences*, 104–105). I should like to pursue this reading because it complements James Hillman's claim that the lonely figure of the old man who has been cast out of his home and knows the melancholy truth of life coming to an end prefigures the return of the fertility god "who invents agriculture" and can "master the geometry of ploughing, the essence of seeds."[34]

Ah Goong the Procreator

Ah Goong is a tragicomic parody of the God in Genesis, whose "big bang" created the universe and whose milky trail of semen sowed the stars of the night sky.[35] He also resembles Abraham, the Jewish patriarch of an archetypal clan of diasporic wanderers and sojourners, who did not father a family until his old age. As Elaine Kim has observed, an aging population of male sojourners on their own gave rise to serious concerns that the Chinese in America would die out.[36] Likewise, Abraham must wait ninety-nine years before God fulfills the fateful covenant, assuring him that he will become "the father of a multitude of nations" and be "most fruitful" (Genesis, 17:3–6). Contemplating the end of his patrilineal line, Abraham must find his comfort in the stars, as does Ah Goong, who lies awake at night identifying the constellations over the Sierra Nevada Mountains. "Look up to heaven and count the stars if you can. Such will be your descendants" (15:5–6). God's promise to Abraham is tinged with the sad knowledge of racial persecution and subjugation that permeates *China Men*. "Know this for certain, that your descendants will be exiles in a land not their own, where they will be slaves and oppressed for four hundred years." Yet Abraham is consoled to hear that he will live to "a ripe old age" (15:13–16). Hong Kingston leaves us with the same consoling thought at the close of *China Men*. "In one hundred and six years, what has given you the most joy?" reporters ask the venerable patriarch in the penultimate intertext, "The Hundred-Year-Old Man." His answer is that of an old man who has acquired the wisdom of King Lear that "ripeness is all" (V.ii.11). "What I like best is to work in a cane field when the young green plants are just growing up," as if to acknowledge that it is only through lifelong contemplation of past roots and their new shoots that humans grow in depth and maturity. "In the end," said Tu Fu, a poet whom Hong Kingston's parents read aloud at home "I will carry a hoe" (*CM*, 306; Chin, "Writing the Other," 98).

Let There Be Light

Hong Kingston confided to Skenazy that, when she wrote *The Woman Warrior*, she conceived the first chapter ("No Name Woman") as "dark, and the second . . . like sunlight. . . . I also saw it as like the way creation works, you know, first there was the darkness, and then the next day God did the light" ("Kingston at the University," 119–120). This natural pattern of alternating darkness and sunlight also runs through *China Men,* as we can see from the efforts of Brave Orchid to bring Ah Goong "into the sunlight" and the parallel attempt of her daughter to create stories that will fill the "formless void" in her father's life. Some Chinese American critics, such as Frank Chin, believe that Hong Kingston's resulting representation of masculinity and paternity panders to a white racist imagination that cannot acknowledge its own "perversions" and "socially unacceptable fantasies," but instead projects the China Man as a "thing of darkness" (*The Tempest,* V.i.275–76), alien and alienated from itself.[37] Garrett Hongo, however, had a very different response after finishing *China Men.* "If it weren't for Maxine Hong Kingston, I wouldn't have my imaginative life. It was a great moment reading *China Men.* That book released human feeling for me. It humanized me, it released my own stories for me. . . . [It] gave me the inspiration to envision the lives of my own ancestors, particularly the men in my family, in a way that I had been blocked from doing. Her work was liberating, I felt, and it gave me my own grandfathers back" (16–17). A vision of light and darkness that is both creative and destructive and that encompasses the critical polarities of Chin and Hongo can be seen at play in one of the daughter narrator's earliest memories of her father, and it is recounted at the start of the last major section of *China Men,* "The Brother in Vietnam."

> My tall parents even taller standing on ladders and covering the windows with black curtains, playing theater in the bright interstice, had been thinking about war. The curtains fell long and black, but the inside of the room shone. My father cut a picture out of a magazine and pinned it on the wall. The yellow light came from it. "You look like this," he said, or "This girl looks like you." She was shining because of her golden hair, a golden girl. It couldn't have been the blonde curls that made her look like me, so it must have been the round face with the fat cheeks. "Shirley Temple also looks like this girl." (264)

Daddy's Golden Girl

At one level, this memory projects an image intrinsic to the incestuous subnarrative of "No Name Woman" and *The Woman Warrior* more generally—that of Daddy's golden girl vulnerable to gender exploitation or, worse, sexual abuse. As Vikki Bell underlines, "From Mary Pickford and Shirley Temple to Tatum O'Neal, the little girl of the silver screen may have changed her costume, cut her curls . . . but her relationship to men remained unaltered . . . she still sacrificed for, pursued or reformed a father figure."[38] Her grown-up, "baby doll" version, Marilyn Monroe, shows the father figure's continuing sexual interest in the female star who acts like his girl child. At another level, the daughter's memory reflects her father's internalization of a white, soft-spoken, "American-feminine" ideal, one that she will feel pressured to emulate as a teenager and that contrasts with the strong, loud, and bossy persona of Chinese women like Brave Orchid (*WW*, 155). Indeed, "The Father from China" depicts BaBa as a China man who tries to refashion himself into the suave lady's man in American movies—the gentleman who prefers blondes. "At a very good store, he paid two hundred dollars cash for . . . the most expensive suit he could find. In the three-way mirror, he looked like Fred Astaire." His laundry partner takes a photo of him to send the family hicks back on the farm in China—"dancing down the New York Public Library steps" as if Ginger Rogers was waiting for him at the bottom (63–64).[39] At a tearoom, he continues to indulge this white, film fantasy by choosing a "blonde dancing girl" as his partner and noting admiringly in the dance hall mirrors that "they looked like the movies" (65). The slim and pale faced blonde is the personification of the pure white womanhood that American antimiscegenation laws protected from Chinese concubinage and yellow racial contamination (Kim, *Asian American Literature*, 6–10).

Yet, in "The American Father," the daughter narrator learns that her mother was equally entranced by blondes—"'Look how beautiful,' they both exclaimed when a blonde walked by"—and that BaBa named her "after a blonde gambler who always won" (243–244); however, the name he gives the first of his children to be born on American soil does not necessarily confirm his visual identification with white subjectivity. It may also reflect the parent's magic wish that Luck will be a Lady in her life. The picture of the blonde pin-up girl he shows his little daughter can also be read as the token of a brief interlude when life was good (61), he was carefree, and both he and his wife still felt they had a fair chance of making it in America. It is significant that the daughter narrator cannot remember whether her father compares her to the blonde pin-up or the other way around. "'You look like this,' he said, or 'This girl looks like you'." The second possibility, that her father saw the blonde's resemblance to his daughter, may be an example of what Freud called "deferred action." Eng explains that this "describes a psychic process by means of which conscious views and meanings are revised at a later time to accommodate new experiences that emerge from unconscious thoughts and experiences" (79). The daughter narrator's vision or revision of a shining "golden girl" radiating a "yellow light" that makes the room glow, though the windows are covered with blackout curtains and war clouds the horizon, lies at the heart of this passage and is central to its dual symmetry of creation and destruction, light and dark. As Linda Kauffman so perceptively remarks, "To see creation and destruction at the same time" is "to understand why the god of war is also the god of literature."[40]

The resemblance the daughter narrator perceives here is not visual or racial so much as metaphorical and mystical.[41] Her vision of a golden child has intertextual links to Fa Mu Lan's clairvoyant glimpse of her mentors as "two people made of gold dancing the earth's dances" (*WW*, 31) that synchronize light and darkness. Indeed, the woman warrior's description of how "the man and the woman grow bigger and bigger, so bright. All light" until they are transfigured into "tall angels in two rows" (*WW*, 32) corresponds to the narrator's early memory in *China Men* of her mother and father as "tall parents even taller standing on ladders" (*CM*, 264). On their tall ladders, the parents may appear to the small child like the angels on top of a Christmas tree, especially as her next vivid memory is of her brother being born on Christmas day. The sixteenth-century English poet Robert Southwell imagined the Christ child appearing to him on Christmas day as a "burning babe." Though it is highly unlikely that Hong Kingston had this poem in mind as an intertext when she wrote her passage, the visionary figure of a burning babe does make an appearance as a symbol of hope at the close of "The Grandfather of the Sierra Nevada Mountains."[42] Ah Goong is spotted "carrying a child out of the fire" that burned down San Francisco and that made "paper sons" legal Americans at last. "Every China Man was reborn out of that fire a citizen" (150–151). The daughter narrator is also reborn as she recuperates her early visual memories and reconceives herself as "a golden girl" encircled by parents who dance her a bright future. BaBa and MaMa would go on to produce five more children in the new world. Reunited in *China Men*, after a separation of many years, and "new" parents again, after the death of their first two children in China, these joint gods of creation look down from their tall ladder on the daughter they have made. In the shining room of revisited memory, what they see is good.

Life in Death: The Myth of Demeter the Mother and Her Daughter Persephone

The daughter's symbolic rebirth occurs on a silent and holy night that stands in stark contrast to a world at war and to the unholy birth that is the genesis of death and destruction in "No Name Woman."[43] For daughters who have been victimized, cultural myths that mirror and dignify their suffering can be therapeutic. Women who have turned to female spirituality for consolation or who find inspiration in its symbolic narratives have felt drawn to the mythic story of Demeter and Persephone (Jacobs, 144–145, 157–158). Its accounts of the mother who brings her daughter Persephone back from the underworld after she has been abducted, raped, and impregnated by the patriarchal figure Hades is especially apropos for daughters who may have suffered incest or abuse at the hands of their fathers. What is particularly relevant to my reading of the passage above is the symbolic name the daughter was given in the pre-Christian rites or mysteries of Eleusis that celebrated her rescue by her mother Demeter. Persephone was known as "she who shines in the dark." Her name gives a mythic depth and luster to the daughter narrator who basks briefly in the glow of her father's regard and who is visualized as a shining light amid the darkness and horror of war. As Eng so pertinently remarks, "Memories recalled during the light of day have the political [and we might now add spiritual] potential to take us someplace where we have never been before" (79)—in this case, a very ancient place indeed.

The visionary apex of the mother-daughter mysteries of Eleusis was the *Epopteia*—or state of having seen—thought to have commemorated the holy birth of a son and to have been staged dramatically as a sudden apparition of light out of unseeing darkness. Votaries were forbidden to reveal what they beheld, as the daughter narrator of "No Name Woman" is sworn to secrecy about the mystery of her aunt. *What* the initiates saw was less important than *how* the vision transformed their way of seeing and understanding. Similarly, the daughter's revisions of memory in *China Men* enable her to see her own birth in a different and more favorable light and, as a consequence, celebrate the birth of her two youngest brothers without the customary, though understandable, resentment that surfaces time and time again in *The Woman Warrior*. Mae Henderson regards creative writing as a dialogic and intertextual encounter not only with literary and imaginary others but with psychic Otherness allowing the subject to "see the other, but also to see what the other cannot see."[44] In other words, the daughter narrator may have become the eyes for her father—seeing what he lacked the insight and feeling to envisage and looking as she wished to be perceived.

The Mystery of Death in Life

In the mysteries of Eleusis, the central vision of holy birth was preceded by ritual banishment in which piglets, sacred to the mother Demeter and symbols of her violated daughter, were sacrificed, possibly by drowning.[45] In a parallel movement, *The Woman Warrior* begins with the banishment of "the precious only daughter," after she falls pregnant, to an "outcast table" in the house (14) and finally to the pigsty outside. Here she gives birth to a daughter whom she regards as "lovely as a young calf, a piglet, a little dog" (21), before drowning her in the family well. Raoul Vaneigem relates how affected Confucius was by the sight of piglets he noticed during his emissary travels in China. "I saw some piglets sucking on their dead mother. After a short while they shuddered and went away. They had sensed that she could no longer see them and that *she was not like them any more.* What they loved in their mother was not her body, but whatever it was that made her body live." [46]

The piglets made Confucius ponder how the parent shields the child from full awareness of mortality. Gerard Manley Hopkins described this awareness as "the blight man was born for" (l. 14), but Confucius saw that even lesser creatures in the animal world felt it with dread. In the direct and uncomplicated manner of all young things, the piglets can sense that the unresponsive mother is dead to them. A good deal of the daughter narrator's energies in the two books go into making her parents recognize her, and especially, into bringing her father back from the unseeing and dead land in which he dwells to the consternation of his family. After the birth of her youngest brother—the runt of the family—in *China Men*, the daughter narrator begins to realize that her father's denials, blank looks, and dreadful silences, as well as her mother's evasive answers, were often motivated by their protective instincts as parents. "Adults were always diverting us from the awful. They wanted to protect us, as I wanted to protect the baby, who a moment ago had been nothing and could easily slip back" (266). The piglets Confucius reputedly saw are object lessons in the horrible fact that life feeds off not only death, but what has been alive only moments before (Van Buren, 45).

BaBa's Journey into Exile

When BaBa set out on the road for the Gold Mountain in 1924, he did not know that he would never see his mother alive again, but she did, and shuddered as he went away. "'Don't go,' said Ah Po. 'You're never coming back.' And then she wept, having spoken his life" (*CM*, 48). He and his wife will not find a mountain piled high with gold in California, only the Chinese laundryman's "sheet mountain, a white shirt mountain, a dark shirt mountain, a work-pants mountain, a long underwear mountain, a short underwear mountain" surrounded by little hills of socks and handkerchiefs for good measure (*WW*, 97–98). In the elegiac intertext that follows her account of his life in America, "The Li Sao"—which she translates as "Sorrow after Departure and Sorrow in Estrangement"—the daughter compares her father to a figure he much admired, Ch'ü Yüan, "China's earliest known poet, a Homer" who wrote of his enforced exile from his homeland during the warring states period between the third and fourth centuries B.C.E. She explains that, "because he had expressed an unpopular opinion, [which was to advise the king against war] Ch'ü Yüan, also called Ch'ü P'ing, meaning 'Peace,' was banished. He had to leave the Center; he roamed in the outer world for the rest of his life, twenty years. He mourned that he had once been a prince, and now he was nothing" (256).[47]

In drawing this comparison, the daughter expressed her complicated feelings for her father. She wished to ennoble BaBa by likening him to a great poet, a great patriot, and a great pacifist and remind the reader of his high cultural credentials, though he was classified as an illiterate and uneducated "coolie" on his entry to America (*CM*, 45). But, in likening her father to a poet who "saw the entire world, but not his homeland" (257), who endured lifelong banishment, and who was doomed to drown himself, she also suggests that his fate may have born a perilous resemblance to that of his sister in "No Name Woman." Ironically, although he enforces his sister's perpetual punishment, which is to be erased from the living memory of the family, he follows her down the road to banishment. His daughter may have feared that he might also be tempted to put an end to his suffering and, like his sister and Ch'ü Yüan, take his own life.

Restoring the Father to Life

After his suicide, Ch'ü Yüan's poetic disciples stood by the riverbank crying, "Return, O Soul" (259). The daughter narrator fears that her own father is a "dead man walking"—a man who has lost his soul in America—and is equally concerned to devise some means of calling him back to life. In her narrative of "The Father from China," she tries to recuperate a Chinese cultural imaginary that gave meaning to his early life and delineate his psychic affiliation with this figurative world, even if he never returned physically to his homeland. She takes up his story at puberty, the age that is so potent and critical in both "No Name Woman" and "White Tigers." She depicts his journey at the age of fourteen to sit for "the qualifying test for the last Imperial Examination ever given" (24) in 1905 not only as an arduous initiation but also as a trial run for the epic journey he will later undertake to the New World and for the mental ordeal he will face during his interrogation by immigration officers at the detention center on Angel Island.[48]

Reclaiming the Father as a Poet

The stakes were high, for the Imperial Examinations could lead to a plum job in the civil service and the prospect of rank and title in the Chinese government (*CM*, 28). The top honors required the mental feats of a great oral poet such as Ch'ü Yüan. BaBa had two natural advantages: he was "very good at gambling," and he had a phenomenal memory (23). In America, he would capitalize on the first talent and dispense with the other "by forgetting the Chinese past" (14). While he remained in China, however, memory did not "hurt," but improved, his chances (Rabinowitz, 69). Though the well of remembrance and inspiration would later be blocked for him in *The Woman Warrior* and, intermittently, throughout *China Men*, he found the poetic words he had committed to memory "came tumbling out, like water, like grain" during his oral examination in front of a panel of mandarin scholars (27). He would go on to demonstrate his knowledge of Chinese characters and skill in calligraphy during a mammoth three-day writing session where he constructed "each word from top to bottom, left to right, water strokes, dots for flames, tailing gondolas for the boat words" and where he "wrote in many styles including The Beauty Adorns Her Hair with Blossoms and The Maid Apes Her Mistress" (28).[49] Little did he know that his mastery of the "feminine" arts of ornate and embellished writing would ill equip him for the sojourner's life of hard labor. "'I'm going as a worker if I can't go as a teacher,' BaBa said. His brothers laughed at him. Those frail hands lifting sledgehammers?" (48). BaBa did not have the last laugh. His skill with pen and ink, though, would come in unexpectedly handy when he managed a gambling house in Stockton and kept "track of the gamblers' schemes of words" and their lucky combinations of characters. "They had bet on those words. You had to be a poet to win, finding lucky ways words go together" (*CM*, 241; Rabine, 489–490).

Poetry as a Quest for Passionate Life

Vaneigem sees poetry as the radical action "which brings new realities into being" and suggests that what makes a man a poet is his "passionate quest for exuberant life" (200, 237), and it is in such a spirit that BaBa set out on foot for the imperial qualifying test. As he walked, he would see the landscape unfold its poetry like a scroll painting. He would look up at the trees above his head and read in their branches words of inspiration and encouragement. "'The snow goose of ambition stirs its wings,' Tu Fu had said on his way to the tests. 'I ride the great snow goose of my ambition'" (24).

If poetry is "the high point of the great gamble on everyday life" (Vaneigem, 200), BaBa's "great gamble," his one and only shot at the last Imperial Examination ever given, did not take him far. He would return home to the thankless job of village schoolmaster. The homeboys he taught had no sensibility or ear for verse. They "spoiled the songs of birds" that had enchanted him on his journey out. They obliged him to shrink "poems to fit the brains of peasant children, who were more bestial than animals" (39). Like his high school teacher son after him in "The Brother in Vietnam," he would find that teaching was destroying the pleasure and pride that he took in the intertextual skills of reading and writing (CM, 39, 279–280).[50] He would also find, to his horror, that "the boys were forcing him to turn literature into a weapon against them" (37). Guan Goong reigned as god of war and not literature in his classroom. Indeed, his daughter traces his nightmares and the bloodcurdling screams that disrupted his sleep back to the hateful experience of teaching students who "ran amok," "played war," and turned the school into "a crazy house" (39). She would describe her father losing all control as he thrashed a delinquent student with his rod. She would show her sympathy for the mounting frustration that drove him to this frenzy by making a pointed intertextual comparison between her father beating the boy until he felt like a rag doll in "The Father from China" and her bullying of a "China doll" classmate in "A Song for a Barbarian Reed Pipe" (CM, 40; WW, 156–160).

Hong Kingston would poignantly reminisce to Skenazy, "My father had a beautiful calligraphic hand, and when he was younger he was a poet, and has a lot of classical poetry memorized. He quite often draws his poetry, paints it; he also often says, 'I don't know why the poetry doesn't come to me any more. I love poetry so much.' . . . I find that incredibly sad, as a writer, that he waits for poems to come and they don't" ("Kingston at the University," 154–155). Sadder still, "The Father from China" suggests poetry stirred his blood as far back as early childhood. Even as a little boy, BaBa continually "'hummed' poems," his chest swelling with song, "playing with big words" while his older brothers teased him as a sissy and "poetry addict" (23–24). Had he won recognition as a poet and top honors as a mandarin scholar, "he would have had an easier life then and not come to the Gold Mountain. He did not 'fly' to Canton or Peiping" (28). In the original legend of the poet Ts'ai Yen, she looked up at the sky and saw migrating geese flying in the formation of the ideograph for home.[51] The "great snow goose" of BaBa's ambition barely lifted off the ground before it circled home and returned him to the job of village teacher. There "the word *poetry*... hit them like a mallet stunning cattle" (36), and his students began to kill the passionate inner life and aspirations centered around verse. He had been trained for a life of scholarly reflection in which "knowledge fell into place, moved from head, from heart, down his arm and out the fingers to converge at the tip of the brush" (27). Hong Kingston explained to Skenazy that the classical Chinese poet was "somebody who can write and sing and paint his poem. See how integrated that is? All those parts of your body are connected. You're not fragmented" ("Kingston at the University," 147). In the classroom BaBa could not connect with his students nor make them see how poetry illuminates the correspondences in the world. Where before poetry was an exercise that coordinated his body and composed his thoughts, whose words flowed out of what filled his heart (Matthew, 12.34–35), now it became "a mortification in his mouth" (36–37).

BaBa would "fly," but it was not on the soaring wings of his early ambition. He would flee the boys who harassed him and the murderous and suicidal thoughts that increasingly tormented him. "He shot them with an imaginary pistol. . . . Sometimes while standing in front of the bad boys, he pointed the imaginary pistol at his own head, and blew it open. . . . He also imagined lifting his arms and flying over their heads, out the door, and into the sky" (40–41). The men's stirring stories of the Gold Mountain would replace the poetry that had once uplifted him and send him out on the road into exile. Yet he would travel with the adventures of Yüeh Fei, the Patriot, for his guidebook (56), as the March girls would take Bunyan on their long pilgrim journey through life (*Little Women*, 12). His daughter would show her intertextual identification with him on this long journey by grafting Yüeh Fei's story onto Fa Mu Lan's. In carving the story of a poet her father revered into the body of *The Woman Warrior*'s text, Hong Kingston was indirectly paying tribute to the pain he had suffered in defense of poetry. Whereas Yüeh Fei's mother carved only four characters into his flesh, Fa Mu Lan's father cuts row upon row of words down her back until it is livid with wounds (*WW*, 38). "Character" is the English word for Chinese ideographs, but it also designates distinguishing or outstanding traits of personality. Norman Holland notes that this latter definition of "character" derives from the Greek *kharax*, meaning a pointed stake for inscribing a line or branding a surface.[52] Chinese characters are traditionally formed with soft brush strokes. Fa Mu Lan's father, however, switches from the soft ink brush used by a scholar-poet like BaBa to a thin, sharp knife that scores lasting marks closer to the Western understanding of character as tempered by experience and suffering. Parents who had the luxury of being doting mothers and fathers exercising a light hand in their original home may become heavy-handed immigrants particularly anxious to turn their children into tough survivors, even at the risk of inflicting lifelong scars. As the narrator says in "No Name Woman," her mother "tested our strength to establish realities. Those in the emigrant generations who could not reassert brute survival died young and far from home" (13).

Poetry's Grand Freedom

During his forced detention on Angel Island, the father would ironically recover a sense of "poetry's grand freedom" (Vaneigem, 193) when "he read the walls, which were covered with poems" of protest against incarceration, the unfair immigration laws, and the loneliness and isolation that rolled in with the thick fog over San Francisco Bay (55). He would write a "wonderful poem" in the darkness of the night "about wanting freedom," using his spit and tears as a prisoner to mix the ink (56). He would unexpectedly find the literary company he had sought at the imperial qualifying test, men who talked about books and about poetry as though they were vitally important (25). "'What is a poem exactly?' asked an illiterate man, a Gold Mountain Sojourner who had spent twenty years in America and was on his way back to his family. 'Let me give it a try,' he said" (57). Without realizing it, BaBa was learning—or his daughter was teaching him retrospectively—that you don't have to succeed as a mandarin scholar or a great oral bard like Ch'ü Yüan to have the gift of poetry. Indeed, she is correcting a major mistake that he made as a rural schoolmaster of boys who "spoke in the brute vulgate," which was to presume that "he had made a bad mistake translating literature into the common speech" (37). As I have shown in this intertextual study of *The Woman Warrior* and *China Men*, Hong Kingston's literary project involved "free translation" of the common speech of her family, and her intertextual writing aimed to keep the cadences of their oral dialect, oral poetry, and oral storytelling alive and to bridge the artificial division between high and low culture (Ching Sledge, "Oral Tradition," 145–147).

The Father's Further Poetic Discoveries

In America the father developed an eclectic interest in the moody modern verse of the Rainy Alley Poet and another Parisian sojourner Wang Tu Ching, in the protofeminist poetry of the old-timer Yüan Mei, and in the bitter laundry verses of the Chicago poet Wen I-to (61–63).[53] His efforts to place poetry as a vital activity at the center of everyday life would earn him the scorn of family and friends. His colleagues would use it as an excuse for cheating him out of his share of their New York laundry. "You were always reading when we were working" (73). His wife would complain, "The only thing you're trained for is writing poems. . . . I know you. . . . You poet. You scholar. You gambler. What use is any of that?" (247) and conveniently forget that, when a doctor in China, she had read the pulse of her patients like a poem of rhymed verse. "She stopped at a girl whose strong heart sounded like thunder within the earth, sending its power into her fingertips. . . . My mother could find no flaw in the beat; it matched her own, the real rhythm . . . of earth-sea-sky and the Chinese language" (*WW*, 76–77). No one at the time seemed to appreciate how extraordinary it was for a learned scholar to depart from classical tradition and explore contemporary Chinese poetry. Only his daughter comes to his defense and suggests, in *China Men*, that his interest in the poetry of cultural exile, racial protest, and immigrant discontent might be the political act of a freethinker. Like Ch'ü Yüan, her father turns to poetry in exile as a form of passive resistance. But then, as she was at pains to show in both "The Great Grandfather of the Sandalwood Mountains" and "The Grandfather of the Sierra Nevada Mountains," his Cantonese descent line was composed of "revolutionaries, nonconformists, people with fabulous imaginations" (*CM*, 87).

The Centrality of Poetry in the Father's Life

When her father finally succeeded in buying his own Chinese laundry in Stockton, he would "ink each piece of our own laundry with the word *Center*, to find out how we landed in a country where we are eccentric people" (*CM*, 14–15). The word he chose as a laundry tag is a translation of the character *zhong*, meaning center or middle. Where Goellnicht argues that this inscription "signifies BaBa's desire to return physically to China" ("Tang Ao in America," 238), my intertextual reading of *The Woman Warrior* and *China Men* traces instead his grim acceptance of the fact that he can never go back. Indeed, BaBa hushes his wife, fresh off the boat in New York, who asks when and if they can return. "'When do you think we'll go back to China? Do you think we'll go back to China?' 'Shh,' he said. 'Shh'" (*CM*, 71). So completely has he broken off relations with his past that his American-born children will wonder whether he ever really lived in China or simply "look[s] and talk[s] Chinese" (14).[54] Goellnicht proposes further that the father longs to recuperate the centric position of the Confucian patriarch and scholar and to escape eccentric marginalization as an immigrant worker in America (239). As I have already indicated, however, "The Father from China" shows that he never achieved this centric position. He tried and failed honorably in the attempt to "win the top honors" of a mandarin scholar.[55] What made him feel marginalized was not failing to achieve top place on the exams. It was losing the battle of literacy with his Chinese students and then the battle of ignorance with the American immigration officials who classified him as an illiterate "coolie" (CM, 28, 39, 45).

More important for my intertextual reading of the father, his laundry "name" tag contains a crucial allusion to the poetry that once constituted the *center* of his life. Indeed, the only full "free days" his daughter recollects him enjoying were absorbed in the study and discussion of figurative language with other scholars. He took the poet's love of discovery with him to the Gold Mountain. While other Californians prospected for gold, he carried on a more eccentric search for the hidden veins of connection between words. Though he often appears to be a hard and unfeeling father in *China Men*, BaBa did not lose his passion for verse. In his family he was always known as a "poet," even when his wife hurled the word at him as a term of blame and not praise; however, as Marilyn Chin remarked to Hong Kingston, both the serious writer and reader must live with the consciousness of marginality (93). The literary training so central to BaBa's formation of character and worldview meant "nothing" to others. Yet his daughter understands how poetry maketh the man. Indeed, as Vaneigem points out, "poetry is what the Greeks call *poiein*, 'making,' but 'making' restored to the purity of its moment of genesis—seen, in other words, from the point of view of the totality" (199–200). In an act of pure love, she now gives her father back this totality by reconsidering his whole life in the light of his love of poetry and suggesting that it set him apart and distinguished him as a "prince" among men like Ch'ü Yüan (256).

This finally is how the daughter narrator of *China Men* wishes her father to be remembered, or to paraphrase Kristeva, imagines him. Hong Kingston's mother would not let her husband forget that he "*used* to be a poet" (Skenazy, "Kingston at the University," 155). Hong Kingston's father told her that she was "living the life that he wanted to live" (Perry, 188). In "The Father from China," the daughter reminds the father of his early passion for poetry. In "The American Father," she shows most memorably that it is not the gambling house he managed in Stockton but the world he introduced her to there, a world made "plain and very beautiful" by poetry, that constitutes "the best of the father places" (240–241). At the same time, she suggests that the loss of this place in his life for poetry, and not the loss of his job per se, was a major cause of his later depression. In this place where life becomes plain and very beautiful,[56] she also takes hold of her father's hand for the first and only time in the two books.

To understand how much it means for the daughter to hold her father's hand at last in *China Men*, we must return to *The Woman Warrior* and reclaim the moment when she honored the mother who "led us out of nightmares and horror movies" and made her feel loved (73). At the start of *China Men*, the father is in no fit state to do the same for his children. He is the captive of nightmares and indeed prompts his daughter to imagine all manner of horrors. "We invented the terrible things you were thinking" (14). In "The Adventures of Lo Bun Sun," she allegorizes the desire that compels the older and more mature narrator of *China Men*—which is to take her father by the hand and lead *him* to a place of safety that he cannot find without her help. In her intertextual retelling of Robinson Crusoe, she depicts the "Friday" character, Sing Kay Ng, as finding his father not once but twice in the tale, and finally "leading his father by the hand as if he were a lady" (232–233).

In the succeeding section, "The American Father," she reshapes the dramatic moment when child and father finally make tangible contact. Now the elegant hand and long fingers—which his mother boasted were made to hold the scholar's pen—have been coarsened by years of hard manual labor and feel "splintery with calluses" to his daughter's touch (240). She unconsciously tried to reproduce the feel of her father's hand by her rough, tomboy behavior earlier in *The Woman Warrior*. "I wanted tough skin, hard brown skin. I had callused my hands" (158). Where her father's callused hand may have conditioned her to fight as a girl, it was also "a beautiful calligraphic hand" (Skenazy, "Kingston at the University," 154) that showed her how to see, to read, and to write. Indeed, when *The Woman Warrior* is intertextually factored into the reading of *China Men*, the father shows a different hand—with the calluses no longer simply the occupational trademark of the manual worker but the signature of the swordsman and calligrapher who remained conscious of his descent from "a family of eighty pole fighters" (*CM*, 28; *WW*, 50).[57]

She proudly recollects in "The American Father" how her father walked her down the "one small block" that constituted Stockton's Chinatown,[58] "pointed out sights," and taught her to look for the precious meaning hidden within her own hometown. "He named the plants, told time on the clocks, explained a neon sign in the shape of an owl. . . . He read signs, and I learned the recurring words: *Company, Association, Hui, Tong.* He greeted the old men with a finger to the hat" as he saluted his own children when they were little and impatiently waited his return home at the beginning of *China Men* (240, 7). She may also imagine that the Chinatown elders "whisper when he goes by" what was rumored about the "old busboy" in *The Woman Warrior*. "He's a swordsman who's killed fifty. He has a tong axe in his closet" (53).

When the father arrived with his daughter at the gambling house, he gave her "pen and ink" and guided her hand as she linked words of her own and traced "the lines and loops connecting the words" (241). She now uses these words to intertextually link—ink—her narrative life with her father's. Their walk together through Stockton's Chinatown to his gambling house recapitulates his own journey of youthful promise and hope through the China countryside to the mandarin qualifying test, where he was greeted by scholars who "quietly conversed" and "talked about winning and losing" the Imperial Exams (25, 28). What the mandarin scholars told him as a young man of fourteen become future strokes of luck, that is to say, calligraphic words that connect the past and the present, one generation to the next, and that the daughter can repeat as a consolation to her aging father. "Failing wasn't such a shame. Kai Li-shih hid in the gambling houses but became a poet nevertheless. Tu Fu, the Earthly Poet, sang about how he failed his third, fifth, and sixth tries" (28). At the end of "The American Father," she depicts her father taking up his hoe like Tu Fu, the Earthly Poet (306). She takes leave of him as he philosophically plants trees in his garden "that take years to fruit" (255) and sowing seed that grows to maturity in her own two narratives. Her father can rest in peace at last.

Conclusion

Respect for the power of poetry, the poetic correspondences that mysteriously weave the loving and consoling connections to others in life, and Hong Kingston's father and mother are all of a piece when *The Woman Warrior* and *China Men* are intertextually read back into relationship to one another. Hong Kingston invests great meaning in intertextuality's correlative activities of reading and writing. She told Shelley Fisher Fishkin that one of the first things she "ever noticed and loved about reading is that words can get through all kinds of barriers; they can get through skin color and culture" (163). The callused palms of her daughter narrator, the "splintery" hands of her father, the muscled body of her mother, and her parents' hard lives of punishing, physical labor (*CM*, 240; *WW*, 97) are reminders of the seemingly insuperable barriers she faced—not only of race, ethnicity, and culture, but also gender and generational differences, reinforced by obdurate silence and secrecy. Reading gave her the strength of conviction to believe that she could penetrate these barriers armed only with the words of the writer. She first exercised her power as a storyteller to fight with her parents and dispute their efforts to strike her aunt's name from the book of life. Over the course of the two books, however, she gradually turns to their defense, and her narratives begin to register a growing sympathy for their poignant, quixotic, and sometimes foolhardy gallantry.[59] In this intertextual study of *The Woman Warrior* and *China Men*, I have tried to show how the daughter narrator honored the hidden heroism of her family—so memorably exemplified by the fortitude both her mother and father showed during their years of grueling work in America.

Hong Kingston pointed out that she came to identify less with the militant courage of the woman warrior Fa Mu Lan than with the survival skills of Ts'ai Yen—the daughter of a scholar, the hostage of barbarians, and a captive soldier who cultivated the art of self-defense and poetry (Bonetti, 36–37; Skenazy, "Kingston at the University," 131–133). Though the author cited her increasing pacifism to explain her later shift in sympathy to Ts'ai Yen, I think that she was further drawn to this legendary figure because she saw her as a new hybrid warrior—a *s/wordfighter*—who combined the daughter's prowess with words, the mother's fighting talk, and the father's acute appreciation for poetry. Ts'ai Yen rode across the vast wastelands of Hun territory, and the daughter narrator rides into the Land of Women in *The Woman Warrior* and on into the Land of Men in *China Men*. Ts'ai Yen learned from her captors that the arrows of battle could be fixed with knock-whistles to make sounds of terror and death, but the reeds of these knock-whistles could also serve as flutes to pipe during the brief interludes of peace.[60] Her voice becomes not only her defensive weapon but her positive response to the men who are both her captors and only companions in the desert. Like a soprano in Chinese opera, she lifts her voice in "a song so high and clear, it matched the flutes" (*WW*, 186). Ts'ai Yen's song carries what Vaneigem eloquently calls "a clear consciousness of its poetry" (194). It also makes a political statement: that the writer must summon up the courage of the fighter—the courage she discovered finally in both her parents—to sing her stark song alone yet in a pure, high voice that reaches to others. In fact, Ts'ai Yen's song provides one answer to the question that the father is asked in China Men—"What is a poem exactly?" (57). They are words that have the spirit to pierce the hearts of those hardened, maimed, or wounded by the exhausting battles and power struggles of life.[61] Hillman calls them "words that carry soul accurately, where thought, image, and feeling interweave" (29)—as they do in intertextual writing and reading.

When Hong Kingston finished her two books, she felt that she had "gone as deeply into men's [and women's] psyches as I can" and concluded that she didn't find men and women "that different" (Pfaff, 17). Both women and men readers have quarreled with her vociferously over such a conclusion, and my own book was born out of a belief that this divisive gender criticism would end only when *The Woman Warrior* and *China Men* were shown intertextually to be connected, indeed, in their internal logic, inseparable from one another, like the family, friends, and associates who form an indestructible part of us. As the Freudian thinker Joan Riviere wisely and humbly acknowledged, our individual lives have been immeasurably enriched by relations with the men and women who were "emotionally important to us" and "are still with us and inseparable from us—the unconscious truth behind the words being that they are *in us* and part of us and therefore inseparable and available to us" (318, 320). I urge those who have been touched by Hong Kingston's work to avail themselves of the opportunity to see this inseparable truth by reading *The Woman Warrior* and *China Men* as they were first intended—indeed, as we were all intended to be— which is together.

Notes

1. Sigmund Freud, "Family Romances," in *On Sexuality: Three Essays on the Theory of Sexuality and Other Works*, vol. 7, edited by Angela Richards, translated by James Strachey (London: Penguin Books, 1991), 222.

2. See Cora Kaplan's discussion of the neurotic fantasies of the family romance, "Wicked Fathers: A Family Romance," in *Fathers: Reflections by Daughters*, edited by Ursula Owen, (New York: Pantheon, 1985), 146–147, and Leslie W. Rabine's discussion of the Freudian family romance in *China Men* in "No Lost Paradise: Social Gender and Symbolic Gender in the Writings of Maxine Hong Kingston," *Signs* 12 (1987), 480–482.

3. Marianne Hirsch argues, "The death or elimination of the father, the brother, the husband, the male lover . . . has become either a precondition or an important preoccupation of female plots." See *The Mother/Daughter Plot: Narrative, Psychoanalysis, Feminism* (Bloomington: Indiana University Press, 1989), 129. Boose and Flowers set out to redress the invisibility of the father-daughter narrative in their *Daughters and Fathers* (Baltimore: Johns Hopkins University Press, 1989). See their introductory remarks (2).

4. Jessica Benjamin ("A Desire of One's Own: Psychoanalytic Feminism and Intersubjective Space," in *Feminist Studies/Critical Studies: Issues, Terms and Contexts*, edited by Teresa de Lauretis [Bloomington: Indiana University Press, 1986]) refers to the intermediate experience of "being and playing *alone* in the presence of the other" (94).

5. Sue Ann Johnston suggested some parallels with Carroll's Alice books, in

"Empowerment through Mythological Imaginings in *Woman Warrior,*" *Biography—Hawaii* 16 (1993), 139, as does King-Kok Cheung, in *Articulate Silences: Hisaye Yamamoto, Maxine Hong Kingston, Joy Kogawa* (Ithaca, N.Y.: Cornell University Press, 1993), n. 21, 102. I will explore the correspondences at greater length below.

6. See Lewis Carroll's play on nominalism (the view that universals are mere names and do not correspond to reality) in his chapter on Humpty Dumpty and the wood where things have no names, in *Through the Looking-Glass and What Alice Found There, The Annotated Alice,* edited by Martin Gardner (London: Penguin Books, 1970), 225–227, 268–270 (which I will cite parenthetically).

7. In "Poet and Patriarch in Maxine Hong Kingston's *China Men,*" in *Autobiography and Questions of Gender,* edited by Shirley Neuman (London: F. Cass, 1991), Joseph Fichtelberg argues (181) that "this 'black sparkling eye of the planet' (239), so resonant with maternal imagery, redeems that other well poisoned, in *The Woman Warrior,* by the narrator's nameless aunt."

8. Kali Israel, "Asking Alice: Victorian and Other Alices in Contemporary Culture," in *Victorian Afterlife: Postmodern Culture Rewrites the Nineteenth Century,* edited by John Kucich and Dianne F. Sadoff (Minneapolis: University of Minnesota Press, 2000), 263, 260–262, 268, 275 n. 8, and 281.

9. In her Penguin edition of Louisa May Alcott's *Little Women* (New York: Penguin Books, 1989), xxxi (which I will cite parenthetically), Elaine Showalter notes that the novel was originally published in two volumes, the first in October 1868 and the second in April 1869. In 1880, they were combined into one book. Diane Simmons, in *Maxine Hong Kingston* (New York: Twayne Publishers, 1999), assumed that Hong Kingston was referring to Alcott's *Little Men* when she recalled coming across a "funny-looking little Chinamen" who made her feel her racial Otherness and exclusion from the white American canon (8).

10. In *Racial Castration: Managing Masculinity in Asian America* (Durham, N.C.: Duke University Press, 2001) David Eng, 57 notes how Hong Kingston revises the racist term "Chinaman" by devising a book title that creates "pluralization and space between *China* and *Men*" (57).

11. See the full electronic text of *Rose in Bloom,* Louisa May Alcott: Teacher Resource File (http://falcon.jmv.edu/~ramseyil/alcott.htm), chap. 2, "Old Friends with New Faces," chap. 9, "New Year's Calls," and chap. 13, "Both Sides."

12. Barbara Sicherman, "Reading *Little Women:* The Many Lives of a Text," in *Women's America: Refocusing the Past,* edited by Linda K. Kerber and Jane Sherron De Hart, 5th ed. (New York: Oxford University Press, 2000), 255, 253–254.

13. See Showalter's comments in her introduction to *Little Women* (xi) and Hong Kingston's discussion of the transcendentalists with Kay Bonetti ("An Interview with Maxine Hong Kingston" [1986], in *Conversations with Maxine Hong Kingston,* edited by Paul Skenazy and Tera Martin [Jackson: University Press of Mississippi, 1998], 39). Hereinafter, I shall refer to this collection of interviews as *Conversations.* See Elliott Shapiro's discussion of Hong Kingston's "dialogic relationship with the Euro-American canon" in "Authentic Watermelon: Maxine Hong Kingston's American Novel," *MELUS* 26 (2001), 11.

14. Louisa May Alcott, chap. 6, "A Firebrand," *Little Men* (New York: Signet Classic, 1986), 86.

15. Lynda M. Zwinger, *"Little Women:* The Legend of Good Daughters," in *Daughters, Fathers and the Novel: The Sentimental Romance of Heterosexuality* (Madison: University of Wisconsin Press, 1991), 61.

16. See Deborah L. Madsen, *The Woman Warrior and China Men.* Vol. 9 in *Gale Study Guides to Great Literature: Literary Masterpieces,* edited by R. Bland Lawson (Farmington Hills, Mich.: Gale, 2001), 21–27, for her summary of the characters in the two books.

17. This is Eng's description (60).

18. A birth date of 1915 would make him only nine when he goes out on the road in 1924. As Frederic Wakeman points out, even 1891 would have made him only fourteen when he sat the last Imperial civil service examination in 1905. See "Chinese Ghost Story" (in *Critical Essays on Maxine Hong Kingston,* edited by Laura E. Skandera-Trombley [New York: G. K. Hall, 1998], 209). (Hereinafter, I shall refer to this volume as *Critical Essays.*)

19. See Freud's lectures "Femininity," in *New Introductory Lectures on Psychoanalysis,* translated and edited by James Strachey (London: Penguin Freud Library, 1991), vol. 2: 162–163, where he argues that "the feminine situation is only established . . . if the wish for a penis is replaced by one for a baby, if, that is, a baby takes the place of a penis" and "The Sexual Aberrations" and "Fetishism" (vol. 7: 65–68 and 351–355, respectively), where he shows his fascination with the foot fetish as the simulation of a female penis, "the absence of which is deeply felt" (68) and as "a token of triumph over the threat of castration" (353). In *Racial Castration,* David Eng "analyzes the various ways in which the Asian American male is both materially and psychically feminized" and cites Freud's essay "Fetishism" as describing "a psychic process whereby the man attempts to obviate the trauma of sexual difference by seeing at the site of the female body a penis that is not there to see" (2).

20. David Willbern summarizes the theories of female development Freud proposed in "Femininity" and other essays on the theory of sexuality. See "Filia Oedipi: Father and Daughter in Freudian Theory," in *Daughters and Fathers,* edited by Lynda E. Boose and Betty S. Flowers (Baltimore: Johns Hopkins University Press, 1989), 77–79.

21. See Dorothy Dinnerstein, *The Mermaid and the Minotaur: Sexual Arrangements and Human Malaise* (New York: Harper Perennial, 1991), esp. 127, 149, where she deconstructed the psychological tendency to find fault with women, especially in their role of maternal caregivers. Janet Liebman Jacobs, *Victimized Daughters: Incest and the Development of the Female Self* (New York: Routledge, 1994), 15–26, also analyzes why daughter victims of paternal incest often displace their feelings of hatred and betrayal onto their mothers.

22. Rachel Lee, "Claiming Land, Claiming Voice, Claiming Canon: Institutionalized Challenges in Kingston's *China Men* and *The Woman Warrior,*" in *Reviewing Asian America: Locating Diversity,* edited by Wendy L. Ng, Soo-Young Chin, James S. Moy and Gary Y. Okihiro (Pullman: Washington State University Press, 1995), sees

this high-pitched voice as "the image of a woman thoroughly dispossessed of home and community" (156–157).

23. See Diane Simmons, "Maxine Hong Kingston's Woman Warrior and Shaman: Fighting Women in the New World," *Femspec* 2.1 (2000), who comments on the contradictions in the woman warrior (54). Although she rises up to support patriarchy, she is also a shameful reminder of how impotent male society has become if it must turn to a mere woman as a savior. Louise P. Edwards explores these contradictions at length, in *Men and Women in Qing China: Gender in the Red Chamber Dream* (Leiden: E. J. Brill, 1994), 92,102–103, 106, 112.

24. See Robert G. Lee, "*The Woman Warrior* as an Intervention in Asian American Historiography," in *Approaches to Teaching Kingston's* The Woman Warrior, edited by Shirley Geok-lin Lim (New York: Modern Language Association of America, 1991), 57.

25. See Geoffrey Chaucer's "The Pardoner's Tale," *The Canterbury Tales, The Works of Geoffrey Chaucer,* edited by F. N. Robinson, 2nd ed. (Boston: Houghton Mifflin, 1961), ll. 731–732, p. 152, and Kathryn Hellerstein, "In Exile in the Mother Tongue: Yiddish and the Woman Poet," in *Borders, Boundaries, and Frames: Essays in Cultural Criticism and Cultural Studies,* edited by Mae G. Henderson (London: Routledge, 1995), 72, who asks the question that haunts Chaucer's wandering Jew—where and what is "the country of my bones?"

26. Sigmund Freud, "The 'Uncanny,'" in Sigmund Freud, *Art and Literature,* edited by Albert Dickson, translated by James Strachey (London: Penguin Freud Library, 1990), vol. 14: 368.

27. Teresa C. Zackodnik, in "Photography and the Status of Truth in Maxine Hong Kingston's China," *MELUS* 22 (1997): 55–69 (reprinted at http://vweb. hwwilsonweb.com, and cited here [4]), notes how Ah Po tries to erase her husband from the family's formal group photo.

28. One possible reading of the no name woman's actions is that she wished to have a child of her own like her father Ah Goong and was willing to risk everything to satisfy this reproductive need.

29. See Angelika Bammer, "Mother Tongues and Other Strangers: Writing 'Family' across Cultural Divides," in *Displacements: Cultural Identities in Question* (Bloomington: Indiana University Press, 1994), 98.

30. In "The Most Popular Book in China" (in *Maxine Hong Kingston's The Woman Warrior: A Casebook,* edited by Sau-ling Cynthia Wong [New York: Oxford University Press, 1999]), Frank Chin satirizes *The Woman Warrior* as a "picture of Joan of Arc as a man forced to dress and act like a girl and castrated after ceremonial incestuous relations with his father to satisfy the perverse sexual lusts of her parents" (24).

31. Mary Gordon, "Mythic History: Review of *China Men,*" *New York Times Book Review,* 24 (June 15, 1980), 1, 24.

32. Madeleine Sorapure, "Representing Shame: The Culture of Confession," in *Writing Lives: American Biography and Autobiography,* edited by Hans Bak and Hans

Krabbendam (Amsterdam: VU University Press, 1998), 110–112. King-Kok Cheung notes Frank Chin's denunciation of the Christian confessional form used by writers of autobiographical fiction like Hong Kingston. See *"The Woman Warrior* versus *The Chinaman Pacific,"* in *Conflicts in Feminism,* edited by Marianne Hirsch and Evelyn Fox Keller (New York: Routledge, 1990), 237–238.

33. Tomo Hattori, "China Man Autoeroticism and the Remains of Asian America," *Novel* 31.2 (1998), 215–236 (reprinted at http://vweb.hwwilsonweb.com, pp. 1–11, esp. 9).

34. James Hillman, "Mythology as Family," in *The Essential James Hillman: A Blue Fire,* edited by Thomas Moore, reprint (London: Routledge: 1994), 211.

35. See Leigh Gilmore's discussion of Hong Kingston's creation story in "No Name Woman," in *Autobiographics: A Feminist Theory of Women's Self-Representation* (Ithaca, N.Y.: Cornell University Press, 1994), 163–172, and Cheung's in *Articulate Silences,* 112.

36. See Elaine Kim's remarks in *Asian American Literature: An Introduction to the Writings and Their Social Context* (Philadelphia: Temple University Press, 1982), 103, and her extended discussion of this issue in "'Such Opposite Creatures': Men and Women in Asian American Literature," *Michigan Quarterly Review* 29:1 (1990), 69–74.

37. See Frank Chin's argument, in "The Most Popular Book in China" (26–28), and David Eng's excellent summary of Chin's literary and cultural quarrel with Hong Kingston.

38. See Vikki Bell (*Interrogating Incest: Feminism, Foucault and the Law* [London: Routledge, 1993], 77), who quotes Florence Rush, *The Best Kept Secret: Sexual Abuse of Children* (New York: McGraw Hill, 1980), 116–117.

39. Diane Simmons, in *Maxine Hong Kingston,* writes disapprovingly of the father who "lives only for the moment" here and wants to look smart and prosperous. It is true that "Ed's glamorous life in New York proves to be an illusion" (74, 114), but I cannot begrudge him his fleeting pursuit of happiness, especially when the narrator can only recollect him having "seven free days" all to himself—when he took the qualifying test for the Imperial Exam (*CM,* 29).

40. See Linda Kauffman's review of *China Men,* in *Critical Essays,* 226.

41. Academics who privilege verbal over visual intelligence have sometimes overlooked the "great power" (*WW,* 25) vision and visual images have had in determining reality, especially for those with rudimentary linguistic skills such as withdrawn or tongue-tied children or Chinese immigrants with broken English. See Bammer's discussion in *Displacements,* 100–101. In her humane study of *Image as Insight: Visual Understanding in Western Christianity and Secular Culture* (Boston: Beacon Press, 1985), Margaret Miles speaks up for those who are invisible to an articulate ruling class because their "primary mode of understanding and relating to the world is not verbal" (xi).

42. Note that Ah Goong's father, Bak Goong, is entranced in "The Grandfather of the Sandalwood Mountains" by the hopeful Christmas story of "the baby being

born" and identifies with "the childless wise men searching for him and finding him" (113).

43. Sara Ruddick, *Maternal Thinking: Towards a Politics of Peace* (London: Women's Press, 1990), remarks that birth has often been appropriated metaphorically "in the service of death," its language perverted to celebrate acts of destruction (204–205).

44. Mae Gwendolyn Henderson, "Speaking in Tongues: Dialogics, Dialectics, and the Black Woman Writer's Literary Tradition, in *Women, Autobiography, Theory: A Reader,* edited by Sidonie Smith and Julia Watson (Madison: University of Wisconsin Press), 348–349.

45. For a full account of the Eleusinian mysteries sacred to the mother Demeter and her daughter Persephone, see Anne Baring and Jules Cashford, *The Myth of the Goddess: Evolution of an Image* (London: Viking Arkana, 1991), 368–390, esp. 369, 378, and 381.

46. Raoul Vaneigem includes this quote, which I have been unable to verify, in *The Revolution of Everyday Life,* translated by Donald Nicholson-Smith (London: Rebel Press/Left Bank Books, 1994), 246. The story may be fictitious, like Hong Kingston's, but it is nonetheless instructive.

47. Debra Shostak, "Maxine Hong Kingston's Fake Books," in *Critical Essays* (61–62), summarizes his history as does Simmons, in *Maxine Hong Kingston* (118–119, 24).

48. E. D. Huntley, *Maxine Hong Kingston: A Critical Companion* (Westport, Conn.: Greenwood Press, 2001), compares BaBa's epic journey to that of Aeneas (132). Aeneas, however, carried his father Anchises on his back, whereas it is the daughter narrator who "carries" her father in *China Men.* See Linda Ching Sledge's essay, "Maxine Hong Kingston's *China Men:* The Family Historian as Epic Poet," *Melus* 7.4 (1980), 4, 7–8, 18.

49. As Rabine notes "Writing belongs to men privileged to express the feminine within them" (491).

50. As Mary Gordon remarks in her review of *China Men,* "His pedagogical failures ring sickeningly true to anyone who has ever had a bad day's teaching" (24). See Fichtelberg's comparison of father and son (181–183).

51. In her "Personal Statement," in Lim's *Approaches to Teaching Kingston's* The Woman Warrior, Hong Kingston regretted not adding this point to "A Song for a Barbarian Reed Pipe" (25). Two years before, in 1989, she had told Skenazy that "there were things that I left out of [Ts'ai Yen's] story. She was far from home and she was lonely among the barbarians, and she would look at the geese going by. In China they call them "home flying geese" because they seem to form . . . Chinese words. . . . She made a song that the geese are writing letters home for her and they are taking her letters home" ("Kingston at the University," in *Conversations,* 132–133).

52. Norman N. Holland, "Not So Little Hans: Identity and Aging," in *Memory and Desire: Aging-Literature-Psychoanalysis,* edited by Kathleen Woodward and Murray M. Schwartz (Bloomington: Indiana University Press, 1986), 52.

53. See Gregory Lee's account of the Rainy Alley Poet in *Dai Wangshu: The Life and Poetry of A Chinese Modernist* (Hong Kong: Chinese University Press, 1989), especially 1–20 and 139–159.

54. Hong Kingston agreed with Rabinowitz's reading of one of the differences between the two books: "China is a landscape inhabited, at least in the narratives, by the women and their myths, and the Gold Mountain, America, is really where the men are and that's where history is" (69). See "Eccentric Memories: A Conversation with Maxine Hong Kingston," in *Conversations*.

55. If the Imperial Exams had not been discontinued, the narrator suggests the father could have hoped to succeed in the relatively "small potato" post of "a scribe or a bookkeeper" (*CM*, 41).

56. Hong Kingston's comment on the song in which Ts'ai Yen imagined that the wild geese were carrying her letters home illustrates the spirit of her poetic insight in this passage of *China Men*. "That is so beautiful. Sometimes life is so evident and ordinary that you fail to recognize something special, you don't see it" (Skenazy, "Kingston at the University," in *Conversations*, 133).

57. The Wudan woman and man warrior in Ang Lee's acclaimed film *Crouching Tiger, Hidden Dragon* touch hands roughened and callused by martial arts and sword fighting, and recognize that the graceful hand movements and controlled strength and swiftness required in calligraphy make it very similar to fencing. Indeed in calligraphy, the name of the woman warrior Shu Lien resembles a sword. Readers will also recall that Fa Mu Lan's father uses the thin blade, which is the mark of a skilled swordsman, to cut the calligraphic words of revenge into her back (*WW*, 38).

58. In an interview with Skenazy appropriately entitled "Coming Home," Hong Kingston remarked that despite the smallness of Stockton's Chinatown, it was an "amazing" place with a palpable "communal spirit" radiating out from its center (114). In *Conversations*.

59. Hong Kingston indicated to William Satake Blauvelt ("Talking with the Woman Warrior," in *Conversations*) that the reading of literature was a disaster for characters like Don Quixote because "they went out into the real world to try to apply their knowledge"—and failed—as did her father in *China Men* (79).

60. See Hong Kingston's discussion of the arrow knockwhistles with Skenazy ("Kingston at the University," in *Conversations*, 132–133). Here she says that Ts'ai Yen took the reeds that were used for the whistles and made them into flutes. On the closing pages of *The Woman Warrior* (185–186), the narrator depicts the barbarians as the makers of flutes and Ts'ai Yen as the maker of lyrical poetry that ironically captures her captors' sounds.

61. "How could it be otherwise," Raoul Vaneigem maintains, "when poetry and power are irreconcilable" because "prestige and humiliation, authority and submission [are] the only music to which the will to power can dance" (200, 239).

Works Cited

Ahern, Emily M. "The Power and Pollution of Chinese Women." In *Women in Chinese Society*, edited by Margery Wolf and Roxane Witke, 193–214. Stanford, Calif.: Stanford University Press, 1975.

Alcott, Louisa May. *Little Men*. New York: Signet Classic, 1986.

———. *Little Women*. Edited by Elaine Showalter. New York: Penguin Books, 1989.

———. *Rose in Bloom*. Louisa May Alcott: Teacher Resource File. Posted at http://falcon.jmv.edu/~ramseyil/alcott.htm.

Arens, W. *The Original Sin: Incest and Its Meaning*. New York: Oxford University Press, 1986.

Bak, Hans, and Hans Krabbendam, eds. *Writing Lives: American Biography and Autobiography*. Amsterdam: VU University Press, 1998.

Bakhtin, M. M. *The Dialogic Imagination: Four Essays*. Edited by Michael Holquist. Translated by Caryl Emerson and Michael Holquist. Austin: University of Texas Press, 1981.

Bammer, Angelika. "Mother Tongues and Other Strangers: Writing 'Family' across Cultural Divides." In *Displacements: Cultural Identities in Question*, edited by Angelika Bammer, 90–109. Bloomington: Indiana University Press, 1994.

———, ed. *Displacements: Cultural Identities in Question*. Bloomington: Indiana University Press, 1994.

Baring, Anne, and Jules Cashford. *The Myth of the Goddess: Evolution of an Image*. London: Viking Arkana, 1991.

Bell, Vikki. *Interrogating Incest: Feminism, Foucault and the Law*. London: Routledge, 1993.

Benjamin, Jessica. "A Desire of One's Own: Psychoanalytic Feminism and Intersubjective Space." In *Feminist Studies/Critical Studies: Issues, Terms and Contexts*, edited by Teresa de Lauretis, 78–101. Bloomington: Indiana University Press, 1986.

Blau, Herbert. "The Makeup of Memory in the Winter of Our Discontent." In *Memory and Desire: Aging-Literature-Psychoanalysis*, edited by Kathleen Woodward and Murray M. Schwartz, 13–36. Bloomington: Indiana University Press, 1986.

Blauvelt, William Satake. "Talking with the Woman Warrior" [1989]. In *Conversations with Maxine Hong Kingston*, edited by Paul Skenazy and Tera Martin, 77–85. Jackson: University Press of Mississippi, 1998.

Bonetti, Kay. "An Interview with Maxine Hong Kingston" [1986]. In *Conversations with Maxine Hong Kingston*, edited by Paul Skenazy and Tera Martin, 33–46. Jackson: University Press of Mississippi, 1998.

Boose, Lynda E. "The Father's House and the Daughter in It: The Structures of Western Culture's Daughter-Father Relationship." In *Daughters and Fathers*, edited by Lynda E. Boose and Betty S. Flowers, 19–74. Baltimore: Johns Hopkins University Press, 1989.

Boose, Lynda E., and Betty S. Flowers, eds. *Daughters and Fathers*. Baltimore: Johns Hopkins University Press, 1989.

Brée, Germain. "Foreword." In *Life/Lines: Theorizing Women's Autobiography*, edited by Bella Brodzki and Celeste Schenck, ix–xii. Ithaca, N.Y.: Cornell University Press, 1998.

Brodzki, Bella, and Celeste Schenck, eds. *Life/Lines: Theorizing Women's Autobiography*. Ithaca, N.Y.: Cornell University Press, 1988.

Brownmiller, Susan. "Susan Brownmiller Talks with Maxine Hong Kingston, Author of *The Woman Warrior*." In *Maxine Hong Kingston's* The Woman Warrior: *A Casebook*, edited by Sau-ling Cynthia Wong, 173–179. New York: Oxford University Press, 1999.

Byatt, A. S. *Possession: A Romance*. London: Vintage, 1991.

Camden, Vera J., ed. *Compromise Formations: Current Directions in Psychoanalytic Literature*. Kent, Ohio: Kent State University Press, 1989.

Campbell, Joseph, with Bill Moyers. *The Power of Myth*. Edited by Betty Sue Flowers. New York: Doubleday, 1988.

Chan, Jeffrey Paul. "The Mysterious West (and Diane Johnson's Reply)." In *Critical Essays on Maxine Hong Kingston*, edited by Laura E. Skandera-Trombley, 84–87. New York: G. K. Hall, 1998.

Chan, Jeffrey Paul, Frank Chin, Lawson Fusao Inada, and Shawn Wong, eds. *The Big Aiiieeeee*. New York: Meridian, 1991.

Chaucer, Geoffrey. "The Pardoner's Tale." In *The Canterbury Tales: The Works of Geoffrey Chaucer*, 2nd ed. Edited by F. N. Robinson, 150–155. Boston: Houghton Mifflin, 1961.

Cheung, King-Kok. *Articulate Silences: Hisaye Yamamoto, Maxine Hong Kingston, Joy Kogawa*. Ithaca, N.Y.: Cornell University Press, 1993.

———. "*The Woman Warrior* versus *The Chinaman Pacific*: Must a Chinese American Critic Choose between Feminism and Heroism?" In *Conflicts in Feminism*, edited by Marianne Hirsch and Evelyn Fox Keller, 234–251. New York: Routledge, 1990. (Reprinted in *Critical Essays on Maxine Hong Kingston*, edited by Laura E. Skandera-Trombley, 107–124. New York: G. K. Hall, 1998, and in *Maxine Hong Kingston's* The Woman Warrior: *A Casebook*, edited by Sau-ling Cynthia Wong, 113–133. New York: Oxford University Press, 1999.)

Chin, Frank. "The Most Popular Book in China." In *Maxine Hong Kingston's* The Woman Warrior: *A Casebook*, edited by Sau-ling Cynthia Wong, 23–28. New York: Oxford University Press, 1999.

Chin, Marilyn. "Writing the Other: A Conversation with Maxine Hong Kingston"

[1989]. In *Conversations with Maxine Hong Kingston*, edited by Paul Skenazy and Tera Martin, 86–103. Jackson: University Press of Mississippi, 1998.

Chodorow, Nancy. *The Reproduction of Mothering: Psychoanalysis and the Sociology of Gender*. Berkeley: University of California Press, 1978.

Chu, Patricia. "'The Invisible World the Emigrants Built': Cultural Self-Inscription and the Antiromantic Plots of *The Woman Warrior*." *Diaspora* 2:1 (1992): 95–115.

Cirlot, J. E. *A Dictionary of Symbols*, 2nd ed. Translated by Jack Sage. London: Routledge, 1993.

Cixous, Hélène. "The Laugh of the Medusa." Translated by Keith Cohen and Paula Cohen. In *New French Feminisms*, edited by Elaine Marks and Isabelle de Courtivron, 245–264. Hemel Hempstead, Herts.: Harvester Wheatsheaf, 1981.

Cixous, Hélène, and Catherine Clément. *The Newly Born Woman*. Introduction by Sandra M. Gilbert. Translated by Betsy Wing. Vol. 24 of *Theory and History of Literature*, edited by Wlad Godzich and Jochen Schulte-Sasse. Minneapolis: University of Minnesota Press, 1991.

Clayton, Jay, and Eric Rothstein. "Figures in the Corpus: Theories of Influence and Intertextuality." In *Influence and Intertextuality in Literary History*, edited by Jay Clayton and Eric Rothstein, 3–36. Madison: University of Wisconsin Press, 1991.

———, eds. *Influence and Intertextuality in Literary History*. Madison: University of Wisconsin Press, 1991.

Culley, Margo, ed. *American Women's Autobiography: Fea(s)ts of Memory*. Madison: University of Wisconsin Press, 1992.

Dinnerstein, Dorothy. *The Mermaid and the Minotaur: Sexual Arrangements and Human Malaise*. New York: Harper Perennial, 1991.

Doane, A. N. "Oral Texts, Intertexts, and Intratexts: Editing Old English." In *Influence and Intertextuality in Literary History*, edited by Jay Clayton and Eric Rothstein, 75–113. Madison: University of Wisconsin Press, 1991.

Edwards, Louise P. *Men and Women in Qing China: Gender in the Red Chamber Dream*. Leiden: E. J. Brill, 1994.

Eliot, T. S. "Little Gidding—1942," *Four Quartets*, 214–223. *Collected Poems, 1909–1962*. London: Faber and Faber, 1963.

Eng, David L. *Racial Castration: Managing Masculinity in Asian America*. Durham, N.C.: Duke University Press, 2001.

Felman, Shoshana. *What Does a Woman Want? Reading and Sexual Difference*. Baltimore: Johns Hopkins University Press, 1993.

Fichtelberg, Joseph. "Poet and Patriarch in Maxine Hong Kingston's *China Men*." In *Autobiography and Questions of Gender*, edited by Shirley Neuman, 166–185. London: F. Cass, 1991.

Fisher Fishkin, Shelley. "Interview with Maxine Hong Kingston" [1990]. In *Conversations with Maxine Hong Kingston*, edited by Paul Skenazy and Tera Martin, 159–167. Jackson: University Press of Mississippi, 1998.

Freud, Sigmund. *Art and Literature.* Vol. 14. Edited by Albert Dickson. Translated by James Strachey. London: Penguin Freud Library, 1990.

———. *New Introductory Lectures on Psychoanalysis.* Vol. 2. Edited and translated by James Strachey. London: Penguin Freud Library, 1991.

———. *On Sexuality: Three Essays on the Theory of Sexuality and Other Works.* Vol. 7. Edited by Angela Richards. Translated by James Strachey. London: Penguin Freud Library, 1991.

———. *The Interpretation of Dreams.* Vol. 4. Edited by Angela Richards. Translated by James Strachey. London: Penguin Freud Library, 1991.

Friedman, Susan Stanford. "Weavings: Intertextuality and the (Re)birth of the Author." In *Influence and Intertextuality in Literary History,* edited by Jay Clayton and Eric Rothstein, 146–178. Madison: University of Wisconsin Press, 1991.

Froula, Christine. "The Daughter's Seduction: Sexual Violence and Literary History." In *Daughters and Fathers,* edited by Lynda E. Boose and Betty S. Flowers, 111–135. Baltimore: Johns Hopkins University Press, 1989.

Frye, Joanne S. "*The Woman Warrior:* Claiming Narrative Power, Recreating Female Selfhood." In *Faith of a (Woman) Writer,* edited by Alice Kessler Harris and William McBrien, 293–301. Westport, Conn.: Greenwood Press, 1988.

Gardner, Martin, ed. *The Annotated Alice: Alice's Adventures in Wonderland and through the Looking Glass.* By Lewis Carroll. London: Penguin Books, 1970.

Gay, Peter. *Freud: A Life for Our Time.* New York: Doubleday Anchor, 1988.

Genette, Gérard. *Palimpsests: Literature in the Second Degree.* Translated by Channa Newman and Claude Doubrinsky. Foreword by Gerald Prince. Lincoln: University of Nebraska Press, 1997.

Gilmore, Leigh. *Autobiographics: A Feminist Theory of Women's Self-Representation.* Ithaca, N.Y.: Cornell University Press, 1994.

Goellnicht, Donald C. "Father Land and/or Mother Tongue: The Divided Female Subject in Kogawa's *Obasan* and Hong Kingston's *The Woman Warrior.*" In *Redefining Autobiography in Twentieth-Century Women's Fiction: An Essay Collection,* edited by Janice Morgan, Colette T. Hall, and Carol L. Snyder, 119–134. New York: Garland, 1991.

———. "Tang Ao in America: Male Subject Positions in *China Men.*" In *Critical Essays on Maxine Hong Kingston,* edited by Laura E. Skandera-Trombley, 229–245. New York: G. K. Hall, 1998.

Goldenberg, Naomi R. *Resurrecting the Body: Feminism, Religion, and Psychoanalysis.* New York: Crossroad, 1993.

Gordon, Mary. "Mythic History: Review of *China Men.*" *New York Times Book Review* 24 (June 15, 1980): 1, 24.

Haaken, Janice. "The Recovery of Memory, Fantasy, and Desire in Women's Trauma Stories: Feminist Approaches to Sexual Abuse and Psychotherapy." In *Women, Autobiography, Theory: A Reader,* edited by Sidonie Smith and Julia Watson, 352–361. Madison: University of Wisconsin Press.

Hand, Seán. "Missing you: Intertextuality, transference and the language of love."

In *Intertextuality: Theories and practices,* edited by Michael Worton and Judith Still, 79–91. Manchester: Manchester University Press, 1990.

Harris, Alice Kessler, and William McBrien, eds. *Faith of a (Woman) Writer.* Westport, Conn.: Greenwood Press, 1988.

Harvey, Elizabeth D. *Ventriloquized Voices: Feminist Theory and English Renaissance Texts.* London: Routledge, 1992.

Hattori, Tomo. "China Man Autoeroticism and the Remains of Asian America." *Novel* 31.2 (1998): 215–236. (Reprinted at http://vweb.hwwilsonweb.com, pp. 1–11.)

Hawthorne, Nathaniel. *The Scarlet Letter and Selected Tales.* London: Penguin Classics, 1986.

Hellerstein, Kathryn. "In Exile in the Mother Tongue: Yiddish and the Woman Poet." In *Borders, Boundaries, and Frames: Essays in Cultural Criticism and Cultural Studies,* edited by Mae G. Henderson, 64–106. London: Routledge, 1995.

Henderson, Mae G. "Speaking in Tongues: Dialogics, Dialectics, and the Black Woman Writer's Literary Tradition." In *Women, Autobiography, Theory: A Reader,* edited by Sidonie Smith and Julia Watson, 342–351. Madison: University of Wisconsin Press.

———, ed. *Borders, Boundaries, and Frames: Essays in Cultural Criticism and Cultural Studies.* London: Routledge, 1995.

Hillman, James. *The Essential James Hillman: A Blue Fire.* Edited by Thomas Moore. London: Routledge, 1994.

Hirsch, Marianne. *The Mother/Daughter Plot: Narrative, Psychoanalysis, Feminism.* Bloomington: Indiana University Press, 1989.

Hirsch, Marianne, and Evelyn Fox, eds. *Conflicts in Feminism.* New York: Routledge, 1990.

Holland, Norman N. "Not So Little Hans: Identity and Aging." In *Memory and Desire: Aging-Literature-Psychoanalysis,* edited by Kathleen Woodward and Murray M. Schwartz, 51–75. Bloomington: Indiana University Press, 1986.

———. *The Dynamics of Literary Response.* New York: Oxford University Press, 1968.

Hong Kingston, Maxine. *China Men.* New York: Vintage Books, 1989.

———. "Cultural Mis-readings by American Reviewers." In *Critical Essays on Maxine Hong Kingston,* edited by Laura E. Skandera-Trombley, 95–103. New York: G. K. Hall, 1998.

———. *The Woman Warrior: Memoirs of a Girlhood among Ghosts.* London: Picador, 1981.

Hongo, Garrett. "Introduction: Culture Wars in Asian America." In *Under Western Eyes: Personal Essays from Asian America,* edited by Garrett Hongo, 1–32. New York: Doubleday Anchor, 1995.

———, ed. *Under Western Eyes: Personal Essays from Asian America.* New York: Doubleday Anchor, 1995.

Hopkins, Gerard Manley. "Spring and Fall: To a Young Child." 50. *Poems and Prose.* Baltimore: Penguin, 1963.

Horton, Karen. "*Honolulu* Interview: Maxine Hong Kingston" [1977]. In *Conversa-*

tions with *Maxine Hong Kingston,* edited by Paul Skenazy and Tera Martin, 5–13. Jackson: University Press of Mississippi, 1998.

Hoy, Jody. "To Be Able to See the Tao" [1986]. In *Conversations with Maxine Hong Kingston,* edited by Paul Skenazy and Tera Martin, 47–66. Jackson: University Press of Mississippi, 1998.

Huntley, E. D. *Maxine Hong Kingston: A Critical Companion.* Westport, Conn.: Greenwood Press, 2001.

Hutcheon, Linda. "Creative Collaboration: Introduction." In *Profession 2001,* edited by Phyllis Franklin, 4–6. New York: Modern Language Association of America, 2001.

Irigaray, Luce. *je, tu, nous: Toward a Culture of Difference.* Translated by Alison Martin. New York: Routledge, 1993.

Islas, Arturo, with Marilyn Yalom. "Interview with Maxine Hong Kingston" [1980]. In *Conversations with Maxine Hong Kingston,* edited by Paul Skenazy and Tera Martin, 21–32. Jackson: University Press of Mississippi, 1998.

Israel, Kali. "Asking Alice: Victorian and Other Alices in Contemporary Culture." In *Victorian Afterlife: Postmodern Culture Rewrites the Nineteenth Century,* edited by John Kucich and Dianne F. Sadoff, 252–287. Minneapolis: University of Minnesota Press, 2000.

Jacobs, Janet Liebman. *Victimized Daughters: Incest and the Development of the Female Self.* New York: Routledge, 1994.

Johnson, Diane. "Ghosts." In *Critical Essays on Maxine Hong Kingston,* edited by Laura E. Skandera-Trombley, 79–83. New York: G. K. Hall, 1998.

Johnson, Kay Ann. *Women, the Family, and Peasant Revolution in China.* Chicago: University of Chicago Press, 1983.

Johnston, Sue Ann. "Empowerment through Mythological Imaginings in *Woman Warrior.*" *Biography—Hawaii* 16.2 (1993): 136–146.

Kaplan, Cora. Wicked Fathers: A Family Romance." In *Fathers: Reflections by Daughters,* edited by Ursula Owen, 133–151. London: Virago, 1983.

Kauffman, Linda. "China Men." In *Critical Essays on Maxine Hong Kingston,* edited by Laura E. Skandera-Trombley, 223–226. New York: G. K. Hall, 1998.

Kim, Elaine H. *Asian American Literature: An Introduction to the Writings and Their Social Context.* Philadelphia: Temple University Press, 1982.

———. "'Such Opposite Creatures': Men and Women in Asian American Literature." *Michigan Quarterly Review* 29.1 (1990): 68–93.

Kristeva, Julia. *About Chinese Women.* Translated by Anita Barrows. London: Marion Boyars, 1977.

———. *Desire in Language: A Semiotic Approach to Literature and Art.* Edited by Leon S. Roudiez. Translated by Thomas Gora, Alice Jardine, and Leon S. Roudiez. New York: Columbia University Press, 1980.

———. "Julia Kristeva Interview with Rosalind Coward," *ICA Documents* (1984): 22–27.

———. *Julia Kristeva Interviews.* Edited by Ross Mitchell Guberman. New York: Columbia University Press, 1991.

————. *The Kristeva Reader.* Edited by Toril Moi. Oxford: Blackwell, 1992.

————. *Tales of Love.* Translated by Leon S. Roudiez. New York: Columbia University Press, 1987.

Kucich, John, and Dianne F. Sadoff, eds. *Victorian Afterlife: Postmodern Culture Rewrites the Nineteenth Century.* Minneapolis: University of Minnesota Press, 2000.

Lee, Gregory. *Dai Wangshu: The Life and Poetry of a Chinese Modernist.* Hong Kong: Chinese University Press, 1989.

Lee, Rachel. "Claiming Land, Claiming Voice, Claiming Canon: Institutionalized Challenges in Kingston's *China Men* and *The Woman Warrior.*" In *Reviewing Asian America: Locating Diversity,* edited by Wendy L. Ng, Soo-Young Chin, James S. Moy, and Gary Y. Okihiro, 147–159. Pullman: Washington State University Press, 1995.

Lee, Robert G. "*The Woman Warrior* as an Intervention in Asian American Historiography." In *Approaches to Teaching Kingston's* The Woman Warrior, edited by Shirley Geok-lin Lim, 52–63. New York: Modern Language Association of America, 1991.

Leonard, John. "In Defiance of 2 Worlds." In *Critical Essays on Maxine Hong Kingston,* edited by Laura E. Skandera-Trombley, 77–78. New York: G. K. Hall, 1998.

Lessing, Doris. "What Good Times We All Had Then." In *Fathers: Reflections by Daughters,* edited by Ursula Owen, 79–88. London: Virago, 1983.

Li, David Leiwei. "Re-presenting *The Woman Warrior:* An Essay of Interpretative History." In *Critical Essays on Maxine Hong Kingston,* edited by Laura E. Skandera-Trombley, 182–203. New York: G. K. Hall, 1998.

Lim, Geok-lin, Shirley. "'Growing with Stories': Chinese American Identities, Textual Identities (Maxine Hong Kingston)." In *Teaching American Ethnic Literatures: Nineteen Essays,* edited by John R. Maitino and David R. Peck, 273–291. Albuquerque: University of New Mexico Press, 1996.

————. "The Tradition of Chinese American Women's Life Stories: Thematics of Race and Gender in Jade Snow Wong's *Fifth Chinese Daughter* and Maxine Hong Kingston's *The Woman Warrior.*" In *American Women's Autobiography: Fea(s)ts of Memory,* edited by Margo Culley, 252–267. Madison: University of Wisconsin Press, 1992

————, ed. *Approaches to Teaching Kingston's* The Woman Warrior. New York: Modern Language Association of America, 1991.

Ling, Amy. "Maxine Hong Kingston and the Dialogic Dilemma of Asian American Writers." In *Critical Essays on Maxine Hong Kingston,* edited by Laura E. Skandera-Trombley, 168–181. New York: G. K. Hall, 1998.

Loewald, Hans W. "The Waning of the Oedipus Complex." In *Papers on Psychoanalysis,* 384–405. New Haven, Conn.: Yale University Press, 1980.

Lorde, Audre. "Poetry Is Not a Luxury." In *Sister Outsider: Essays and Speeches,* 36–39. Freedom, Calif.: Crossing Press, 1984.

Madsen, Deborah L. The Woman Warrior *and* China Men. *Gale Study Guides to Great Literature: Literary Masterpieces.* Vol. 9. Edited by R. Bland Lawson. Farmington Hills, Mich.: Gale, 2001.

Maitino, John, and David R. Peck, eds. *Teaching American Ethnic Literatures: Nineteen Essays*. Albuquerque: University of New Mexico Press, 1996.

Marks, Elaine, and Isabelle de Courtivron, eds. *New French Feminisms*. Hemel Hempstead, Herts.: Harvester Wheatsheaf, 1981.

Marvell, Andrew. "The Garden." *Complete Poetry*. Edited by George de F. Lord, 48–50. New York: Modern Library, 1968.

Matus, Jill. *Toni Morrison*. Manchester: Manchester University Press, 1998.

Miles, Margaret. *Image as Insight: Visual Understanding in Western Christianity and Secular Culture*. Boston: Beacon Press, 1985.

Miller, Elise. "Kingston's *The Woman Warrior*: The Object of Autobiographical Relations." In *Compromise Formations: Current Directions in Psychoanalytic Literature*, edited by Vera J. Camden, 138–154. Kent, Ohio: Kent State University Press, 1989.

Miller, Nancy K. "Arachnologies: The Woman, the Text, and the Critic." In *The Poetics of Gender*, edited by Nancy K. Miller, 270–295. New York: Columbia University Press, 1986.

———, ed. *The Poetics of Gender*. New York: Columbia University Press, 1986.

Morante, Linda. "From Silence to Song: The Triumph of Maxine Hong Kingston." *Frontiers: A Journal of Women's Studies* 9.2 (1987): 78–82.

Morgan, Janice, Colette T. Hall, and Carol L. Snyder, eds. *Redefining Autobiography in Twentieth-Century Women's Fiction: An Essay Collection*. New York: Garland, 1991.

Mylan, Sheryl A. "The Mother as Other: Orientalism in Maxine Hong Kingston's *The Woman Warrior*." In *Women of Color: Mother-Daughter Relationships in Twentieth-Century Literature*, edited by Elizabeth Brown-Guillory, 132–152. Austin: University of Texas Press, 1996.

Neuman, Shirley, ed. *Autobiography and Questions of Gender*. London: F. Cass, 1991.

Ng, Wendy L., Soo-Young Chin, James S. Moy, and Gary Y. Okihiro, eds. *Reviewing Asian America: Locating Diversity*. Pullman: Washington State University Press, 1995.

Nishime, LeiLani. "Engendering Genre: Gender and Nationalism in *China Men* and *The Woman Warrior*." In *Critical Essays on Maxine Hong Kingston*, edited by Laura E. Skandera-Trombley, 261–275. New York: G. K. Hall, 1998.

Outka, Paul. "Publish or Perish: Food, Hunger, and Self-Construction in Maxine Hong Kingston's *The Woman Warrior*." *Contemporary Literature* 38 (1997): 447–482. (Reprinted at http://wveb.hwwilsonweb.com, pp. 1–16.)

Owen, Ursula. "Introduction." In *Fathers: Reflections by Daughters*, edited by Ursula Owen, 9–14. London: Virago, 1983.

———, ed. *Fathers: Reflections by Daughters*. London: Virago, 1983.

Park, Clara Claiborne. "Ghosts on a Gold Mountain." In *Critical Essays on Maxine Hong Kingston*, edited by Laura E. Skandera-Trombley, 216–222. New York: G. K. Hall, 1998.

Perry, Donna. "Maxine Hong Kingston" [1991]. In *Conversations with Maxine Hong*

Kingston, edited by Paul Skenazy and Tera Martin, 168–188. Jackson: University Press of Mississippi, 1998.

Pfaff, Timothy. "Talk with Mrs. Kingston" [1980]. In *Conversations with Maxine Hong Kingston,* edited by Paul Skenazy and Tera Martin, 14–20. Jackson: University Press of Mississippi, 1998.

Pipher, Mary. *Reviving Ophelia: Saving the Selves of Adolescent Girls.* New York: Ballantine, 1994.

Quinby, Lee. "The Subject of Memoirs: *The Woman Warrior*'s Technology of Ideographic Selfhood." In *Critical Essays on Maxine Hong Kingston,* edited by Laura E. Skandera-Trombley, 125–145. New York: G. K. Hall, 1998.

Rabine, Leslie W. "No Lost Paradise: Social Gender and Symbolic Gender in the Writings of Maxine Hong Kingston." *Signs* 12 (1987): 471–492. (Reprinted in *Maxine Hong Kingston's* The Woman Warrior: *A Casebook,* edited by Sau-ling Cynthia Wong, 85–107. New York: Oxford University Press, 1999.)

Rabinowitz, Paula. "Eccentric Memories: A Conversation with Maxine Hong Kingston" [1986]. In *Conversations with Maxine Hong Kingston,* edited by Paul Skenazy and Tera Martin, 67–76. Jackson: University Press of Mississippi, 1998.

Rajan, Tilottama. "Intertextuality and the Subject of Reading/Writing." In *Influence and Intertextuality in Literary History,* edited by Jay Clayton and Eric Rothstein, 61–74. Madison: University of Wisconsin Press, 1991.

Riffaterre, Michael. "Compulsory reader response: The intertextual drive." In *Intertextuality: Theories and practices,* edited by Michael Worton and Judith Still, 56–78. Manchester: Manchester University Press, 1990.

———. "The Intertextual Unconscious." *Critical Inquiry* 13 (1987): 371–385.

Riviere, Joan. *The Inner World and Joan Riviere: Collected Papers, 1920–1958.* Edited by Athol Hughes. London: Karnac Books, 1991.

Rizzuto, Ana-Maria. *The Birth of the Living God: A Psychoanalytic Study.* Chicago: University of Chicago Press, 1981.

Roberts, Michèle. "Outside My Father's House." In *Fathers: Reflections by Daughters,* edited by Ursula Owen, 103–112. London: Virago, 1983.

Robertson, Nan. "'Ghosts' of Girlhood Lift Obscure Book to Peak of Acclaim." In *Critical Essays on Maxine Hong Kingston,* edited by Laura E. Skandera-Trombley, 88–91. New York: G. K. Hall, 1998.

Rowlands, Barbara. "Terrors of the Night." *South China Morning Post.* December 3, 2001.

Ruddick, Sara. *Maternal Thinking: Towards a Politics of Peace.* London: Women's Press, 1990.

———. "Thinking about Fathers." In *Conflicts in Feminism,* edited by Marianne Hirsch and Evelyn Fox Keller, 222–233. New York: Routledge, 1990.

Ruoff, A. LaVonne Brown, and Jerry W. Ward Jr., eds. *Redefining American Literary History.* New York: Modern Language Association of America, 1990.

Rush, Florence. *The Best Kept Secret: Sexual Abuse of Children.* New York: McGraw Hill, 1980.

Rusk, Lauren. "The Collective Self: Maxine Hong Kingston and Virginia Woolf." In *Virginia Woolf and Her Influences: Selected Papers from the Seventh Annual Conference on Virginia Woolf,* edited by Laura Davis, Jeanette McVicker, and Jeanne Dubino, 181–186. New York: Pace University Press, 1998.

Sabine, Maureen. "'Thou art the best of mee': A. S. Byatt's *Possession* and the Literary Possession of Donne." *John Donne Journal* 14 (1995): 127–148.

Sadoff, Dianne F. "The Clergyman's Daughters: Anne Bronte, Elizabeth Gaskell, and George Eliot." In *Daughters and Fathers,* edited by Lynda E. Boose and Betty S. Flowers, 303–325. Baltimore: Johns Hopkins University Press, 1989.

Schneider, Mark A., and Lewellyn Hendrix. "Olfactory Sexual Inhibition and the Westermarck Effect." Posted at http://www.siu.edu.~sociolfactory.htm, pp. 1–15. (Originally published in *Human Nature* 11:1 [2000]).

Schroeder, Eric J. "As Truthful as Possible: An Interview with Maxine Hong Kingston" [1996]. In *Conversations with Maxine Hong Kingston,* edited by Paul Skenazy and Tera Martin, 215–228. Jackson: University Press of Mississippi, 1998.

Schueller, Malini. "Questioning Race and Gender Definitions: Dialogic Subversions in *The Woman Warrior.*" *Criticism* 31 (1989): 421–437.

Seshachari, Neila C. "Reinventing Peace: Conversations with Tripmaster Maxine Hong Kingston" [1993]. In *Conversations with Maxine Hong Kingston,* edited by Paul Skenazy and Tera Martin, 192–214. Jackson: University Press of Mississippi, 1998.

Shapiro, Elliott H. "Authentic Watermelon: Maxine Hong Kingston's American Novel." *MELUS* 26 (2001): 5–28.

Shih, Shu-mei. "Exile and Intertextuality in Maxine Hong Kingston's China Men." In *The Literature of Emigration and Exile,* edited by James Whitlark and Wendell Aycock, 65–77. Lubbock: Texas Tech University Press, 1992.

Shostak, Debra. "Maxine Hong Kingston's Fake Books." In *Critical Essays on Maxine Hong Kingston,* edited by Laura E. Skandera-Trombley, 51–74. New York: G. K. Hall, 1998.

Shu, Yuan. "Cultural Politics and Chinese-American Female Subjectivity: Rethinking Kingston's *Woman Warrior.*" *MELUS* 26 (2001): 199–223.

Sicherman, Barbara. "Reading *Little Women:* The Many Lives of a Text." In *Women's America: Refocusing the Past,* 5th ed., edited by Linda K. Kerber and Jane Sherron De Hart, 246–258. New York: Oxford University Press, 2000.

Simmons, Diane. *Maxine Hong Kingston.* New York: Twayne Publishers, 1999.

———. "Maxine Hong Kingston's Woman Warrior and Shaman: Fighting Women in the New World," *Femspec* 2.1 (2000): 49–65.

Skandera-Trombley, Laura E. "A Conversation with Maxine Hong Kingston." In *Critical Essays on Maxine Hong Kingston,* edited by Laura E. Skandera-Trombley, 33–48. New York: G. K. Hall, 1998.

———. "Introduction." In *Critical Essays on Maxine Hong Kingston,* edited by Laura E. Skandera-Trombley, 1–30. New York: G. K. Hall, 1998.

———, ed. *Critical Essays on Maxine Hong Kingston.* New York: G. K. Hall, 1998.

Skenazy, Paul. "Coming Home" [1989]. In *Conversations with Maxine Hong Kingston,* edited by Paul Skenazy and Tera Martin, 104–117. Jackson: University Press of Mississippi, 1998.

———. "Kingston at the University" [1989]. In *Conversations with Maxine Hong Kingston*, edited by Paul Skenazy and Tera Martin, 118–158. Jackson: University Press of Mississippi, 1998.

Sledge, Linda Ching. "Maxine Kingston's *China Men*: The Family Historian as Epic Poet." *MELUS* 7.4 (1980): 3–22.

———. "Oral Tradition in Kingston's *China Men*." In *Redefining American Literary History*, edited by A. LaVonne Brown Ruoff and Jerry W. Ward Jr., 142–154. New York: Modern Language Association of America, 1990.

Slowik, Mary. "When the Ghosts Speak: Oral and Written Narrative Forms in Maxine Hong Kingston's *China Men*." In *Critical Essays on Maxine Hong Kingston*, edited by Laura E. Skandera-Trombley, 246–260. New York: G. K. Hall, 1998.

Smith, Jeanne R. "Cross-Cultural Play: Maxine Hong Kingston's *Tripmaster Monkey*." In *Critical Essays on Maxine Hong Kingston*, edited by Laura E. Skandera-Trombley, 334–348. New York: G. K. Hall, 1998.

Smith, Sidonie. "Filiality and Woman's Autobiographical Storytelling." In *Maxine Hong Kingston's The Woman Warrior: A Casebook*, edited by Sau-ling Cynthia Wong, 57–83. New York: Oxford University Press, 1999.

Smith, Sidonie, and Julia Watson, eds. *Women, Autobiography, Theory: A Reader*. Madison: University of Wisconsin Press.

Sorapure, Madeleine. "Representing Shame: The Culture of Confession." In *Writing Lives: American Biography and Autobiography*, edited by Hans Bak and Hans Krabbendam, 106–114. Amsterdam: VU University Press, 1998.

Steele, Jeffrey. "The Call of Eurydice: Mourning and Intertextuality in Margaret Fuller's Writing." In *Influence and Intertextuality in Literary History*, edited by Jay Clayton and Eric Rothstein, 271–297. Madison: University of Wisconsin Press, 1991.

Suzuki-Martinez, Sharon. "Trickster Strategies: Challenging American Identity, Community, and Art in Kingston's *Tripmaster Monkey*." In *Reviewing Asian America: Locating Diversity*, edited by Wendy L. Ng, Soo-Young Chin, James S. Moy, and Gary Y. Okihiro, 161–170. Pullman: Washington State University Press, 1995.

Thompson, Phyllis Hoge. "This Is the Story I Heard: A Conversation with Maxine Hong Kingston and Earll Kingston." *Biography—Hawaii* 6.1 (1983): 1–12.

Topley, Marjorie. "Marriage Resistance in Rural Kwangtung." In *Women in Chinese Society*, edited by Marjorie Wolf and Roxane Witke, 67–88. Stanford, Calif.: Stanford University Press, 1975.

Turner, Victor W. *The Ritual Process: Structure and Anti-Structure*. London: Routledge and Kegan Paul, 1969.

Van Buren, Jane Silverman. *The Modernist Madonna: Semiotics of the Maternal Metaphor*. London: Karnac Books, 1989.

Vaneigem, Raoul. *The Revolution of Everyday Life*. Translated by Donald Nicholson-Smith. London: Rebel Press/Left Bank Books, 1994.

Wakeman, Frederic, Jr. "Chinese Ghost Story." In *Critical Essays on Maxine Hong*

Kingston, edited by Laura E. Skandera-Trombley, 207–215. New York: G. K. Hall, 1998.

Waller, Margaret. "Intertextuality and Literary Interpretation." In *Julia Kristeva Interviews*, edited by Ross Mitchell Guberman, 188–203. New York: Columbia University Press, 1991.

Whitlark, James, and Wendell Aycock, eds. *The Literature of Emigration and Exile* (Lubbock: Texas Tech University Press, 1992).

Whitman, Walt. *The Complete Poems*. Edited by Francis Murphy. London: Penguin Classics, 1996.

Willbern, David. "*Filia Oedipi:* Father and Daughter in Freudian Theory." In *Daughters and Fathers*, edited by Lynda E. Boose and Betty S. Flowers, 75–96. Baltimore: Johns Hopkins University Press, 1989.

Williams, A. Noelle. "Parody and Pacifist Transformations in Maxine Hong Kingston's *Tripmaster Monkey: His Fake Book*." In *Critical Essays on Maxine Hong Kingston*, edited by Laura E. Skandera-Trombley, 318–333. New York: G. K. Hall, 1998.

Wolf, Arthur P. *Sexual Attraction and Childhood Association: A Chinese Brief for Edward Westermarck*. Stanford, Calif.: Stanford University Press, 1995.

———. "The Women of Hai-shan: A Demographic Portrait." In *Women in Chinese Society*, edited by Margery Wolf and Roxane Witke, 89–110. Stanford, Calif.: Stanford University Press, 1975.

Wolf, Margery. "Women and Suicide in China." In *Women in Chinese Society*, edited by Margery Wolf and Roxane Witke, 111–141. Stanford, Calif.: Stanford University Press, 1975.

Wolf, Margery, and Roxane Witke, eds. *Women in Chinese Society*. Stanford, Calif.: Stanford University Press, 1975.

Wong, Sau-ling Cynthia. "Autobiography as Guided Chinatown Tour? Maxine Hong Kingston's *The Woman Warrior* and the Chinese American Autobiographical Controversy." In *Maxine Hong Kingston's* The Woman Warrior: *A Casebook*, edited by Sau-ling Cynthia Wong, 29–53. New York: Oxford University Press, 1999. (Reprinted in *Critical Essays on Maxine Hong Kingston*, edited by Laura E. Skandera-Trombley, 146–167. New York: G. K. Hall, 1998.)

———. *Reading Asian American Literature: From Necessity to Extravagance*. Princeton, N.J.: Princeton University Press, 1993.

———, ed. *Maxine Hong Kingston's* The Woman Warrior: *A Casebook*. New York: Oxford University Press, 1999.

Woodward, Kathleen, and Murray M. Schwartz, eds. *Memory and Desire: Aging-Literature-Psychoanalysis*. Bloomington: Indiana University Press, 1986.

Woolf, Virginia. *A Room of One's Own*. London: Grafton, 1988.

———. *The Voyage Out*. London: Grafton, 1986.

Worton, Michael, and Judith Still. "Introduction." In *Intertextuality: Theories and practices*, edited by Michael Worton and Judith Still, 1–44. Manchester: Manchester University Press, 1990.

————, eds. *Intertextuality: Theories and practices.* Manchester: Manchester University Press, 1990.

Wright, Elizabeth. *Feminism and Psychoanalysis: A Critical Dictionary.* Oxford: Blackwell, 1992.

Yeats, William Butler. "The Magi." *Selected Poems.* Edited by M. L. Rosenthal, 49. New York: Macmillan, 1965.

Yu, Ning. "A Strategy against Marginalization: The 'High' and 'Low' Cultures in Kingston's *China Men.*" *College English* 23 (1996): 73–87. (Reprinted at http://vweb.hwwilsonweb.com, pp. 1–7.)

Yuan, Yuan. "The Semiotics of China Narratives in the Con/texts of Kingston and Tan." *Critique* 40 (1999): 292–303. (Reprinted at http://vweb.hwwilsonweb.com, pp. 1–6.)

Zackodnik, Teresa C. "Photography and the Status of Truth in Maxine Hong Kingston's *China Men.*" *MELUS* 22 (1997): 55–69. (Reprinted at http://vweb.hwwilsonweb.com, pp. 1–7.)

Zwinger, Lynda M. *Daughters, Fathers, and the Novel: The Sentimental Romance of Heterosexuality.* Madison: University of Wisconsin Press, 1991.

Index

Eliot, T.S., 54–55
Elliott, Charles (editor), 74; and Alfred A. Knopf (publishing company), 40
Eng, David, 78, 167, 169, 171, 182, 185, 187

Fa Mu Lan, 8, 31, 72, 74–75, 86, 91–92, 94, 99–100, 119–120, 133, 138, 140–143, 157, 164, 174, 179, 186, 192–193, 198. *See also* Incest: in *The Woman Warrior*; "White Tigers"; *Woman Warrior, The*: battle of the sexes in; *Woman Warrior, The*: feminism in; *Woman Warrior, The*: heroism in; Women: symbolism of their bodies
Father (Ba Ba): as cipher, 6, 28–29, 45, 97, 100–101, 113; depression of, 95, 97, 102, 116, 180; early life as Bibi, 12, 177–179; education, 111, 179, 189–191; exile from the center, 13, 189, 194–195; as imaginary father, 117, 195; as immigrant worker, 88, 90, 94, 164, 190, 195; as laundryman, 48–49, 90, 95, 97, 98, 119, 144, 166, 188–189, 194; likeness to Ch'u Yuan, 189–190, 193, 194–195; links to his sister (no name woman), 8–9, 81, 83, 88–92, 97, 146, 189; as mandarin scholar, 13, 30, 48–49, 80, 97, 98, 156, and his memory, 79–80, 190; as poet, 13, 30, 98, 190–197; as savior, 13, 158, 179–180; as schoolmaster, 191; as sojourner, 86, 188, 190; suicidal thoughts of, 92, 189, 192; symbolic murder of, 13, 83. *See also* *China Men*; Kristeva, Julia: and theory of the imaginary father; Grandfathers; *Woman Warrior, The*: traces of the father in
"Father from China, The" (*China Men*), 73, 87, 90, 94–96, 98, 168, 170–171, 179, 185, 189, 191, 195
Felman, Shoshana, 49
Fisher Fishkin, Shelley, 197
Flaubert, Gustave, and *Madame Bovary*, 37–38
Flowers in the Mirror. *See* Li Ruzhen
Friedman, Susan Stanford, 23, 51–52, 54
Freud, Sigmund: "Family Romances," 10,

131, 155–156, 178; femininity, 171–172; fetishism, 172; *The Interpretation of Dreams*, 41–43, 54; reality principle, 17; the talking cure, 148; "The Theme of the Three Caskets," 9, 114–116; "The 'Uncanny,'" 176

Genesis, 183–184
Genette, Gerard, 93
Ghosts: definition of, 3, 21, 47; in *The Woman Warrior*, 112, 114, 128, 137–139
"Ghostmate, The" (*China Men*), 138, 167
Gilmore, Leigh, 126
Ginsberg, Allen, 78
Goellnicht, Donald C., 85, 90, 91, 194–195
Gold Mountain: in *China Men*, 12, 71, 167, 168, 173, 188, 191–192, 195; in *The Woman Warrior*, 87, 95
Gordon, Mary, 181
"Grandfather of the Sierra Nevada Mountains, The" (*China Men*), 73, 87, 126, 168, 171, 173, 176, 183, 186, 194
Grandfathers: definition of, 44–45, 111, 165, 167; Ah Goong, 12–13, 70, 87, 88, 96, 123, 126, 127, 168–178, 186; Ah Goong and his sexual pathology, 181–183; Bak Goong, 73, 176; Kau Goong, 35, 111, 112, 142; Say Goong, 44, 140, 158–159. *See also* *China Men*; *China Men* and *The Woman Warrior*: patriarchy in; Incest; *Woman Warrior, The*: traces of China men in
Grandmothers: Ah Po, 12, 96, 172–179, 188; Mad Sao's mother, 175
"Great Grandfather of the Sandalwood Mountains, The" (*China Men*), 73, 96, 167, 176, 194

Haaken, Janice, 11, 140. *See also* Incest
Hattori, Tomo, 182
Hawthorne, Nathaniel, and the intertextual influence of *The Scarlet Letter*, 11, 36–37, 44–45, 132, 163
Henderson, Mae G., 187
Hillman, James, 183, 198
Holland, Norman N., 53. *See also under* Intertextuality: theories

About the Author

Maureen Sabine is associate professor and senior lecturer in the Department of Comparative Literature at The University of Hong Kong, Pokfulam. Her current research areas are women's autobiographical writings, feminist cultural studies, and early modern love poetry.

Production Notes for
*Sabine / Maxine Hong Kingston's Broken Book of Life:
An Intertextual Study of* The Woman Warrior *and*
China Men

Cover and interior designed by the production
staff of the University of Hawai'i Press with
text in Giovanni and display in Amber

Composition by Josie Herr in QuarkXPress

Printing and binding by The Maple-Vail Book
Manufacturing Group

Printed on 60 lb. Sebago Eggshell